Inequality in Financial Capitalism

Recently, the issue of inequality has regained attention in the economic and political debate. This is due to both an increase in income inequality, in particular among rich countries, and an increasing interest in this issue by researchers and politicians. In the last three decades, income inequality among rich countries increased. This period also witnessed the growth of "financial capitalism", characterised by the strong dependency of economies on the financial sector, by the globalisation and intensification of international trade and capital mobility, and by the "flexibilisation" of labour markets and the reduction of wage shares.

From the 1980s to the present day, this book considers the theoretical aspects of inequality (its foundations, definitions, approaches and origins) and examines empirical evidence of income inequality in a wide range of advanced economies. The key arguments in this volume are that income inequality increased during this period because labour and welfare became seen as costs to be compressed in "financial capitalism" rather than as a fundamental part of aggregate demand to be expanded. However, the welfare state is not a drain on economic performance and competitiveness, nor is it a barrier to economic efficiency. Instead, it is demonstrated that in countries that adopt "welfare capitalism", welfare state expenditure not only contributes to a reduction in inequality but also fosters economic growth.

Inequality in Financial Capitalism is of great importance to those who study economics, political economy, labour economics and globalisation.

Pasquale Tridico is a professor at the Roma Tre University in Rome, Italy. He is director of the two-year master's degree in labour market, industrial relations and welfare systems and director of the master's in human development and food security. He is lecturer of labour economics and economic policy, and is the Jean Monnet Chair of Economic Growth and Welfare Systems. He is also general secretary of the European Association for Evolutionary Political Economy (EAEPE).

Routledge Frontiers of Political Economy

For a full list of titles in this series, please visit www.routledge.com/books/series/SE0345

Inequality in Financial Capitalism

Pasquale Tridico

Routledge
Taylor & Francis Group

LONDON AND NEW YORK

First published 2017
by Routledge
2 Park Square, Milton Park, Abingdon, Oxon OX14 4RN

and by Routledge
711 Third Avenue, New York, NY 10017

First issued in paperback 2018

Routledge is an imprint of the Taylor & Francis Group, an informa business

British Library Cataloguing in Publication Data
A catalogue record for this book is available from the British Library

Library of Congress Cataloging in Publication Data
Names: Tridico, Pasquale, 1975– author.
Title: Inequality in financial capitalism / Pasquale Tridico.
Description: 1 Edition. | New York: Routledge, 2017. | Includes index.
Identifiers: LCCN 2016045390 | ISBN 9781138944121 (hardback) |
ISBN 9781315672083 (ebook)
Subjects: LCSH: Income distribution. | Equality—Economic aspects. |
Social policy. | Financial institutions—Social aspects. | Welfare state.
Classification: LCC HB523 .T75 2017 | DDC 339.2—dc23
LC record available at https://lccn.loc.gov/2016045390

ISBN 13: 978-1-138-33598-1 (pbk)
ISBN 13: 978-1-138-94412-1 (hbk)

Typeset in Times New Roman
by codeMantra

To my little son, Francesco
With the hope that he will grow up in a more just and fair world

Contents

Figures

Tables

Preface

The objective of the book is to identify the determinants of the increase of income inequality that rich countries experienced in the last three decades. My hypothesis is that in the age of *financial capitalism*, and at least since 1980, along with the financialisation of the economy, inequality increased because capital-labour relations dramatically changed: labour flexibility increased, wage share declined, trade unions lost power hence labour market institutions weakened, and public social spending started to retrench and did not compensate for the vulnerabilities created by the globalisation process.

The new governing economic paradigm, analysed in the first part of the book, called "financial capitalism", is characterised by the strong dependency of economies on the financial sector, by the globalisation and intensification of international trade and capital mobility, and by the "flexibilisation" of labour markets. In this context, I argue, income inequality increased because labour, which is the most important source for income, is seen by the supply-side approach, as a cost to be compressed rather than as a fundamental part of aggregate demand to expand. In turn, the worsening of income distribution contributed to the scarce dynamic of GDP, or in other words to what has been called "the secular stagnation".

In parallel, financial rents and financial compensation and profit increased since the 1980s. A flexible labour market with compressed wages needed to be supplemented by available financing. Financial tools were developed to sustain consumption, which otherwise was compressed by low and unstable wages. In this framework emerged also the 2007 financial crisis, analysed extensively in the second part of the book, first in the United States and then in Europe. Moreover, the welfare state represented another cost to be compressed, following the rhetoric of competitiveness and advocating the so-called "efficiency thesis" against the "the compensation thesis". Hence, wage share declined as well as consumption.

The book also proposes a new classification of welfare models, such as welfare capitalism and financial capitalism. This classification is drawn on the basis of the examination of five dimensions of economic and labour relations: (1) income distribution, (2) labour flexibility, (3) financialisation, (4) social spending, and (5) wage shares. Contrary to the efficiency thesis argument, I show that in countries that belong to the first category, welfare state expenditure not only contributes to reduce inequality, but it also fosters economic growth. My econometric exercises and the empirical evidences, run on a panel from 1980 up to today, on a group of thirty-four rich countries belonging to OECD show clearly these processes and confirm my hypotheses.

The structure of the book

The book is divided into two parts. The first part concerns the theoretical aspects of inequality, its foundations, definitions, approaches and origins. In this part, the main ideas of the determinants of income inequality in "financial capitalism" will be put forward, covering a time span of at least three decades (1980–2014). The second part deals with empirical evidences and policies suggestions, and it focuses in particular on the financial and economic crisis, which started in 2007 in advanced economies and its connections with inequality. This crisis, and also the long GDP stagnation, is considered to be the consequence of the financial-led model built in the previous three decades, which has at its core the increase of income inequality.

Acknowledgements

This book is a result of several years of research and studies, during my many research visits in several universities in Europe and in the United States, at least since my first research visit to New York University (NYU), as a Fulbright scholar during 2010–11. During this period of five to six years, I met many people with whom I discussed and commented my work or inspired my writings. I am indebted to them. I am grateful to Larry Wolf, director of the Center for European Studies at NYU who hosted and supported my visiting during my Fulbright Scholarship; I am also grateful to the US-Italy Fulbright Commission for the scholarship I received in 2010–11. I am grateful to Richard Wolf from New School, with whom I enjoyed talking to about the tremendous consequences in US of the financial crisis and whose public talks inspired my work. I am also grateful to Branko Milanovic who I met during my second visit at NYU in 2014 while he was at City University of New York. With Branko I discussed an idea, which I develop in the book, about historical forces driving within and between inequality in the world. I am indebted to Pascal Petit and Esther Sasson Jeffers who supported me during my research visit to the Paris 8 University in the fall of 2011 within the framework of the COST project "Systemic Risks, Financial Crises and Credit – the roots, dynamics and consequences of the Subprime Crisis". I am grateful to Mirosława Klamut, Ewa Pancer-Cybulska and Łukasz Olipra who supported my research and teaching visits several times between 2011 and 2013 at Wroclaw University of Economics within the framework of the Kuznia Kadr project and of the Erasmus mobility project. I am grateful to Hardy Hanappi, Bernhard Rengs and Manuel Scholz-Wäckerle, with whom I enjoyed discussions and from whom I benefited of great comments and help during my research and teaching visits at the University of Technology in Vienna in 2013 and in 2014, within the framework of the COST project and of the Erasmus mobility project. I am grateful to Andrea Bernardi with whom I enjoyed discussing the lines of my book, and from whom I received support during my research and teaching visits at the Manchester Metropolitan University within the framework of the Erasmus mobility project during the fall and the winter of 2014–15. I am grateful to the European Commission and in particular to the Jean Monnet team from which I received a grant during 2013–16 (N. 542598-LLP-1–2013-IT-AJM-CH), which in large part supported my research and this book. I am grateful to my home institution, the Roma Tre University and the Department of Economics, which sponsors my work and allows for the necessary flexibility that my research requires in combination with my teaching obligation. Here I am indebted to Sebastiano Fadda who always supported my work, and from whom I always benefited from great comments and discussion. Moreover, I wish to thank Antonella Mennella and Alessia Naccarato for their comments and suggestions to the econometric parts, and Riccardo Pariboni for letting me use some parts of a joint paper (Pariboni and Tridico 2016). Parts of this book were presented as papers at several conferences in Europe and in the US. I am indebted to the people who commented on my works in particular at the last five EAEPE conferences in Genoa (2015), Nicosia (2014), Paris (2013), Krakow (2012) and Vienna (2011). Last but not least, I am grateful to my wife, Iryna, for her love and support during these years: since I met her in Poland at the end of 2011 I shared with her ideas and project of the book, and I received support and love, which were crucial for me for overcoming the "blank days" and the discourage which eventually occurred in particular in 2015 when I was close to abandoning the idea of this book. Without her, this book would be an unfinished project. Finally, in 2016, during the last months of my writing, my effort on the book was happily accompanied by our newborn and little child, Francesco, to whom I am already indebted for giving me a new perspective on world issues. To him this book is dedicated, with the hope that he will grow up in a more just and fairer world.

Introduction

Income inequality, labour market and uneven development during financial capitalism

Main ideas

In this introductory chapter, I explain the main ideas and the main hypotheses of the book along with the main links and mechanisms of transmission between labour market, financialisation, financial-led growth regime and inequality.

The objective of the book is to identify the determinants of the increase of income inequality that rich countries experienced in the last three decades. I will refer mostly to the Organization for Economic Cooperation and Development (OECD) countries, and sometimes, more in particular, to the US and Western Europe. I will not bring about new data on inequality. The increase of inequality is today well documented by both mainstream and heterodox organisations and authors from different perspectives. I will instead focus on a particular idea and a particular mechanism of transmission of inequality, and I will prove how this mechanism works and leads to inequality.

The main working hypothesis of the book is that in the age of "financial capitalism" (which will be defined extensively), and at least since 1980, along with the financialisation of the economy, inequality increased because labour flexibility increased, trade unions lost power hence labour market institutions weakened, and public social spending started to retrench and did not compensate for the vulnerabilities created by the globalisation process. The change, however, was not exogenous but was caused by a political change since the end of the 1970s which imposed a new economic paradigm or consensus favouring globalisation and finance. The important technical progress that was occurring was also functional to that change. However, technological progress is not a cause of inequality: the way technological progress affects income distribution is shaped by economic and social decisions. Both globalisation and finance increased pressure on labour, changed capital-labour relations, and allowed for an increase in labour flexibility and a weakening of labour market institutions and social policy, which in turn led to a reduction in the wage share. The increase of income inequality was just the natural consequence of this process. The schematic mechanism reported in the following box illustrates this idea.

Working hypothesis

*1970s: Ideological switch, political change and technical progress →
1980s: capital expansion → globalisation and financialisation → change
in capital-labour relations → 1990s and 2000s: labour flexibility, weakening of labour market institutions and adverse social policies → recovery
of profits and soar of financial rents and compensations → wage share
reduction → **INEQUALITY** → moderation of aggregate demand → scarce
GDP dynamics → secular stagnation*

As the Marxian literature showed, inequality is functional to *capitalism*;
more than that, in *financial* capitalism, as I will show, inequality emerges as
crucially important and, at the same time, is the cause of financial instability
and crises.

The issue of inequality has regained attention in the economic and political
debate. This is due to both an increase in income inequality, in particular among
rich countries (as shown in Figure I.1), and an increasing interest in this issue by
researchers and politicians after three decades of institutional changes, which
shaped a new capitalism's model in most advanced economies. Public opinion,
in the last years, in particular since the financial crash in 2007–08 became very
sensitive about the issue of inequality, which is, as already stated, increasing
dramatically in rich countries. Policymakers, international organisations and
academicians are also devoting huge attention to inequality, both in theoretical
and in policy terms. Inequality was ignored for a long period by mainstream
economics, which reached a consensus around the Kuznets curve and similar
works. The increase in inequality is also challenging the neoclassical approach,
which does not see inequality as a main issue in economics. It is more considered
a moral or a social issue, not very much concerning the economic sphere or harm-
ing the economic performance.

Today, the richest 10 per cent of the population in the OECD countries earn
about ten times the income of the poorest 10 per cent; in the late 1980s, the richest
10 per cent earned about 7 times the income of the poorest 10 per cent (OECD,
2014). At a global level, the top 1 per cent of the population own 48 per cent of
global wealth (about US$120 trillion).[1] Most of this wealth is concentrated in
Europe and North America (US$140 trillion out of US$250 trillion). According
to a recent report by Oxfam, the richest 85 people in the world – the likes of Bill
Gates, Warren Buffett, and Carlos Slim – own about US$70 trillion, more wealth
than the roughly 3.5 billion people who make up the poorest half of the world's
population.

Global wealth in 2015 amassed at US$250 trillion, while global income
(i.e. GDP) was about US$76 trillion. In the United States, the country among ad-
vanced economies, which best represents the transformation towards a new model

of capitalism since the 1980s, with a more uneven society, the top 10 per cent (1 per cent) of people own about 70 per cent (38 per cent) of wealth in the economy. Data in terms of income (rather than wealth) follow the same trend in proportion: the top 10 per cent (1 per cent) of people own about 47 per cent (20 per cent) of income in the economy (Piketty, 2014).

These numbers tell us the great divide of the society and the strong uneven development taking place both within countries and between countries. These numbers also indicate an important difference to take into account between *wealth inequality* and *income inequality,* being the later is the principal focus of this book. The first refers to the difference in the accumulation of assets (such as land, money, financial and non-financial assets, and other resources).[2] The second refers to income distribution and has to do with both the functional income distribution (which concerns the way capital and labour shares are distributed in terms of total profits and total wages over GDP, as factors of production compensations), and the personal income distribution (which concerns the dispersion of income across households – who can be capitalists, i.e. profit-earners, and workers, i.e. wage-earners). In simple terms, the wage share is the total wage compensation (number of employees by the nominal wages) over the GDP; the profit share, which, similarly, is the total profit compensation, can easily be obtained as a residual: GDP – wage share.

The personal income distribution (or the personal income inequality) is generally captured best by the Gini coefficient, which logically is an indicator of income distribution and inequality. Considering also that the distinction between wage-earners and profit-earners is not always very clear, the use of personal income inequality (and of its popular measure – i.e. the Gini coefficient), being wider, encompasses in general terms the concept of income inequality, since it represents the dispersion of individual incomes and not of aggregate incomes (which sometimes is difficult to aggregate or to classify; see also Fadda 2016).[3]

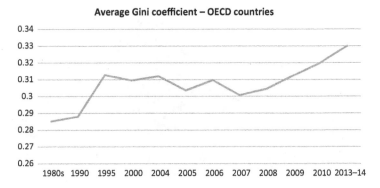

Figure I.1 The increase of income inequality.
Source: OECD online database, 2016.

Empirically, it can be observed that the increase of income inequality in rich countries has to do with both the reduction of the *wage share* and the increase of *personal income dispersion* in the last two to three decades. These two concepts are strongly correlated: when wage share decreases, *ceteris paribus,* the total personal income distribution, obviously, will be more uneven, as Fadda (2016: 24) argues.[4] Figure I.2 shows the correlation between inequality (Gini coefficient) and wage share (adjusted)[5] during a long period (1990–2013) among a group of thirty-four OECD countries and clearly indicates this relationship: when wage share shrinks, inequality increases.

The increase of income inequality, in particular among advanced economies, contradicts the famous Kuznets' curve (1955) according to which inequality increases in the initial phase of the development process and then decreases when economies become richer. Piketty (2014) already noticed this; and in his recent book, he rejects the idea of the Kuznets' bell curve. On the contrary, he proposes a horizontal "S" curve. However, Piketty focuses on a historical perspective and only on few countries, while I will focus on the years that are probably the ones where inequality increased the most – i.e. from the 1980s to present – trying to explain the most immediate causes of inequality in the last years among a larger group of countries. During this period, the world changed, the structure of rich economies was reshaped, and in most of these countries, the huge technological progress created strong and long waves of transformations. Before that, since the end of the 1970s, the political changes created the basis also for a new paradigm of political economy, first in the U.S. and in the U.K. and later in most advanced and emerging economies.

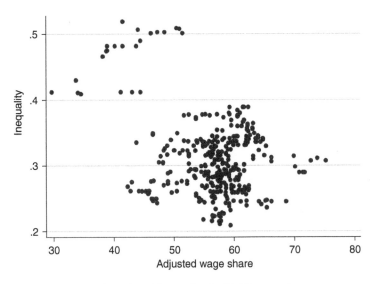

Figure I.2 Wage share (adjusted) and inequality in OECD countries.
Source: An elaboration on OECD and ILO data. Panel 1990–2013.

I particularly underline the importance of the following six changes for the process of globalisation and financialisation shaping a new economic regime:

1   The political (and to some extent also ideological) change that occurred during the 1980s, particularly in the United States and Great Britain with the new administrations of Reagan and Thatcher. These two political leaders were able to shape, to some extent, the international political consensus globalisation required. This change was later promoted with the help of major international organisations, such as the International Monetary Fund (IMF) and the World Bank (WB), which had close ties with the Washington administration (Stiglitz, 2002), along with a new political economic doctrine that became known as the "Washington Consensus".

2   The financial deregulation that occurred in particular under the stimulus and policies of the Reagan and Thatcher administrations and later in many advanced and developing economies. Financial deregulation contributed to both the expansion of capital globally, in search of higher profits, and the intensification of finance and financial tools as an integral aspect of the economy. Economies across the globe soon became attracted to the process of financialisation.

3   The fall of the Berlin Wall in 1989 and the following dissolution of the Soviet Union in 1991, which ended the Cold War and the ideological divide between Eastern and Western Europe and in a way between the Eastern and Western World. The inclusion of the former communist economies in the global economy, or to be more precise, in the economic system of Western Europe, North America and other few advanced economies also played a crucial role.

4   The deepening of the European Union integration process, which culminated in the Maastricht Treaty, introducing capital mobility along with the liberalisation of trade, services, goods and labour in an important and large market.

5   The tremendous challenges posed by the technological progress that brought about the ICT Revolution and all the other great innovations introduced in transport and in telecommunications, substantially reducing transportation costs.

6   The takeoff (during the 1980s and 1990s) of several emerging economies – often identified with the term BRIC[6] – in terms of economic growth and other development indicators.

The new paradigm of political economy emerging during the processes of globalisation and financialisation, which will be called throughout the book "financial capitalism", is characterized by the strong dependency of economies on the financial sector, by the globalisation and intensification of international trade and capital mobility, and by the "flexibilisation" of labour markets. From an economic policy perspective, the change resulted in the withdrawal of the state from the economy (i.e. the minimization of its economic intervention) and the dominance of supply-side policies (i.e. labour flexibility, tax competition for firms and capital).

This paradigm favours pro-rich growth, as in most advanced economies the top 1 per cent (or top 10 per cent) of populations get the highest share of income.[7] The paramount example is the United States, where in the past two to three decades most of the benefits of the economic growth accrued to the richest people, as Table I.1 shows.

In this context, I argue that income inequality increased because labour, which is the most important source for income, is seen by the supply-side approach as a cost to be compressed rather than as a fundamental part of aggregate demand to expand. In the age of financial capitalism, characterized by the intensification of globalisation and financialisation, labour-capital relations are changing, and, in most of the cases, labour represents the weaker part. From one side, within the conflict between labour and capital, trade unions lost power, and labour market institutions, such as labour protection against firing, unemployment subsidies, substitution rate for unemployment subsidies, etc. weakened. From another side, labour flexibility, atypical labour contracts and temporary work created unstable jobs and therefore unstable consumption.

In this framework, I must also analyse the 2007 financial crisis, which represents the peak for the financial capitalism model, before the crash. However, as I cover in the second part of the book, policies put forward as remedies for the crises suffer from the same flaws, which generated the crisis. In other words, paraphrasing medical science, it seems that: *doctors (policymakers) wish to cure the disease with the same virus that generated the infection.* The current European (and euro) crisis has similar origins: the change of the European social model, operated through the Maastricht Treaty, put forward the basis for the low economic growth of most of the EU member states. Since 1992–93, deflationary policies and the retrenchment of welfare states, in the context of globalisation and financialisation processes, contributed to both the European secular stagnation, and the increase of income inequality.

Moreover, within the new *financial capitalism* paradigm, the welfare state represents another cost to be compressed. In order to foster firms' competitiveness and economic growth, social spending needs to be reduced, advocates of the

Table I.1 Pro-rich economic growth 1993–2013

Period	Income real growth	Fraction of total growth captured by top 1%	Fraction of total growth captured by bottom 99%
GDP expansion 1993–2010	13.8%	52%	48%
GDP expansion 1993–2000	31.5%	45%	55%
GDP expansion 2002–2007	16.1%	65%	35%
GDP expansion 2009–2012	6%	95%	5%

Source: Saez (2013).

so-called "efficiency thesis" argue. In fact, most of the countries are experiencing a retrenchment of the welfare state or at least a stabilization of the expenses which corresponds, in the age of globalisation and of aging, to a per capita reduction in real terms. However, the efficiency thesis is challenged by "the compensation thesis", which argues that because globalisation increases inequality, welfare state expenditure needs to increase. Some countries, which I will prove in Chapter 3, chose this second approach to cope with the challenges of globalisation and, in fact, in the past decades increased welfare spending and had better economic performance.

The book proposes also a new classification of welfare models, such as welfare capitalism and financial capitalism. These classifications are drawn on the basis of the examination of five dimensions of economic and labour relations: (1) income distribution, (2) labour flexibility, (3) financialisation, (4) social spending, and (5) wage shares. In the countries that belong to the first category, welfare state expenditure not only contributes to reduce inequality, but it also fosters economic growth. On the contrary, the countries in the second category have higher inequality, and in particular during the current economic crisis, they also exhibit worse economic performance. In other words, in this analysis, the welfare state does not appear to be a drain on economic performance and competitiveness or as a barrier to economic efficiency.

Inequality and financial capitalism: a review

The financial and economic model established at the end of the 1970s, during the past three decades in most advanced economies, can be named and captured in different ways from a conceptual point of view: the IMF speaks about "financial deepening" in a positive way, and finance is identified as a positive factor bosting growth through collection of bigger amount of savings and capitals. Critical economists prefer to speak, in particular after the financial crisis of 2007, and to some extent also before (Krippner, 2005) in terms of financialisation of the economy or financialised-capitalism, where capital and savings are used not necessarily to favour and boost productive investments. Instead, they are used to increase asset values in order to favour increase in shares' dividends; or to increase transactions in terms of volume and speed in order to speculate over marginal changes in prices of shares; or to move large sum in order to speculate over marginal chances of currencies; or for pure speculative purposes in order to favour decrease or increase of the values of certain assets or hedge funds. These can be some of the reasons behind the great amount and volume of transactions in the stock exchanges of many advanced and emerging economies today, or Over the Counter (OTC) by passing also the formal and quite loose regulatory of national stock exchanges.

These transactions, which reached at the eve of the financial crisis in 2007 the value of about US$2 trillion each day, are, according to some economists, beneficial for economic growth because they favour saving collection and efficiently allocate investments as Alan Greenspan believed. Greenspan, a former chairman of the US Federal Reserve Board (Fed), was the main force behind American monetary policies between 1987 and 2006 (the exact period when financial capitalism was shaped), and fundamentally he created the monetary regime that the current financial system requires. Greenspan was also a great supporter of sub-prime lending and derivatives, stating: "Derivatives have been an extraordinarily useful vehicle to transfer risk from those who shouldn't be taking it to those who are willing to and are capable of doing so" (US Senate Banking Committee, 2003).

Other economists argue that these financial instruments are not efficient because they do not favour economic growth in the end and are also socially inefficient because they increase inequality and in turn also harm economic growth, since a more unequal society may decrease economic performance and growth (Ostry, 2016). In the best case, they favour a credit boom and a credit-consumption driven growth, which would be, however, fragile and unstable and subject to recurrent crises. At the same time, financial compensation in this model rose enormously and inequality, too. In financial capitalism both (the modest) economic growth and income inequality are financial led.

The relationship between inequality and finance is controversial and can be described at least in two ways, according to most of the current critical political economy literature:

- Inequality → (credit availability) and financial crisis.
  Inequality may weaken aggregate demand and drag on the economy because higher income groups spend a smaller share of their income; moreover, income inequality boosts financial instability because it increases demand for credit and this may destabilize the aggregate demand, in particular during credit rationing time.
- Finance → (financialisation) and inequality.
  Inequality is boosted (i.e. can be considered a dependent variable) by financial development, credit consumption and the financialisation of the economy, which allows for an expansion of the debt, both public and private, the compression of the wage share through downsizing of workforce and distributing of profits among shareholders, flexible labour markets, and the reduction of welfare state that increases income vulnerability and reduces worker purchasing power. This second scenario is more a perspective of long/medium-run where institutions change, a transformation of the structure of the economy occurs and the relationship between capital and labour takes new forms. In this perspective is actually inserted our contribution, and it is described as the relationship between inequality and other variables.

These two lines of relationships between finance (and financial crisis) and inequality are, obviously, interconnected and interdependent, as several authors claim, and often the differences between the two mechanisms described above are overlapping (Wisman, 2013) or, to use the words of Van Treeck (2014), complement each other. One of the first to argue in favour of the interdependencies between financial crisis and inequality is Rajan (2010) who maintains that low- and middle-income consumers have reduced savings and increased private debt in the United States with the increase of income inequality in the 1980s. This allowed to keep, at least temporarily, private consumption and employment high but contributed also to the creation of an unsustainable credit bubble, which burst in 2007.

Elsewhere (Tridico, 2012), I argued that the financial-led growth model, which is characterized in the labour market by a reducing wage share, labour flexibility, precarious and unstable jobs and poor wages (which are at the basis of the worsening of income distribution), encourages the demand for credit to finance consumption. In turn, new demand for credit destabilizes aggregate demand and economic growth. Cynamon and Fazzari (2013) argue in favour of the unsustainable rise in household leverage concentrated in the bottom 95 per cent as the ultimate cause of the Great Recession. They found that inequality affects demand growth and creates a drag on the economy because higher-income groups spend a smaller share of income;[8] while Goda and Lysandrou (2014) argue that economic inequality was boosted by credit consumption, and in turn this affects negatively stable economic growth. These interactions between income inequality and finance can be described within a Marxian analysis as follows: wage compensation, which is shrinking, as many economists report (see for instance Stockhammer, 2013), affects the labour capacity whose value is generally less than the value of the output produced. The excess of supply (which is also the surface of worker's exploitation) is compensated by credit consumption. In this way, Lysandrou (2011) argues, crisis is endemic to capitalism and inequality, and while workers suffer twice from these crises (being exploited and paid less, and being encouraged to increase credit consumption), capitalists gain twice (because they gain from the exploitation, which produces excess of supply, and obtain returns from financial products).

Several authors underline a clear trajectory of a new political economy paradigm which took place after 1980 in US and in Europe and which is at the basis of the worsening of income distribution. This paradigm is shaped by specific and flawed economic policies. Palley (2012) sees three momentums shaping the new model: the first flaw was the growth model adopted after 1980 that relied on debt and asset price inflation to fuel growth instead of wages. The second flaw was the model of globalisation that created an economic gash. The third was the financial deregulation and the house price bubble that kept the economy going by making even more credit available. In this context, while income distribution worsened and debt accumulated, the economy needed larger speculative bubbles to grow. Finally, these bubbles started to burst with the housing sector crash in 2007. Stiglitz (2012), who examines the devastating effects of monetary and budgetary policies and of globalisation on the increase of inequality in the US since the 1980, brings about a similar analysis. Moreover, Stiglitz (2012) warns on the dangerous effects of inequality on democracy.

Wisman (2013) in his analysis concludes that rising inequality was the cause for the current economic crisis. The increase of inequality and wage stagnation has at least three channels through which it originated in the 1980s. First, consumption constraints, which made investments less profitable and favoured instead credit consumption, greater indebtedness and financial speculation. Second, a negative externality started to spill over with workers forced to struggle more to keep a minimum acceptable level of income through longer working hours and greater levels of indebtedness. Third, rich people, most in the financial sector, became even more political influential and able to affect policies such as tax cuts for them, further financial deregulation and welfare reduction.

In Chapter 2, I will test an econometric model that synthesizes most of the causes mentioned above in a single and valid empirical model, stressing in particular the role of financialisation, globalisation, labour market institutions and the retrenchment of welfare state as explanatory variables for income inequality. Hence, the channel of transmission, in my approach, follows more the second line described above: Financialisation → inequality.

Categories and discourses of financial capitalism

Financial capitalism can be defined and described from different perspectives, such as from the financial sector point of view; from the housing sector perspective with its connections with the insurance and mortgage companies; from the CEO and the shareholders' viewpoints; from a corporation point of view and its interests in the expansion and in global markets; from the emerging countries' point of view (i.e. BRICS, MINT), which are considered countries of opportunities because of the large size of their relatively unexploited markets; from the Wall Street and other stock exchanges points of view with their main interests in whatsoever investments, as far as bringing higher returns, higher profits, higher value shares; from the hedge funds point of view where speculation more than investments are the main drivers of behaviours, and financial asset accumulation is the main objective in order to affect financial markets and government decisions; from the government and policy perspectives as far as financial markets are left as much as possible unregulated and free to move capitals; and the list could go on.

In all these cases, however, and in all these perspectives, the features of financial capitalism are consistent and constitute a specific model that is different from the one in place in advanced economies before the 1970s. This model considers first of all financial markets and financial expansion as the drivers of economic growth and policies and institutions should allow for that expansions. It also considers dividends, share values, financial assets, returns and profits as the main incentives for investors who in most cases are anonymous and completely disconnected from the real industrial production. Hence, this model considers also labour and wage compensation as costs to compress as much as possible as an "obstacle" that needs to be tuned in order to fit with the needs of business and of investors.

The main policies and institutions that are used in labour market and in industrial relation in order to adjust labour to the needs of investors are labour and wage flexibility, which in fact became one of the main policies in labour markets of advanced economies in the last twenty to thirty years. Consecutively trade unions need to be weakened in order to eliminate frictions. Capital mobility is well often a real threat against trade unions and labour protections in order to favour and accept labour adjustments. Hence, income inequality is a well-expected outcome of this process, an appendix of the financial capitalism model.

A paradoxical phenomenon is taking place within financial capitalism, which concerns the confrontation between goods market and stock market. In the goods market, competition brings about, in general and in most cases, increasing in size of firms, innovation, productive investments, and market size. In the stock market instead, competition brings about downsize of firms listed in the stock exchanges, reductions of costs, and distribution of more remunerative dividends. This paradox can be explained with the contraposition of "principal and agent": the first acts in the goods market, owns the firms, and does everything in order to increase the size and to get higher profits. Agents in the stock market instead work in order to create rooms for higher dividends for shareholders and higher bonuses for themselves, so they have conflicting interests with the firms. Even in the case of Merger and Acquisition (M&A) in the stock exchange, where apparently the objective is to increase the size, in reality the objective is to increase synergy so that costs (mostly labour costs) can be reduced. In fact the sum of two corporations would not be one resulted in the M&A of the new corporation in terms of employees, labour costs, size, etc.

CEO salaries, in financial capitalism, depend on the increase of value shares, and on the short-term results performance in the stock exchange. Differences of CEO salaries between financial capitalism and the previous regime, which can be called "Fordist capitalism", are huge. In 1950, the average American chief executive was paid about twenty times as much as the typical employee of his firm. Today, the pay ratio between the corner office and the shop floor is more than 500 to 1, and many CEOs do even better. In 2011, Apple's Tim Cook received $378 million in salary, stock, and other benefits, which was 6,258 times the wage of an average Apple employee ($60,000). A typical worker at Walmart earns less than $25,000 a year; Michael Duke, the retailer's former chief executive, was paid more than $23 million in 2012.

This represents the return of a "patrimonial society" (of the time of Balzac and Austin), as Piketty (2014) stated: a small group of wealthy rentiers lives lavishly on the fruits of its inherited wealth and huge amount of land, and the rest struggle to keep up. Where the patrimonial society today is the financial class. For the United States, in particular, this would be a cruel and ironic fate. The egalitarian pioneer ideal has faded into oblivion and the rich countries of today may be on the verge of becoming the Old Europe of the twenty-first-century's globalised economy.

Before the financial crash of 2007, generous monetary policies were in place. This increased opportunity in the financial sector. Increased speculation, increased value shares, increased asset prices and dividends contributed to the financial bubble; it allowed for the boom in the housing sector and for the emerging of the huge business in the insurance sector connected with the housing sector. This lasted until a little before the bubble burst in 2007. After that, and with the objective to restore confidence and revitalize investments and financial markets, more generous monetary policies were restored, through massive injections of liquidities in the financial markets known as quantitative easing (QE) implemented by the Central Banks of most of the advanced economies (the Fed, the Bank of England and the Bank of Japan initially, the European Central Bank a bit later). Generous policies and QE favoured financial speculations more than real investments and did not allow, so far, for the well-known "Keynes effect" to take place with minor consequences in terms of GDP growth and employment. On the contrary, the gap between the financial compensation in the financial sector and the labour compensation increased even more, and income inequality worsened also after the crisis. This because in financial capitalism, investment behaviour is not driven by macroeconomic policies (such as the Keynes effect) but by discourses and narratives appealing in the financial markets, stories able to convince speculators, hedge funds owner and managers, feeling and perverse "animal spirits" (Erturk *et al.*, 2008).

In financial capitalism, the cost of living for middle class increased with respect to the "Fordist time" where the middle class and workers in advanced economies enjoyed higher productivity gains and growing salaries. In financial capitalism, labour productivity did not go to workers; rather it went to the financial sector, and this contributed also to increased inequality.

In this context, also housing became an asset over which to speculate in financial capitalism. In many cases, houses are bought not necessarily to live, as happened mostly in the Fordist time, but as an asset through which speculate, expect higher returns, and in some cases also causing increase in prices. Moreover, expenses for social housing decreased hugely among advanced economies in the last two to three decades, in order to favour more room for a private business and higher remuneration in the sector. Obviously, in these cases, as in many others, conflict of interests between governments and corporations interested in the business of housing (insurance companies, mortgage companies, building construction companies) are clear.

Some emerging economies are "managed" by their governments, like big corporations with customers rather than countries with citizens. This is the case in particular for small or weak emerging economies like Singapore, Thailand, and Malaysia. While big emerging economies such as BRICS or MINT (Mexico, Indonesia, Nigeria, Turkey) are considered big assets to exploit through the intervention of fiscal structural adjustments whose programs are administered by IMF and WB with the objective to implement neoliberal policies able to fit with the financial capitalism model such as: capital mobility, privatization, fiscal discipline, public deficit and debt reduction, labour market flexibility, etc.

Since 1980, and in particular since the Thatcher and Reagan administrations in the UK and the US, financial capitalism was shaped in policy terms. First in the UK and the US and later in other advanced economies, a set of neoliberal policies boosting financialisation and globalisation were implemented, such as deregulation of the financial sector, liberalization of trade, capital mobility, wage flexibility, privatization, structural adjustments, retrenchment of welfare states, the creation of a second pillar in the pension system – i.e. the pension funds with the clear aim to collect easy savings.

A proxy I use in this book to describe financialisation, which refers to the rise of financial claims and incomes versus the real sector, is the "Market capitalisation" (also known as capital market value), which is the share price multiplied by the number of shares outstanding and listed in stock exchanges. Listed domestic companies are the domestically incorporated companies listed on the country's stock exchanges at the end of the year. Listed companies do not include investment companies, mutual funds, or other collective investment vehicles.

Figure I.3 describes the increase of financialisation in advanced countries between the 1980s and the eve of the financial crash in 2006. The only exception here (which however confirms our expectations) is Japan, which in fact experienced the current stagnation observed in most of today's advanced economies, already before, since the end of 1980s. Japan had its main financial crash in the mid-1980s, the bubble burst and then financialisation, which had reached a high level, started to decline. A similar path can be observed two decades later in the rest of the advanced economies. Financialisation increased along with instability. It is interesting to note the trend of the market capitalisation of listed companies before and after the crisis. The data shows how companies protected themselves, withdrawing from stock exchanges as the crisis began. Before that, the financial euphoria and the manias, in the Kindleberger way (2005), convinced many firms to be listed in the stock exchanges and to engage in speculative trading. Now that the crisis of confidence dampened the euphoria, the percentage of firm capitalisation in the stock exchange has decreased dramatically, and as Kindleberger (2005) predicts, panics have substituted themselves for manias. Clearly, a "reversed V" is visible in Figure I.3, with the average capitalisation in 2006, on the eve of the crisis, peaking around 120 per cent of GDP, while the average in 2002 and in 2009 was 70 per cent and 73 per cent, respectively.

In this context of financial bubbles and bursts, the effects on economic growth are important, in terms of economic recession and stagnation. Interesting enough is the reduction of market capitalisation after the financial crash of 2007–08.

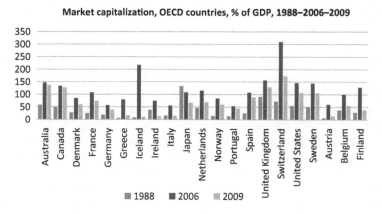

Figure I.3 Financialisation, 1988–2009.
Source: Own elaboration, IMF data.

How is financialisation connected to inequality? This is an important question that this book aims to answer. In short, financialisation worsens income distribution through two channels:

1   It favours the aggressive implementation of the principle "downsize and distribute" so that corporations' managers have as the only objective to maximize and *distribute* dividends for the shareholders at the cost of squeezing production, cutting wages and *downsizing*. Moreover, assets are wasted in speculation strategies rather than in productive investments.
2   It favours an aggressive short-term strategy of corporations' managers interested mainly to sell products and to the maximization of bonus and profits in the short terms at the expenses of the wage bill.

Labour market institutions and in particular labour flexibility are functional to these strategies. I will explore in detail, in the rest of the book, these aspects and the relationship between financialisation and inequality.

An interpretation of the secular stagnation in financial capitalism

Financialisation (a process that involves a set of institutions and financial tools) and labour flexibility (a set of labour market institutions that increase freedom of entrepreneurs to fire and hire workers and to cut wages) are two general categories of institutional forms that have been going hand in hand in particular during the last two decades, although not everywhere, and that were introduced across the world by countries in different degrees in order to guarantee the expansion of the globalisation process, which is believed by most policymakers and governments to boost the national economy. As I will show, economic performance in financial capitalism is in general not better than during the previous regime of accumulation. Economists started to speak, in different ways and with different justifications, about "the secular stagnation" to underline that GDP in the new century will not grow (or is not growing) as much as in the second half of the previous century (Summers, 2016). In my approach, secular stagnation and income inequality are strongly connected. They are two faces of the same coin. In turn, secular stagnation and income inequality are depending on the financial capitalism model and its mechanisms. The model describes the mechanisms and the connections of the financial led-growth model (or the financial capitalism model) with both inequality and secular stagnation and will be our guideline throughout the whole book (see Figure I.4).

Labour flexibility increased almost everywhere in Europe and in advanced economies in the last twenty years. A flexible labour market with compressed wages and precarious jobs needs to be supplemented by available financing. Hence, financial tools were developed to sustain consumption, or better to say credit consumption, which otherwise was compressed by low and unstable wages. It is difficult to establish a causal relationship, though, between financialisation and labour

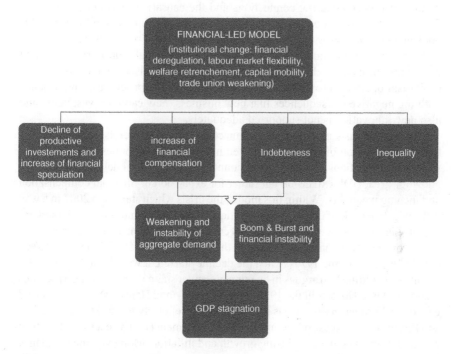

Figure I.4 The model – an interpretation.

flexibility. However, a stronger correlation between these two institutional forms is evident. Private (and also public) indebtedness in this context increased along with huge gains in the financial sectors, not only by top managers and owners but also by brokers and dependent workers of the financial sector (Peet, 2011).

A large number of financial tools were invented to finance consumption, to postpone payments, to extend credit, and to create extra consumption. Interestingly enough, evidence shows that while income inequality increased in the US and in other advanced economies dramatically in the last thirty years, consumption inequality did not increase, just because borrowing opportunities allowed for workers to consume using credit channels.

On the other hand, this kind of "credit consumption" in the context of the financial-ed model was needed by the economies; otherwise, the saving glut in Asia and the low-income capacity of domestic workers would leave firms with un-bought goods and services and would create aggregate demand imbalances. Workers could now afford to buy cheap goods from China and, thanks to financial innovation and cheap money, expensive houses, luxury cars, and other durable goods at home. Such a model of consumption is however unstable as the financial crash of 2007–08 showed. Paradoxically, the causes of the crisis lie within the financial-led model: it creates credit consumption, which causes both its development and its failure. In this context, the connections and the causation mechanisms between financialisation → inequality → financial crisis are of primary importance in this book and become one of the most important objectives of my analysis.

At the same time, huge allocation of assets for speculation purposes, credit consumption, easy credit for housing and all other tools invented in financial capitalism operate a crowding out effect with respect to productive investments, with the negative consequences that new business, new capital investments and also new innovation is not supported adequately.

The current crisis is intrinsically connected with the model itself. And also the (secular) stagnation of GDP, which lasted in advanced economies since the 1980s with some exceptions, is intrinsically connected with this model, which does not allow for great GDP expansion but rather for expansion of financial compensation and income inequality. Within this model, the crisis which started in 2007 in a way is the negative peak of the secular stagnation, while the normal is the GDP moderation, as Figure I.5 suggests, because 1980 economic growth in advanced economies was below 2 per cent on average. During the golden ages (1950–73), it was between 4 and 5 per cent. In the 1970s, when the decline started, it was about 2 per cent.[9]

Summers (2016: 2–3) argues in favour of a secular stagnation, recalling a previous theory of Alvin Hansen in the 1930s. In Summers' (and Hansen's) view, advanced economies' propensity to save is increasing and propensity to invest is decreasing, and this produces excess of savings (S) over investment (I). The excess of S in turn acts as a drag on demand, reducing growth and inflation. Moreover, the imbalance between S and I pulls down real interest rates (R) stimulating from one side credit consumption from another side alternative ways to save such as buying houses. When economic growth is somehow achieved, as in the US between 2003–07, this comes from dangerous levels of borrowing that translates excess of S into unsustainable levels of I in the housing sector, which produced the housing bubble. A similar leverage occurred also in other sectors and in other advanced economies, with the well-known phenomenon of credit consumption, which sustained, when occurred, economic growth for a while. Systemic risk increased, bubbles emerged and then burst, as Minsky (1986) predicted, and the financial crisis was a natural consequence when panic suppressed the euphoria (Kindelberg, 2005).

GDP growth per capita

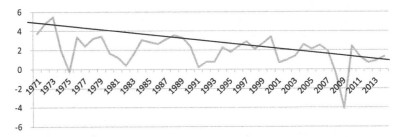

Figure I.5 Economic growth in OECD countries.
Source: Own elaboration on OECD data.

However, I argue, Summers' argument is not fully convincing. Moreover, the imbalance between S and I is not an irreversible tendency. First of all, excess of savings is a consequence of an excess of income going to the wealthiest part of the society, which has a lower propensity to consume – i.e. the capitalists, to use a classical or Kaldorian terminology (Kaldor, 1956, 1961). A smaller fraction of their income is spent, and a higher one is saved. Second, the imbalance is a consequence of lower wages for workers and in turn of lower consumption and demand by them. In this sense, greater savings levels have been driven by increase in inequality. Third, it is a consequence of a retrenchment tendency of public expenditure and welfare expenditure occurring among advanced economies in the last two decades and intensifying in the last years after the crisis, known as fiscal adjustments and austerity program (see also Hein 2015). Finally, from the investment side, the reduction of I has been driven by slower growth of labour force, and by the availability of cheap capital good which increases the value of saving.

Hence, in my view, the solution to the secular stagnation can be found from one side in the fiscal policy and government deficit rather than in monetary policy and quantitative easing, which would absorb the excess of S. From another side, income distribution policies and wage increases would compensate the negative drag on the aggregate demand operated by excess of S. Finally, a program of public investment would increase the stock value of I.

The secular stagnation is intimately related to policies and features that shaped the financial-led model. In the context of financial capitalism, perverse incentive schemes within financial institutions and extra bonuses for managers, "super-managers" and brokers contributed to excessive risk taking and to huge financial compensation. Increasing risky trades made fortunes for financial intermediaries, who were rewarded according to the short-term expansion generated by these risky activities rather than the long-term profitability of investments. Benchmarks became the delivery of exceedingly high expected quarterly earnings in terms of dividends and share prices for investors. This hugely increased financial pressure generated manias and reinvigorated the bubbles.

Moreover, in financial capitalism, the supposed benefits of globalisation in terms of economic growth compensated, allegedly, for the social costs of inequality, and therefore policymakers were not paying so much attention to inequality. Trickled down effects were supposed to occur and to deliver later benefits to all, including reducing inequality. Today, after the financial crisis, inequality is becoming more and more a structural problem to blame for the pain and for the causes of the financial and economic crisis. It is more and more considered a factor which created economic imbalances and which can therefore harm economic performance, too. I will develop my contribution in this direction: not only is inequality functional to capitalism, as in the Marxian tradition but also inequality is generated by *financial* capitalism, and at the same time is the cause of its imbalances and unsustainability. Inequality is one of the causes, if not the most important, of the financial crisis; one of the most important factors to blame for the current economic imbalances in rich countries; a structural economic disease which not only causes social costs and rises moral issues but also lowers economic performance.

There is no trade-off between economic growth and inequality, simply because with inequality there is no growth. This has been observed in the last three decades and today the IMF, which in the past advocated capital mobility (globalisation), financial deregulation (and financialisation), and structural adjustments (austerity), acknowledges the failure of its program supporting globalisation, financialisation and austerity. This program was not able to deliver economic growth. Instead it brought about the worsening of income inequality, as Figure I.6 suggests.

The secular stagnation, which has been characterizing advanced economies in the last two to three decades, is also the result of this policy triangle suggested by IMF and internationalized after the Chile economic boom. As Ostry *et al.* (p. 39) states:

> The benefits in terms of increased growth seems fairly difficult to establish when looking at a broad group of countries. The costs in terms of increased inequality are prominent. Such costs epitomize the trade-off between the growth and equity effects of some aspects of the neoliberal agenda. Increased inequality in turn hurts the level and sustainability of growth.

More in detail, with reference to the austerity policies, Ostry *et al.* (2016) states that a consolidation of 1 percentage point of GDP worsens the Gini index by 1.5 per cent within five years. The effects of capital inflows on inequality are also very important: an increase of capital mobility of 1 per cent of GDP bring about a worsening in the Gini of 3 per cent over the next five years.

Therefore, the conclusion is that the neoliberal policies, so ineffective in delivering growth, cause a worsening of inequality. The famous trade-off theory (going back to Kuznets) according to which the cost to have more growth would be a greater inequality is completely invalidated. Instead, the outcome is the worse in both of these dimensions.

Figure I.6 The IMF policy triangle for secular stagnation and inequality.

Econometric results and empirical evidences of this book clearly show these processes. The econometric exercises, and most of the empirical evidence runs on a panel from 1980 up to today, on a group of thirty-four rich countries belonging to OECD, confirm my hypothesis: the increase of inequality in the last two to three decades seems to be caused by an increase of financialisation, an increase of labour flexibility, the weakening of trade unions, and the retrenchment of welfare states, in other words to the change of the economic model, which represents also the basis over which the so-called "secular stagnation" manifested.

Notes

1 Credit Suisse, Global Wealth Report 2015.
2 An extensive definition of wealth, by Piketty (2014) is any asset that can be traded and that generates a financial return in a society at a given moment in time, as well as monopoly rights over ideas (patents) and media (copyright), and houses and properties. Piketty's proxy for the total capital of the society uses this wide definition of wealth.
3 For instance, very often "workers" in the financial sector are also compensated with stock options, shares and other assets rather than in cash salary. As well as it happens that sometimes workers are self-employed or are independent workers, in which cases their remunerations formally are not a salary but a profit.
4 The reduction of wage share, or more generally the (non)constancy of factor shares, is an important theoretical aspect, which I will discuss extensively in the next chapter.
5 "Adjusted" wage share considers also in the share self-employment (ILO projections), contrary to the "unadjusted" wage share.
6 Brazil, Russia, India and China.
7 This was well documented by Piketty (2014) and Saez (2013). Striking it richer. The evolution of top income in the United States. University of Berkley, mimeo.
8 Cynamon and Fazzari (2013) found that in particular after the 2007–08 financial crisis, in the US, the top 5 per cent spent a smaller share of income and the following stagnant recovery would be explained by the demand drag on the economy.
9 The term "secular stagnation" is different from the term "great moderation", which indicates the drop in price volatility, inflation and the reduction of variation in the GDP business cycle that occurred in the US and in most advanced economies since the 1980s. In contrast with the previous period (1950–73), known as the golden age, the great moderation is characterized by supply-side policies, trickled down policies, debt-led growth, self-regulating market, globalisation and inequality. In the golden age, those characteristics were contrasted respectively by demand-side policies, full employment policies, wage-led growth, strong financial regulation, balanced trade, shared productivity gains and prosperity.

Part I

Definitions, approaches and origins of income inequality

1 Theories, methods and varieties of inequality

The social origins of inequality

The very foundation of the problem of inequality is the concept of social welfare. According to the utilitarian approach, social welfare is the sum of individual welfare. Social welfare improvements are not possible (or would not be "Pareto efficient") by re-distributing resources from one individual to another, because a "Pareto" improvement is a situation in which it is impossible to make someone better off without making someone else worse off. On the other hand, an egalitarian approach would consider re-distribution of resources to avoid the situation where an individual could become richer by taking advantage of the fact that the other is in poor health or in poor education or is handicapped (Sen, 1973). In this latter approach, the application of the Rawls' criterion would be the best policy; the aim is not individual welfare but the level of welfare in the society. If one individual (A) has a lower level of welfare than another (B), and if B can be made better off by re-distributing resources from A, then the Rawls' criterion of justice requires that B should have sufficiently more income to make B's utility equal to A's. In Rawlsian thinking, inequalities have to be adjusted by following two principles: (1) offices and positions must be open to everyone under conditions of *fair equality of opportunity*, and (2) they have to be of greatest benefits for the least-advantaged members of the society (Rawls, 1971: 303). To be applied, these criteria require more than meritocracy. 'Fair equality of opportunity' requires not only that positions are distributed on the basis of merit but also that all have equal opportunity, in terms of education, health, etc. to acquire those skills on the basis of which merit is assessed. The application of these principles would, in the end, produce much greater advantages for the society as a whole.

Another way to look at the problem of inequality is through social peace and cohesion. Sen (1973) saw inequality as strictly linked to the concept of rebellion, and indeed the two phenomena are linked in both ways. Inequality causes rebellion, but it may happen that income inequality may increase after a rebellion where it brings power to a specific apparatus or a nomenclature or a social class; this has happened many times in history when, for instance, rebellions were led by army generals or by elites of nobles. In several transition economies, inequality increased after a "rebellion" that brought to power oligarchs. In particular, in the former Soviet Union, inequality increased dramatically after the 1991 August Coup, which deposed Soviet president Mikhail Gorbachev and dissolved the URSS. In some African countries, such as Congo and Sudan, the same happened: rebellions, carried out by generals and warlords, deposed previous authoritarian or less authoritarian regimes, but such a change brought about an increase in inequality. Nowadays, economists try to capture a causality nexus (inequality → rebellion → inequality) through the use of some modern governance indicators such as political stability. The link between political stability and inequality is demonstrated in numerous empirical works such as Alesina and Perrotti (1996) and Easterly (2001), where it emerges that income inequality increases during political instability.

An interesting explanation of inequality in the Americas is put forward by Sokoloff and Engerman (2000), who, in order to explain inequality in wealth, human capital and political power, suggest an institutional explanation, historically founded, which lies in the initial roots of the factors of endowment of the respective colonies. In general, political institutions set up by the Spaniards and Portuguese in Latin America were different from the ones set up by the British in North America. Moreover, the latter sent educated people and skilled work forces, along with the lords, to the New World, and these started to build their own future; while the Spaniards and the Portugueses did not encourage massive migration from the motherland but sent landlords who basically exploited slaves from Africa.

One of the first cross-country works on inequality was made by Kuznets (1955). He showed that in the early stage of economic growth income tends to be unequally distributed among individuals. In the early stage of a growth process, over time, the distribution of income worsens. In the later stages, national income starts to be more equally distributed. Hence, inequality declines in the end, after the country has accomplished the U-shaped trajectory. Several later empirical studies confirmed this relationship (Chenery and Syrquin, 1975; Ahluwalia, 1976). The reason for such a relationship was attributed to structural changes, which at the beginning of the "transition" brought about job losses and inequalities.

Nevertheless, the implicit trade-off behind the Kuznets' curve (economic growth/ inequality) and the idea that an increase in inequality is sometimes necessary for a rapid growth has been often criticized (Atkinson, 1999). Milanovic (1994) puts forward n alternative hypothesis to explain why income inequality differs among countries; he shows that inequality decreases in richer societies because social attitudes towards inequality change as those societies get richer, and inequality is less tolerated. Birdsall and Sabot (1994) showed, contrary to the Kuznets' hypothesis, that inequality may be a constraint for growth and, if inequality is lowered, then a country could have a GDP per capita 8.2 per cent higher than a country with income inequality 1 standard deviation higher.

Voitchovsky (2005: 273) suggests a similar hypothesis, however, stressing *the shape* of the distribution and suggests that inequality at the top end of the distribution is positively associated with growth, while inequality lower down the distribution is negatively related to subsequent growth. Moreover, empirical evidence in cross-countries analysis, from Latin American to East Asian Countries, pose the question why Latin America has high inequality and low growth and, on the contrary, why East Asia has high growth and low inequality. Birdsall and Sabot (1994) suggest that it is a matter of policies and social attitude towards inequality. In Latin America, dictators, generals and the ruling classes acted, for long time after World War II, with little respect for the poorest part of their society, implementing fiscal and trade policies that provided little benefits to the poor. On the contrary, in East Asia, the ruling classes were more aware of social needs and implemented policies such as land reforms, public housing, public investments in rural infrastructures and public education, which had a positive effect on both growth and income distribution; better educated people can get a better job and earn more; public investment in the rural sector can bring farmer productivity and income higher; public housing and other social services can increase the purchasing power of people; and so forth.

Varieties of (economic) inequality

The concept of inequality, which in most cases interest economists, is the inequality of opportunity and the inequality of outcome. Roughly speaking, the first type of inequality has to do with the "external circumstances", which are beyond the personal control of individuals and allow for a disadvantage of an individual with respect to another (Atkinson, 2015). They concern family background, social context, and similar. The inequality of outcome concerns instead "internal circumstances" of an individual, such as efforts, skills and similar and for which the individual is (supposedly) responsible.

Neoclassical economics in general neglect economic inequality since it is considered neutral with respect to economic performance. First of all, because neoclassical models analyse (people) compensation in terms of factor of production compensations so that incomes go to factor labour and factor capital according to their shares (which is supposed to be constant in the long run)[1] and to their prices, which is supposed to be affected by the demand and supply, hence by "external" forces. Thus, income distribution is "functional" to the trend and forces of the economy so that if for some reasons demand of capital increase, its prices (profits) go up while labour demand decrease and wages decrease; if demand of capital decreases, profits decreases and wages increase. Labour and capital are supposed to be substitute and their prices flexible so that market forces (demand and supply) allow for continuous adjustment and equilibria with full utilization of resources (no unemployment).[2] If, however, neoclassical economics were to consider between persons' compensations rather than merely factor of production compensation, the whole picture would change. Inequality would immediately appear not only between shares (of labour and capital) but also within shares (among workers, among people and within the society). In this way, also the utilitarian approach, at the basis of the neoclassical mechanism of functional distribution, would be questioned since the interpersonal sum of income (among some bottom group of the society) would be disadvantageous for some groups with respect to others, although the total sum of the income would be the same in the society.

Some economists (Deaton, 2013), however, are interested in the inequality of opportunity as they consider this morally and socially wrong. Other economists, in particular in the last years, further call the attention on the inequality of outcome and the possible remedies against that (Atkinson, 2015; Piketty, 2014). There is a strong justification for this purpose, which is also the justification of this book and its main guide.

First of all, people's lives are not only affected (ex-ante) by family and social context but also (during job and school) by luck, accidents and similar things that would justify ex-post adjustments for both equity and macroeconomic reasons (I shall come back on the macroeconomic reasons later).

Second, rewards for some works and professions can be over (or under) priced and therefore over (or under) compensated by some political forces that act in a particular moment and context so that inequality among people would increase unjustifiably, beyond the traditional neoclassical argument of marginal productivity. This is not only a matter of imperfect competition, as it occurs with mark-up in some sectors, but it is crucially due to the specific economic model and the political paradigm that would allow for a biased income distribution in favour of a particular lobby and of a specific economic sector. This is the case of the financial sector which, within the financial capitalism model, gets all the advantages of economic growth beyond marginal productivity justification (at least in the long run). This is also the main focus of this book, so we shall come back to this central issue.

Third, as Atkinson (2015) argued inequality of outcome crucially influences future inequality of opportunity, so that individuals and families, which are allowed by the already biased and unjust circumstances listed above to gain extra compensation and to become richer, will affect future initial conditions of their children with greater advantages with respect to other children, so that Atkinson concludes, "If we are concerned about inequality of opportunity tomorrow, we need to be concerned about inequality of outcome today" (Atkinson, 2015: 11).

Fourth, the relevance of power and of politics that is crucially shaping the dimension of inequality through formal rules, power and institutions set the "rules of the game", which affect income distribution such as minimum wage, welfare support, or rule concerning (de)regulation for specific sectors, such as finance, anti-monopoly rules, and or support for specific sectors, such as export-oriented sectors and agriculture subsidies.

Economic inequality is usually defined in terms of income inequality and it is captured by differences in incomes, in factor compensations, wages, and money. However, inequality is much more than that. It includes inequality of access to resources, inequality in education, social inequality, class inequality, political inequality, etc. (see De Muro, 2016). These types of inequality, contrary to income inequality, are difficult to measure, so economists usually prefer to deal with the latter. However, very often, at the basis of income inequality, there is the inequality exactly of those types listed above (Bastia, 2013). Similarly, following the Fraser (1995; 2005) analysis, inequality is a combination of three material and immaterial dimensions in the context of globalisation; these dimensions are as follows:

1   Representation (political dimension)
2   Redistribution (economic dimension)
3   Recognition (cultural dimension)

In the first dimension, misrepresentation is unjust, and it is a source of inequality that brings about power inequality and lack of participation in the decision-making process. Another source of inequality is obviously economic inequality (i.e. income inequality) which has to do with lack of redistribution and therefore brings about income differentials and income inequality. This is the dimension on which this book is focused, and I will deal mostly with this type of inequality. Last but not least, the cultural dimension of income inequality has to do with recognition of diversities and equal rights, to different social categories, with respect to religion, race, gender, ethnicity, etc.

All of these three categories of inequality may act in the sense to generally restrict access to resources, discriminating among people, excluding particular groups, creating differences from the beginning, and lack of equal opportunities, generating and consolidating persistent socioeconomic differences which will be crystalized and perpetuated in future.

Considering the second dimension, redistribution, since the new model of financial capitalism took place, and in particular in the last twenty to thirty years when globalisation and financialisation intensified, restrictions to education, public goods such as health, infrastructure, and welfare in general increased. This may have worsened access to resources for goods, which are now market-ised, since the poorer parts of the society may not afford market prices. Hence, equal opportunities squeezed, and inequality increased.

Probably not the same can be said as far as political and cultural inequality are concerned. After the Second World War, in fact, at global level, political rights and civil liberties expanded. People participation in politics may have increased, and also cultural diversity is more tolerated. This does not mean that political equality and cultural equality are reached. Far from that. However, at a global level, cultural recognition probably improved and political representation as well. Nevertheless, as far as we focus on the economic dimension of inequality, the trend of income inequality in the last two to three decades was negative, and it increased sharply.

Capital accumulation and inequality in capitalism: a long-term perspective

Inequality is not a new phenomenon at all. From Marx, the literature on inequality has been abundant. Some scholars argue that it is an intrinsic phenomenon of capitalism. The last book of Piketty (2014) follows this line. However, he argues that policies and institutions (and wars) can decrease the tendency of capital accumulation, exploitation and uneven development, which create inequality. The notorious tendency law described by Piketty as a key determinant of income inequality is the following:

$$r > g$$

where r is the rate of remuneration of capital and g is the rate of growth of the economy. If the first is, over a very long run, constantly higher than the second, then income inequality will increase. Institutions, welfare states, taxes and pro-labour policies, as the ones implemented between 1945 and 1975 in most advanced economies, contribute to reduce or to keep lower inequality. Similarly, the wars, since they destroy capital accumulation, have the effects to reduce income inequality, as it has happened between 1914 and 1945. The argument of Piketty overcame the Kuznets' (1955) theory according to which inequality increases in the first phase of capital expansion and GDP growth, and decreases in the second phase when the country reaches a higher level of GDP. Kuznets' argument was based on data that referred to the period between the end of the nineteenth century and the end of the Second World War in the US (moreover, as Kuznets recognized, much of that theory was based on speculation rather than on empirical observed findings). Kuznets noticed that at the end of the period, when the US became richer, inequality was decreasing. The argument Piketty puts forward is completely different, so that against the famous reverse U-shaped Kuznets' curve, he proposed a horizontal S-shaped curve, which indicates that inequality between the nineteenth and twentieth centuries first increased then decreased between 1914 and 1975 for the above explained reasons, and then, after 1975, increased again. Similarly, Milanovic (2016) opposes the Kuznets' curve, a so-called "Kuznets' waves" indicating that inequality rises, falls and then rises again endlessly.

Both authors, Kuznets and Piketty, spoke about income inequality within countries. To this argument, we will contribute stating that inequality increases within countries, but during the same time inequality between countries can decreases. In this latter case, we would speak about global inequality, or differences between GDP per capita among countries, in other words, income divergences. Global inequality has been explored recently by Bourguignon and Morrison (2002); Baten *et al.* (2010); Milanovic (2011), and Milanovic (2016) among the others. The very broad and interesting study of Milanovic (2016) shows that while income inequality increased in advanced economies, global income inequality (differences among countries) decreased in the last years, particularly since 2000. However, Milanovic (2016) argues, that might not continue if China's income per head rises above the global average, and if technological progress does not advance in emerging and developing countries.

A much broader view of the accumulation process is offered by Arrighi (1994) and Braudel (1982). Following these two authors, each accumulation cycle, at the end of its period (which corresponds also to its peak) is characterized by a phase of financialisation where financial capitals, in liquidity means, is abundant and dominating the accumulation phase. This phenomenon occurred at the end of the sixteenth century during the Northern Italian hegemony, where the oligarchy of the Genoese capitalism withdrew from commerce, entered the financial business and supported the Spanish expansion. A similar phenomenon occurred also at the end of the hegemony of Holland, in the middle of the seventeenth century, when the Dutch entered the financial business and became the bankers of Europe. This tendency of a transformation from an industrial capitalism towards a financial capitalism was confirmed during the crisis of 1873–96 when the British capitalism, at the end of the fantastic industrial momentum entered the financial phase. Finally, this transformation has been occurring for the past three decades, at least in the US, the hegemonic country of the fourth cycle of capitalism on the Braudel and Arrighi classifications.

The main point here is that at the end of each cycle of the capital accumulation, returns of the productive expansion starts to declines because of the increased competition between capitalists. Hence, capitals become more flexible and very liquid so as to be employed in the financial sector and speculation. Financial expansion starts and allows for another great expansion of returns. However, as Arrighi (1994) stated, this is already signalling a crisis: the process of capital accumulation is at the end, and entering the financial expansion represents its last momentum. It is the sign of the beginning of the crisis, the alarm.

A closer look at Table 1.1 concerning phase of development and inequality will clarify this argument.

Our argument here is that over a very long run, global (between) inequality and national (within) inequality may have opposite direction depending on the main factors driving economic growth. When the main driver of economic growth in the central geographical area of development (the core) is technology and in particular means of transport like large ships connecting distant countries and continents, so that the periphery accumulates gaps against the core, then inequality becomes mainly global inequality (B in Table 1.1), forces of divergences take place with increasing differentials in terms of GDP per capita among countries. Inequality increases mainly between countries. This is because technological gaps are prevailing and take time to be filled. Leader countries enjoy higher income than followers because productivity advantages accumulate. In the meantime, followers have to build both the technological capacity and also the social capability – i.e. institutions and organisations to emulate leaders (Abramowitz, 1986). During this process, income in the following economies increase at a slower pace so that differences with the leaders increase (Kuznets, 1965). The advantages of technology are distributed better within the leader country and income of all increase. A similar process takes place in the follower countries, which try to catch.

When, on the contrary, the main drivers of economic growth in the core countries are labour, skills, human capital and competences, after a wave of innovation which brought about a process of technological accumulation, then inequality

Table 1.1 Types of inequality and accumulation, a historical perspective

Types of inequality between (B) vs. within (B)	Inequality	Period/ cycle of accumulation	Core	Rival incumbent	Main driver of growth	Main/decisive events	Regime of capital accumulation: main sector	International regime
B	higher	1400–1600	Northern Italy: city-states of: Venice, Florence, Genoa and (later) Spain	Spain/ Holland / Portugal/ France	Technology/ means of transport/ large ship	Venetian trade and conquer/ Florentine banking invention/ Genoese financial intermediaries to Spain	Money and trade	Protectionism
W	lower	1400–1600	Northern Italy: city-state of: Venice, Florence, Genoa and Spain		Technology/ means of transport/ large ship		Money and finance	Protectionism
B	higher	1600–1750	Holland	UK / France	Technology/ means of transport/ large ship	1648: Westfaila Pax	Commerce and trade	Protectionism
W	lower	1600–1750	Holland		Technology/ means of transport/ large ship		Commerce and trade	Protectionism

B	lower	1750–1900	UK	France	Labour	30-year war/industrial revolution	Industry, trade and finance	Openness, international trade
W	higher	1750–1900	UK		Labour		Industry, trade and finance	Openness, international trade
B	higher	1900–1970	US		Technology	Financial crisis 1870/WWI and WWII	Advanced industry	Protectionism
W	lower	1900–1970	US	Germany	Technology		Advanced industry	Protectionism
B	lower	1970–2050	US		Labour/Skills	Oil shock 1970s/financial boom	Finance	Openness, globalisation financialisation
W	higher	1970–2050	US		Labour/Skills		Finance	Openness, globalisation financialisation

Source: Own elaboration.

becomes mainly within countries inequality (W in Table 1.1), with increasing polarization between rich and poor in the countries. In other words, inequality is increasing mainly within countries in this phase. This is because labour, skills and human capital allow for larger degrees of labour exploitation and therefore for faster and larger differences in the functional income distribution between profits and wages. This process occurs both in leader and in follower countries.

However, inequality within countries, shaped by the intensive use of labour, can be politically and institutional determined through the "rules of the games", as I stated above, which set the institutions on the basis of which income distribution is regulated. Obviously in this context, income distribution is not perceived to be "functional" as in the neoclassical mechanism between the factor of production according to the market forces of demand and supply.

The sub-example of the US (a leader country) and of Western Europe (as follower) is very interesting and reflects this approach. The US and Western Europe can be considered the core countries with respect to the rest of the world. Between 1950 and 1975 (a sub-period included in the US hegemony period of 1900–present), an important wave of innovation allowed the US economy to grow and to accumulate technological gaps. Technical progress was the main driver of economic growth both in the US and to some extent also in Western Europe (with some delay). Within countries (in the US and in Europe), income increased for all and inequality decreased. On the contrary, between countries differences, at a global level, increased faster. In the second period, 1975–present, skills, labour and human capital are the main drivers of growth, both in the US (leader) and in Western Europe (follower). In this period, within countries income differences (in the US and in Europe) increased faster and between countries differences, at global level, increased slower or reduced.

Figure 1.1 represents this situation at a global level, reporting world data from 1900 to 2010 concerning average income and income dispersion (standard deviation among countries). It appears clearly that between 1950 and 1975, income dispersion (which is a proxy for *between* countries inequality) is higher than average income. In the second phase (1975–2010), there is a convergence in the sense that income dispersion (*between* countries inequality) decreases towards average income, and *within* countries inequality increased. In the last ten years (2000–10), this process intensifies even more in fact *within* countries inequality increased much more than between countries inequality. This is very consistent with the recent results of Milanovic (2016). Thus, within countries income inequality reaches similar levels than the ones before the Second World War (1900–1945).

With reference to the last cycle of modern capitalistic accumulation, under the US hegemony, in this book we focus on the period that starts with the financial expansion during the 1970s in the core of the process of accumulation – i.e. the US – and later in the capitalistic archipelago connected with the US – i.e. Europe, Canada, Australia, New Zealand and Japan, or more generally the OECD countries.

The global financial expansion of the last thirty years or so is neither a new stage of world capitalism nor the forerunner of a coming hegemony of global

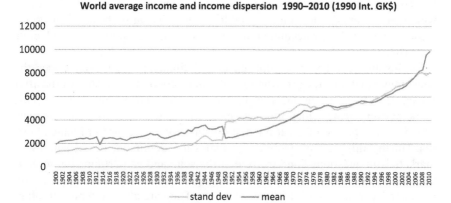

Figure 1.1 World income and disparities.
Source: Own elaboration on Maddison database.

markets. Rather, it is the clearest sign that we are in the middle of a hegemonic crisis. As such, the expansion can be considered a temporary phenomenon that will end more or less catastrophically, in depending on how the crisis will be addressed by the declining hegemonic power (i.e. the US). The only question that remains open in this regard is not whether the present global dominance of financial markets collapses but rather how soon and how catastrophically it collapses (Arrighi *et al.*, 2003).

The current global economic and financial crisis is probably one of the last momentums of the financial expansion, started in the 1970s. This should anticipate the passage to another cycle and to another hegemonic power. Arrighi, in his new edition of the Long XIX century (2009), foresees the increasing role of China and the possibility of China – that is the second largest economy after the United States – to become the engine of a new accumulation cycle which would focus on East Asia, with China being its core. Yet as Pianta (2014) observed in his presentation of the Italian version of the new edition of Arrighi's book, the transition towards China is complicated at least by two reasons.

*   Because of the intrinsic problems of the Chinese economy such as the limited role (although potentially huge) of its internal market so that China continues to export large amounts of goods and capital to the declining country – the United States.
*   The huge US military power.

No signs show that the economic rise of China can make a country hegemonic, able to replace the US at the center of a new world order. As Arrighi (2014) argues, the hegemonic transition appears complicated, but, with the rise of the whole East Asia, a scenario of rebalancing of power and wealth between the regions of the world could occur. In this context, an important role will be played also by collective actions, social movements and democratic forces, which are factors that are almost completely nonexistent in the past transitions towards new cycles of accumulation at the end of each period of productive expansion.

In this book, I focus on this period of financial expansion, under the hegemony of US and the growing role of Asian economies, notably China after Japan. The Arrighi long-term argument fits also with our main focus. This is the period during which productive expansion was substituted by finance. This is also a period of great financial instability and recurrent financial crises. During this period, neoliberal policies are dominant, the hegemony of markets is unquestioned and the role of the state and its participation to market economy is diminishing. In contrast, big corporations, multinationals, are often stronger than states and governments. They are able to impose to other states/governments what in the past they were not able to impose unless by wars, such as limitation of sovereignty in economic and financial issues, free trade zones, free taxes zones, free movement of capitals, labour rights and trade unions limitations, social cuts in social dimensions to increase the size of markets and privatization of public assets in crucial and strategic sectors such as infrastructure, water, and communication to increase their power vis-à-vis the states.

Forces driving inequality: financialisation, globalisation and lack of appropriate policies

After the Second World War, economic growth in most advanced economies occurred under the Keynesian compromise or paradigm of economic policy, which allowed not only for the construction of an important welfare state to provide indirect wages and consumption capability to nearly everybody, but it also allowed to distribute equally productivity gains between workers and firms. Therefore, wage earners increased their income steadily at least until the mid-1970s. The wage share increased and consumption fuelled the positive dynamics of the aggregate demand. At the same time productive investments, both public and private, accompanied this positive trend and supported the demand. Economic growth occurred and demand management policies guaranteed a steady development. Labour productivity was driven, following the Kaldor-Verdoorn approach, by the expansion of aggregate demand, which crated positive spillover and economies of scales.

Since the end of the 1970s, a new paradigm of economic policy, financial capitalism, has emerged or rather was shaped in policy and institutional terms, first in the UK and the US and later in other advanced economies as we stated earlier. The political and economic roots of the financialisation process that brought about a new financial-led growth regime, along with the process of globalisation, can be found in the 1970s. However, they were openly manifested politically in the 1980s. The financial sector has been an early and eager promoter of deregulation in the

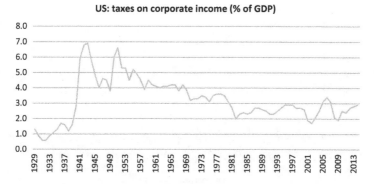

Figure 1.2 Tax corporations in the US.
Source: FREED database.

1980s in the UK and in the US under the Thatcher and Reagan administrations (Petit, 2009; Boyer, 2000), respectively, which Jessop (2002) identifies as transition phases to the post-Fordist financial-led regime. Jessop (2002) argues that new accumulation strategies emerged during that period, a new paradigm of political economy. This new paradigm involved multinational firms, international financial discipline, a more authoritarian state, and a form of popular capitalism. The previous Fordist strategy was replaced by an internationally oriented and financially aggressive strategy, deregulated and concentrated dually on Wall Street and in the City of London.

The main objective of this new paradigm was to restore the profit rate, which did not increase between 1945 and 1975. Financialisation and globalisation were identified as two pillars through which (global) capitalism could return to its original idea, freed from the string imposed by the Keynesian compromise. Financial expansion and globalisation shaped the model of financial capitalism in which states and governments are obliged to fit, to create institutions, to implement policies, to compete with each other through tax competition, attraction of capitals, and social dumping, and to deregulate labour markets and compress labour through labour flexibility.

However, a decline of labour productivity occurred in most advanced economies and among the Greatest economies (G/7) as Figure 1.3 suggests. Financialisation and globalisation did not help to return to the labour productivity growth rate which occurred before the 1970s. Nevertheless, as it was stated, allowed for a recovery of profit rate and financial compensation, which in turn led to an increase in inequality.

Reaganomics and Thatcherism were strategies that aimed to restructure the accumulation system through the deregulation of the financial system (Peck and Tickell, 1992) at the expense of the social compromise realized after the Second World War. Moreover, after the fall of the Soviet Union, Alan Greenspan, who

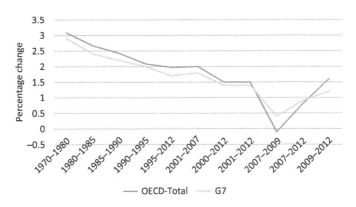

Figure 1.3 Labour productivity per hour.
Source: OECD database.

rose to oversee the US Federal Reserve during the Reagan administration, believed that the world economy could expand greatly through the globalisation of the financial sector (Greenspan, 2007).

In this context, the profit rate, which constantly fell after the Second World War, arrested its decline and started to recover. Figure 1.4 shows a recovery of profit both at world level and in the most advanced economies (in the so-called G7) since the 1980s, in coincidence with the processes of financialisation and globalisation. This is consistent with Arrighi's argument (1994) explained in the previous section, who identifies an alarm for investors in the 1970s mainly due to the decline of profit rate in the manufacturing industrial sector. The deregulation of finance, the expansion of global capital and capital mobility, the process of globalisation and market integration, the change of labour-capital relations (in favour of the capital) allow for an arrest of the decline of the profit rate and a recovery in the profit rate and in particular allow for an increase of dividends and shareholders' payments in the financial sector (see also Figure A1 in the appendix).

Finance allows for both speculation and indebtedness. Financial investments look more lucrative for investors, and households are pushed more and more towards private indebtedness and credit consumption because their income constraints increase consistently in a period of wage stagnation. The dramatic increase of labour flexibility occurring in the age of financial capitalism is functional to the idea of "downsize and distribute", which allows for an expansion of financialisation and the implementation of remuneration schemes for managers based on the firm's short-term performance and on shareholders' objectives, interested uniquely on the maximization of dividends. Corporate managers in advanced economies are increasingly abandoning the pursuit of "new ways to generate productivity gains on the basis of retain and reinvest" and are capitulating "to

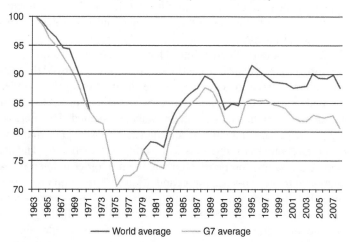

Figure 1.4 World profits.
Source: Michael Roberts, 2015 (https://thenextrecession.wordpress.com).[3]

the new competitive environment through corporate downsizing" (Lazonick and O'Sullivan, 2000).

The example of the US economy, as shown in Figure 1.5, is a paramount example.

The link between globalisation and inequality has been largely explored in the literature since the Stolper and Samuelson theorem, according to which market integration increases inequality and vulnerability as increased international trade raises the incomes of the owners of abundant factors and reduces the incomes of the owners of scarce factors (Stolper and Samuelson, 1941). Since advanced

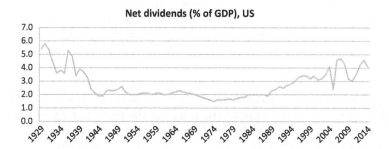

Figure 1.5 Dividends in the US.
Source: FREED database.

industrial countries are more capital-intensive economies and abundant in skilled labour, trade is expected to be beneficial for skilled labour and detrimental to unskilled labour, thus increasing income inequality. For labour-intensive economies, which is typically the case of developing countries, trade is expected to increase regional disparities.

Globalisation and global finance introduced aggressive outsourcing practices and foreign direct investment (FDI) outflows, which has improved the bargaining position of capital relative to labour in higher-income countries. Trade unions lost power, and labour market regulations, such as labour protection against firing, unemployment benefits, and minimum wage, weakened. The increase of the bargaining power of capital against labour had as a consequence that it was easier for capital to obtain tax reductions and welfare retrenchment. The states are willing to embark on tax competition among them in order to keep investments and production at home. This has direct and negative impact on unskilled labour and income distribution, which worsens without welfare support and social institutions. Income inequality increased because labour, which is the most important production factor for income, is seen by the supply-side approach as a cost to be compressed rather than as a fundamental part of aggregate demand to be expanded.

Figure 1.6 suggests a mechanism of cumulative causation, which led to the increase of income inequality and mass unemployment. Following the approach of Arrighi (1994) described earlier, the process starts with the decline of profit rate and of labour productivity in advanced economies in the manufacturing sector. The reactions of firms (and of policy) to those declines developed through two main pillars: the financialisation of the economy and the intensification of globalisation. The first represents to some extent a refuge sector for firms – the finance – in order to invest their liquidity and get higher returns than in the manufacturing sector. The second, globalisation, was the necessary appendix of financialisation. In fact, the process of financialisation was favoured by international openness, market integration and capital mobility, which has shaped the process of globalisation since the end of the 1980s.

Hence, while globalisation and financialisation allowed the declining path of the profit rate to restore, their expansion determined also the increase of income inequality. To be more precise, the restoring of profit rate occurred at the expenses of the squeeze of wage share. The reduction of wage share in advanced economies occurred prevalently through two channels: financialisation and globalisation, which operate in the following directions:

- Financialisation → wage share decline: through the downsizing of employment level, the intensive use of labour, the pursuit of objectives such as distribution of higher dividends to shareholders, and the distribution of higher payoffs in the finance sector, which caused the worsening income inequality.
- Globalisation → wage share decline: capital mobility increased the power relation of capital vis-à-vis labour. Trade unions lost their influence in

bargaining higher wages, higher welfare, and better working conditions. Global tax competition (to attract capital) increased among countries and social policies decreased as well as public expenditure. Unemployment increased and semi-employment (precarious jobs) increased. Weaker institutions in the labour market and labour flexibility allowed continuous adjustment of labour to capital through supply-side policies. Therefore, income inequality increased.

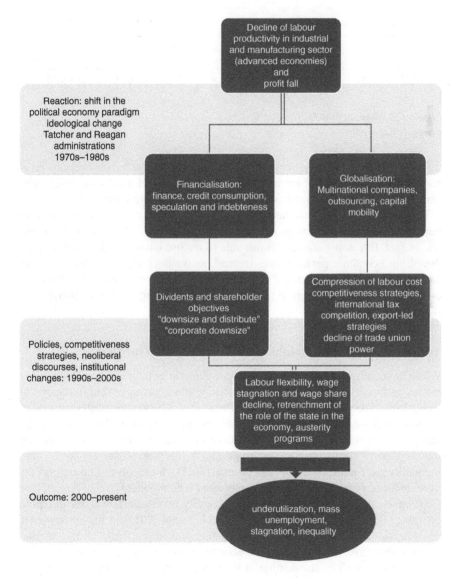

Figure 1.6 Forces driving inequality.

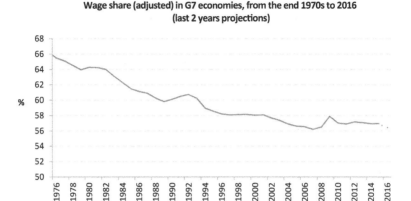

Figure 1.7 Wage share in G7 (on average).
Source: Ameco database.

The interaction of the two channels allowed for a decline in consumption level and in worker income, which became instable and relied mostly on credit consumption. Aggregate demand declined as well as GDP dynamics.

Hence, consequences are negative not only in terms of income distribution but also in terms of unemployment, underutilization and above all GDP dynamics. In fact, this new paradigm is not able to restore labour productivity or produce high economic performance. Instead, as we have argued before, it is the basis for what has been defined as the secular stagnation (Summers, 2016) – in other words, an economic decline along with a worsening of income distribution (Franzini, 2016).

Technological progress, labour productivity and inequality

While financialisation and globalisation are directly or indirectly involved in our model, as forces driving inequality, something more has to be said in regards to technological progress. According to Allison *et al.* (2014) major determinants of growing income inequality within countries appear to be skilled-biased technological change (SBTC) and the growth of incomes of workers in the financial industry, particularly among executives. Other recent explanations for income inequality were put forward by Van Reenen (2011) who seems to find support for trade-induced technological change associated with inequality.

However, the SBTC explanation for inequality is very controversial and quite complex (Pianta and Tancioni, 2008). Stockhammer (2015) in his econometric analysis shows that the technological change had little effects on the decline of wage share over GDP in advanced economies in the last three decades, which was instead caused by the decline of the bargaining power of trade union. The reduction of wage share consecutively contributed to the increase of income inequality rather than the SBTC. Similarly, Galbraith (2012) who, in his recent book, stresses inequality as a cause of the crisis, argues that inequality reflects the concentration of wealth at the very top of the distribution, quite independently from the SBTC. These contributions, which are very relevant for this study, have stressed the link between credit availability (as a consequence of increasing inequality) and financial crises (see for instance Perugini *et al.*, 2015) and inequality as the cause for the current financial crisis (Stockhammer, 2015; Galbraith, 2012).

Hence, it seems that the technological explanation for inequality has little empirical evidence. What really matters, as far as this relation is concerned, is the governance of the technological progress and the institutions that are at the basis for the payoff of its improvement. First of all, evidence among countries is not consistent at all: Scandinavian and other North European countries proved that technological progress is compatible with equity if institutions and appropriate policies are implemented. Similar conclusions are reached by Bogliacino and Lucchese (2015), who analyse the East and West Germany reunification in order to see whether the supply of skills could lead to inequality, and find no evidence on that. Moreover, technological change (and its consequences) can be state-guided as Mazzucato (2013) showed for the case of the US, where every major technological change in recent years traces most of its funding back to the state. Finally, Piketty (2014) and Palma (2009) show that most of income inequality can be attributed to the top 1 per cent of wage earners, particularly within the financial sector, and this is difficult to explain in combination with the SBTC argument. In fact, as Atkinson stated (2015: 3), "Technological progress is not a force of nature but reflects social and economic decisions".

If, however, the SBTC argument is not relevant to explain income inequality within countries, in our approach, the technological dimension is very relevant to explain inequality between countries, as we explained with the help of Table 1.1. When technology and/or means of transportation are the main drivers of economic growth, then inequality is increasing mainly between countries. When the main drivers of economic growth are labour, skills, human competences, then inequality is increasing mainly within countries.

Technological progress remains the main driver of labour productivity, λ, which shapes in turn also economic growth, gY. The simple relation can be captured by the following equation:

$$gY = L * \lambda$$

where L stands for Labour. In turn, λ is defined as Y/hL – i.e. the output divided by the labour input per hours, h (in order to have the hourly labour productivity).

Neoclassical economics attribute differences in wages to differences in labour productivity so that higher labour productivity corresponds to higher wages. Hence, there is a sort of "justified" inequality coming from work effort and labour productivity. This type of inequality is even functional to economic growth since it is the basis, neoclassicals argue, of incentives for work effort. However, heterodox economists argue that institutions, capital-labour relation, power relations, industrial relations, politics, norms and laws stands above technical coefficients of distribution, and determine levels and factors of income distribution. Hence, it would be easily possible to allow for differences in compensation of a factor of 500 or of 1,000 times between poorest and richest earners, without even being able to count for personal labour productivity. Income differentials between chief executives and non-supervisory workers increased tremendously in the past decades in most advanced countries. These differences have nothing to do with differences in labour productivity, while instead are differences determined by board decisions, institutional choices, and so on. Hence, inequality can't be understood independently of politics and of institutions.

However, labour productivity contributes greatly to economic growth. To understand fully the concept of labour productivity, which at first glance appears to be so abstract and distant, the best definition can be given by two dialogues collected over a long period of time, between a traveller and a craftsman, which took place just over a century apart. The first dialogue refers to a context that is still pre-industrial, in the laborious and rich city of Florence, between a famous passer-by, a nineteenth-century traveller and prime minister of an important European nation, visiting the new recently created capital of Italy and a Florentine craftsman with very few tools that would now be defined as archaic. The second dialogue refers to a present-day context, once again in Florence, between a tourist in the city of the Medici and a Florentine craftsman with technologically advanced tools and equipment.

> 19th-century traveller: "How many shoes, sir, do you make in one day?"
> Florentine craftsman: "In one day, I just about manage to prepare the leather and cut the material for one pair of shoes that I will finish by sunset."

> New millennium tourist: "How many shoes, sir, do you make in one day?"
> Florentine craftsman: "In one day's work, if I am fit, motivated and in good spirits, I can make between eight and ten pairs of good-quality shoes."

This dialogue shows that as time has passed and technology has advanced, labour productivity has increased approximately eight to ten times compared with the end of the nineteenth century. This dialogue also shows that labour productivity is simply the amount of goods produced by a worker in one day or in one working hour. It crucially depends on the technological progress and amount of capital and tools available in a certain period actually used by the worker. In 1800, the lack of capital and advanced tools and low level of technological progress kept productivity levels very low and consequently, levels of income were also low. Today, a significant advance in technological progress, which increased considerably, especially in the period immediately after the Second World War, results in much higher labour productivity, a much higher production level and, consequently, a much higher level of income (see Tridico, 2016). Income time series data available through Angus Maddison's database provides us with important information on income levels for this dialogue and consequently clarifies the close links between income level and labour productivity, as shown in Figure 1.8.

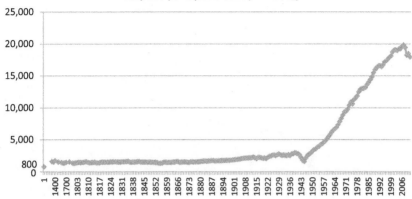

Figure 1.8 Italian GDP in history.
Source: Own elaboration on Maddison database.

During the 1800s, the income level was fairly constant and stood at around $1,500 (in PPP), reaching $1,800 towards the end of the century and almost $3,000 before the Second World War. As is widely known, Italian economic development began after the Second World War and reached $20,000 in more recent years (just before the current financial crisis), approximately ten times more than it was in our traveller's time at the end of the nineteenth century in Florence. A comparison between the income level at the end of the nineteenth century and present-day Italy and the levels of productivity then and now is revealing: labour productivity, as well as income levels, have increased approximately eight to ten times in the same period. We have therefore established a stable, crucial correlation between productivity and income: as productivity increases, so does income. Between the 1400s and up to the end of the 1800s, income fluctuated between $1,500 and $1,800. In this same period, labour productivity was stagnant, whereas it grew slightly between the end of the nineteenth century and the Second World War and steeply increased in the period after the Second World War when the Italians' income increased significantly.

England, or better to say Great Britain (what is today the UK), led the advanced economies groups starting the impressive economic development and the industrial revolution during the XVIII centuries. Labour productivity in this period grew at an impressive pace and per capita income reached $4,000 at the end of the XIX century in the UK (prices are expressed, following Maddison methodology in 1990 Int. GK$). The rest of advanced economies followed with some delay, with the exception of the US, which instead was able to catch up with the UK at the end of the XIX century and overcame the former calorizator in 1904 with a per capita income of $4,464 against $4,450 in the UK (see Figure 1.9).

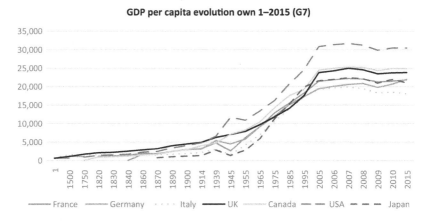

Figure 1.9 Rich countries GDP in history.
Source: Own elaboration on Maddison database.

If income increases when productivity grows, then the crucial issue to be examined remains labour productivity. What makes its potential increase, and what stimulates its growth? We have mentioned technological progress and innovation, and this is definitely the main reason: in a period of great innovation in which new processes and new products are created, new ideas circulate and technological innovation is absorbed, companies introduce new machinery and new tools, and the economy as a whole increases labour productivity and both the production level and the income level. The period after the Second World War was definitely the best period and also the most important in terms of innovation and technological progress: the greatest innovations of all time occurred in this period and encouraged growth in labour productivity through unprecedented industrial development. The period between the Industrial Revolution, which, as we all know, began in England at the end of the eighteenth century, and the First World War provides the necessary conditions for a subsequent wave of modern development and the great innovations of the 1900s. During this period, modern societies witnessed big transformations and went from being industry-based economies to service-based ones. During this period, the biggest contribution to the transformation was a massive increase in labour productivity stimulated by significant technological innovation and all the inventions in this period.

Before the Industrial Revolution in England and earlier still, in the Middle Ages, there was very little technological innovation and it was limited to agriculture and construction. Income was generated and, at best, offered the existing population a means of existence. This state of affairs prompted Malthus (1766–1834) and other economists and demographers who lived before the great technological advances of the nineteenth century to make apocalyptic predictions based on population growth that would have led to the cultivation of increasingly less fertile land with a decrease in food production. This would have resulted in a halt in economic development since the population would tend to increase at a geometric rate – i.e. faster than food production, which increases arithmetically. Malthus was wrong because he had not predicted the great development, initially technical and then economic, that encouraged labour productivity and which began from the nineteenth century onwards in the agrofood industry, in industry in a narrow sense and in the economy as a whole. If we consider the fifty most important inventions of all time, according to a group of scientists interviewed by the *Atlantic*, from the invention of the wheel onwards, twenty occurred during the nineteenth century (with fifteen in the second half), another twenty in the twentieth century and only ten prior to the year 1800. This explains the stagnation of labour productivity and income before the industrial revolution, shown in Figure 1.8.

To a marginal extent, something else contributes to productivity growth. In the example of the dialogue, the Florentine craftsman answered the modern tourist saying that he also needed to be fit, motivated and in good spirits to produce between eight and ten pairs of good-quality shoes and, obviously, needed his machinery and tools. There is therefore, especially in modern times, a need for other factors, factors that are mostly not economic, that help or facilitate productivity: first of all, health, which our nineteenth-century craftsman obviously needed as well, but also motivation and good spirits, factors that are mostly psychological and social but also institutional and can have different origins, exogenous (social, political and psychological) and endogenous (the economic demand which increases the craftsman's motivation – i.e. his pay or wages if he is a worker). In addition to this, the dialogue implicitly shows that there is a need for the craftsman's expertise, his skills and his knowledge, which is something quite different from technological innovation and innovation, and regards his training, cultural knowledge, experience and manual skills, which all have an important effect on his productivity. These are factors that are endogenous to the production process itself since they can be continuously increased through learning by doing and continuous training. Once again, the acquisition of these skills and the necessary cultural and educational knowledge crucially depends on economic and institutional incentives, the rules according to which individuals acquire knowledge, the school and education system and its level of accessibility.

In the most recent economic literature, these arguments are reported as efficiency wage theory, where the effect of higher wages on labour productivity is positive, and *inefficiencies* are reduced. High workers turn over, firing procedure, flexible contracts, low retributions and more in general a conflictual working environment are detrimental for the firm's work culture and negatively affect workers' effort (Shapiro and Stiglitz, 1984). On the contrary, higher wages positively affect workers' efforts. The improvement of workers' conditions contribute to the establishment of more cooperative industrial relations and increase employees' commitment. Hence, *ceteris paribus*, bonus and premium, wages, trust, good environment and good relations within the firms (and between the principal-agent relations) increase labour productivity.[4]

More recently, in particular since 1975, labour productivity, as we saw before, did not increase as fast as before. This occurred mainly in advanced countries, which in the meantime experienced a structural transformation towards the service sector, usually characterized by lower levels of technological intensity and productivity. The problem is that in advanced economies, the tertiary sector employs around 70 per cent of working population, while manufacturing employ around 25 per cent or less and the rest, a very small fraction, is involved in agriculture. So the biggest bulk of the working population works in a sector where productivity gains are more difficult to obtain (Delli Gatti *et al.*, 2012) and this may have negative consequences on wages, income and consumption and therefore on the dynamics of the GDP. Along the excess of saving, the productivity slowdown is often reported as an important explanation for the secular stagnation (Summers, 2016).

However, as I stated also for the excess of saving, the productivity slowdown is not an exogenous variable occurring for natural causes. Labour productivity is endogenous as Kaldor and other classical economists argued. In his 1961 article, Kaldor criticizes the way neoclassical economics deals with technical progress, which is characterized, in his view, as a continuous, exogenous process of improvement in the state of knowledge. As Kaldor notices, since "improved knowledge is, largely if not entirely, infused into the economy through the introduction of new equipment" (1961, p. 207), the rate of shift of the production function cannot be treated as exclusively dependent on chronological time but has to be studied in connection with the rate of accumulation. Kaldor proposes the following technical progress function:

$$\dot{\lambda} = \alpha + \beta \dot{k} \tag{1}$$

This equation determines the rate of growth of labour productivity ($\lambda = Y/L$) and has two components: the first has an exogenous nature and is given by the parameter α, which defines the height of the function and expresses "society's

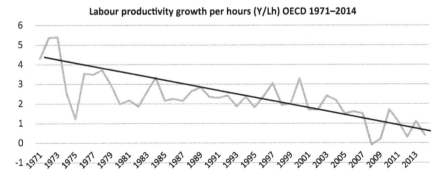

Figure 1.10 Labour productivity.
Source: Own elaboration on OECD database.

'dynamism', meaning by this both inventiveness and readiness to change and to experiment" (ibid., p. 208). The second part of the equation states that the evolution of labour productivity is a positive function of the rate of growth of capital per head k ($k = K/L$). According to Kaldor, given that most technical innovations and improvements are incorporated into machineries and equipment, for any given level of society's dynamism and inventiveness, the economy can absorb only a bounded amount of technical change, which is an increasing function of the speed with which capital is accumulated. Equation (1) can be described with Figure 1.10.

As it is clear from the figure, the technical progress function is convex upwards: the speed of capital accumulation brings forth diminishing returns, mainly because the ideas able to generate the greatest improvements in productivity are exploited first (ibid., p. 208); hence, for high rates of investment (i.e. $\dot{k} > \dot{k}_p$) productivity growth is less than proportional than capital accumulation.

Kaldor (1961) proposes an argument in favour of the convergence of the economy towards the point of intersection of the technical progress curve and the 45° line: on the left of point P, output grows faster than capital; the related increase in the Y/K ratio is likely to induce expectations of a prospective rate of profit higher than the realized one. This will cause an increase in investment (and also a shift leftwards of the accumulation function), until it intersects the technical progress curve at point P, where output and capital grow at the same rate (as a consequence of the same rates of growth of Y/L and K/L, respectively on the vertical and on the horizontal axes in Figure 1.11). In correspondence of this equilibrium point, the capital-output ratio is constant (technical progress is neutral in the sense of Harrod), and the economy experiences continuous increases in the amount of capital per worker, which in presence of growing population and full employment is compensated by a decrease of working hours per worker (Fadda, 2016: 24). The opposite occurs on the right side of point P, with a convergence towards it, and the realization again, thanks to the "neutral" technical progress, of the constancy of factor shares, which is part of the stylized facts denounced by Kaldor (1956).

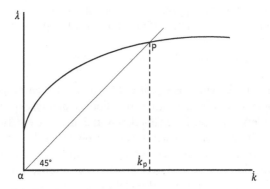

Figure 1.11 Kaldor's 'technical progress function'.

It is interesting to notice here that a strong difference between Ricardo and Kaldor emerges: the first maintains that in order to keep a balanced path of growth with full employment, the advantages of technical progress should go to the profit share, while in Kaldor, exactly the opposite applies – the reduction of working hours should occur in presence of the same wage rate (Kaldor, 1956). The implication of this difference on income inequality is clear.

The constancy of factor shares is also adopted in the neoclassical growth models (for instance Solow, 1956), where with the widespread use of the Cobb-Douglas production function, the factor shares (α and $1-\alpha$) are simply the exponents of K and L (kept constant), and income distribution does not affect economic growth. The stability of factor shares is determined by the assumption of elasticity of substitution between capital and labour, fixed and equal to one.[5] This assumption, along with the inverse relation between profit rate and the intensity of capital, has always been theoretically criticized (Garegnani, 1966) and never in fact was empirically verified (the recent investigation of Piketty [2014] shows that this unit elasticity assumption is empirically unfounded).

Kalecki shows in his economic growth model (Kalecki, 1965) that the wage share is determined by the degree of monopoly and can therefore vary, although he recognizes that Kaldor's stylized facts of constancy of factor share, empirically observed until 1960s, to some extent apply, since no great wage share fluctuations were observed. These findings, in particular the different interpretations of Kalecki and Kaldor with reference to different periods, suggest that the wage share depends also on particular political and social conditions, which can change over time. A similar interpretation is put forward by Kuznets (1933, p. 30) who pointed out that labour share is intimately related to the struggle of labour against capital and to the significant political and social conflicts that center about the relative share of these productive factors.

The recent empirical evidence contradicts the constancy of factor share. In particular, in financial capitalism factor shares are not constant at all, and the wage share keeps shrinking. The work of Paolo Sylos Labini (see. for example. Sylos Labini 1984; 1999) has stressed the connections between labour productivity, income distribution and the dynamics of demand in connection with the wage share. Briefly, Sylos Labini's approach to labour productivity can be illustrated by the following productivity equation (Sylos Labini, 1999, p. 259):

$$\lambda = Y/L = f(\Delta Y) + f(\Delta w - \Delta P_{ma}) + f(\Delta ULC - \Delta P) + \Delta I \tag{2}$$

Labour productivity λ, which is equal to the ratio between output (Y) and the level of employment (L), is a positive function of output expansion (ΔY, also known as Smith effect), a positive function of the difference between w (wages) and Pma (price of machinery) so that if wages grow faster than Pma, λ increases. This is because when wages are cheaper than machineries, investors implement labour intensive strategies, with lower productivity growth (this is also known as Ricardo Effect). The element $\Delta ULC-\Delta P$ (difference between growth of unit

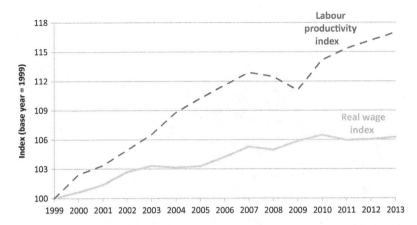

Figure 1.12 The gap: labour productivity and real wage in advanced economies.
Source: ILO 2015, online database.

labour costs and prices – i.e. the absolute cost of labour) captures obviously the wage share, which can be synthetically written as (1–Π). Finally, labour productivity is a positive function of investments (I).

Figure 1.12 shows the gap accumulated in the last years between unit ULC (the labour productivity index in the figure) and the real wage index in advanced economies. This gap contributed dramatically to the reduction of wage share.

The first argument of equation 2, the "Smith effect", describes a mechanism similar to the already introduced Kaldor-Verdoorn effect (see also Pariboni and Tridico, 2016). The second argument – the price of labour relative to the price of investment – is labelled as the "Ricardo effect" and finds its rationale "in the classical notion of induced, factor-biased technical change" (Tronti, p. 210). Sylos Labini, however, focuses his attention on the third element, the productivity-enhancing role of the wage share, which stimulates positive dynamics of the aggregate demand. Moreover, from the entrepreneur's perspective, the pressure exerted by the increasing cost of labour provides a stimulus to reorganize the production process in a more efficient way. This pressure incentives the adoption of technologically advanced equipment and machinery, which allow production to rise without having to increase the number of employees.

Pariboni and Tridico (2016) show how wage share positively affects labour productivity in a sample of OECD countries between 1990 and 2013. They tested a modified Sylos Labini equation, and their findings confirm that relation as their (reproduced) Figure 1.13 shows.

As reported in Lavoie (2014), traces of this intuition date back to Webb (1912), a seminal contribution whose main purpose was to support a proposal for the establishment of a legal minimum wage. The basic idea is that, as long as wage compression is prevented (through, for instance, a minimum wage) entrepreneurs

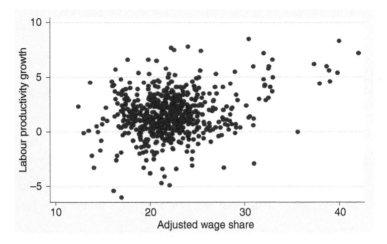

Figure 1.13 Wage share and productivity.
Source: Parboni and Tridico, 2016.

have to find other ways to lower the production costs (through innovation) with respect to their competitors. The institution of a minimum wage can lead to an increase in the real wage and can push out of the market firms that do not keep pace with technological innovations.

On the basis of the brief discussion above, it is possible to conclude that wage compression and a worsening in income distribution not only do not necessarily enhance the external competitiveness and dynamism of a country, but on the contrary, they might create a drag on productivity and inhibit technical change. In this regard, the case of the Southern European countries described in Storm and Naastepad (2015) is paradigmatic: low-wage countries tend to remain stuck in low-tech production segments, specialised in "commodities and destination markets where demand growth is above average" (ibid., p. 968) and exposed to the competition of countries with a permanent advantage in terms of labour cheapness.

Consequences of inequality

To conclude this chapter, I will briefly discuss the consequences of inequality. The question is whether inequality negatively affects economic performance; and second, whether inequality negatively affects government revenues and fiscal performance. Winkelmann and Winkelmann (2010) have already found important answers and a robust inverse relation between the size and the income of the middle class (and economic performance) and inequality, and Larch (2012) found evidence that a more unequal distribution of income can harm fiscal performance of a country. More recently, evidences from the IMF (see Ostry *et al.*, 2014) and the OECD (see Cingano, 2014) have also found that high levels of inequality were associated with lower economic growth, suggesting that there is no "big trade-off" between equality and efficiency. Hence, economic and fiscal policies in the post-2007 financial crisis should take into consideration their distributional implications.

In our approach, inequality is bad for several reasons. First of all, the impact of inequality on aggregate demand: as I have argued, inequality weakens aggregate demand and drags down the economy since higher income groups spend a smaller share of the income; lower demand dynamics produce lower GDP dynamics. The second problem has a genuinely instrumental nature: inequality leads easily to economic instability and financial crisis, in particular when the financial sector tries to compensate the lack of consumption and aggregate demand with credit availability and debt-led growth as several studies show (Galbraith, 2012; Perugini *et al.*, 2015; Stockhammer, 2015; Stockhammer, 2013; Cynamon and Fazzari, 2013). These two problems are the main focus of this book.

Moreover, inequality increases relative poverty, and poverty is associated with high crime, bad health and lower life expectancy. Hence, from this way, human development deteriorates when inequality increases. The example of former Soviet Republics and Eastern European countries, former communist economies, is paradigmatic: with the economic transition towards market economy, inequality increased in most of those countries and human development dimensions (longevity, health) deteriorated, with negative consequences on human development (as witnessed by human development indexes, UNDP, 2000; Tridico, 2011a).

Inequality and poverty are also associated with unequal distribution of political power. Wealthy citizens maintain disproportionate political power compared to poorer citizens. This political imbalance allows for further disequilibria and political instability. Public choices and policies would be controlled and designed by the richest, and this would crystalize differences and immobilize social mobility, with negative consequences again in terms of wages, income, consumption and aggregate demand expressed by the masses of people who suffer from deprivation and poverty. Access to education by the poor would be limited by high prices in the private market and by limited resources in the public sector (see also Birdsong, 2015).

Finally, inequality is problematic for ethical intrinsic reasons and for the sustainability of modern political systems. This problem has to do with social cohesion and democracy: a society strongly unequal may easily evolve towards authoritarian regimes and unstable political systems (Stiglitz, 2012). The examples of several Latin American countries in the past, and of several post-communist countries today, show that this is a very realistic scenario.

Notes

1 As I discuss in the section "Technological progress, labour productivity and inequality" on p. 40, this has scarce evidence and it is also theoretically questioned.
2 At the same time, if profits decrease (increase), capital demand increases (decrease); in parallel, wages go up (go down) and labour demand decreases (increase). This guarantees, in the neoclassical approach, constancy of factor shares and therefore

irrelevance of distribution and inequality for growth and for the stable evolution of the economy on a constant path of growth.

3 Data used in this figure comes from World Penn Tables weighted for the size of GDP.

4 In mainstream literature, this is known as the "wage-efficiency effect" (see, for example, Shapiro and Stiglitz, 1984, and Akerlof and Yellen, 1986; Altman, 1988). See also Lavoie (2014, pp. 304–06) for a discussion of Marxist and radical approaches that share with the efficiency wage literature the emphasis on workers' morale and motivation as a main explanatory factor for productivity.

5 Neoclassical models with a Cobb and Douglas (1928) function having constant elasticity substitution between labour and capital equal to one implies that an increase (decrease) of K/L ratio is associated to a decreases (increase) of r/w (profit/wage) ratio; hence, factor shares remain constant. In this context, income distribution is not at all a problem for economic growth, although wage differentials and income dispersion may (or should) occur in order to guarantee appropriate incentives for agents in the economy.

2 The determinants of income inequality in rich countries

Introduction

The objective of this chapter is to identify empirically the determinants of the increase in income inequality that rich countries have experienced over the last two to three decades. My hypothesis is that along with the financialisation of economies that has taken place since 1990, inequality increased because labour flexibility intensified, labour market institutions weakened as trade unions lost power, and public social spending started to retrench and did not compensate the vulnerabilities created by the globalisation process. In this context wage share declined. Using data from thirty-four OECD countries from 1990 to 2013, I empirically evaluate this hypothesis. My results clearly suggest that the increase in inequality over the last two to three decades is caused by an increase in financialisation, a deepening of labour flexibility, the weakening of trade unions, and the retrenchment of the welfare state.

Over the last two decades at least, income inequality within rich countries, or better to say, among OECD countries has increased; while income inequality between countries based on per capita income likely has decreased recently, income inequality within countries has risen in most OECD and several developing countries over the last two to three decades (Allison *et al.*, 2014). During the same time the Gini Coefficient increased from about 27 per cent to 33 per cent on average. Following to some extent Piketty's (2014) broad conclusions – rejecting the Kuznets paradigm, I focus in this chapter on the years that are probably the ones during which inequality increased the most – i.e. from 1990 to present.

Since the late 1970s, political changes created the basis for a new paradigm of political economy, first in the US and in the UK and later in most advanced and emerging economies. This new paradigm, called "financial capitalism", is characterized by a strong dependency on the financial sector, by the globalisation and intensification of international trade and capital mobility, and by the "flexibilisation" of the labour market (Epstein, 2005; ILO, 2013). From an economic policy perspective, these changes resulted in the partial withdrawal of the state from the economy (i.e. the minimization of its economic intervention) and the dominance of supply-side policies (i.e. labour flexibility, tax competition for firms and capital, etc.; Shield, 2012).

In the age of financial capitalism, labour-capital relations are changing, and in most cases labour represents the weaker part. On the one hand, as a result of the conflict between labour and capital, trade unions lost power, and labour market regulations, such as labour protection against firing, unemployment benefits, and minimum wage, weakened. On the other hand, the expansion of labour flexibility, atypical labour contracts and temporary jobs created unstable jobs and therefore unstable consumption (Jha and Golder, 2008).

Moreover, within the aforementioned new paradigm of political economy, the welfare state represents another cost to compress. In order to improve firms' competitiveness and boost economic growth, social spending needs to be reduced[1] (Allan and Scruggs, 2004; Castells, 2004; Blackmon, 2006). In fact, most countries are experiencing a retrenchment of the welfare state or at least a stabilization of public expenditure. In an age of globalisation and aging, this corresponds to a per capita reduction in real terms (Adema *et al.*, 2011). As a result, wage share shrinks and income inequality increases; the aggregate demand declines (or does not increase), and GDP stagnates.

As I argued in Chapter 1, the link between globalisation and inequality has been investigated since Stolper and Samuelson (1941). Other recent arguments explaining inequality have been challenged by Lemieux *et al.* (2009) and Card *et al.* (2004) among others and more recently by OECD (2011) and Bogliacino and Maestri (2014) who find that labour market reforms appear to be responsible for most of the wage inequality that occurred in the last decade. Chusseau and Dumont (2012) show that globalisation and changes in labour market institutions weakening the welfare state explain the increase of inequality in a group of twelve rich countries.

Atkinson *et al.* (2011) instead, pointed out the changes in taxation that reduced progressivity in particular at the top of the distribution as main drivers of inequality. Similarly, Facundo *et al.* (2013) argue that reductions in the top income tax rate is the most important factor explaining inequality. Liberati (2007) argues that financial openness is negatively associated to government size (and tax rates), and this of course affects redistribution policies (Gastaldi and Liberati, 2011).

In our framework, inequality emerges in financial capitalism as a result of the interaction of financialisation, globalisation, labour market institutions and the retrenchment of welfare state. Although financialisation has to do with wealth (in the sense of capital ownership), it affects both functional income distribution and personal income inequality and therefore we focus on income inequality rather than on wealth inequality. The dominance of finance in advanced economies is connected not only to the development of the financial sector in those economies but also to the huge increase, in the last two to three decades, of the so called "performance related payments" (PRP) of managers with respect to the rest of the economy. However, PRP are not formally part of the profit share but are part of the wage share. As Stiglitz (2012) noticed, this misleading allocation not only overevaluates the wage share, but it also contributes to increase income inequality (or more precisely, wage inequality – which includes PRP).

In our approach, the main channel of transmission is financialisation (and globalisation) → inequality. In particular, finance and shareholders found more convenient for their dividends and compensations in the last two to three decades to follow a business model, which can be synthesized with "downsize and distribute" (i.e. reducing the size of the workforce instead of increasing their investment levels). Policies in this period, such as labour flexibility, welfare retrenchment, tax reduction (and tax competition) and capital mobility, were all functional to that aim. In this context, wage share, in advanced and in particular in financialised countries, decreased, wage stagnated or decreased and income inequality increased. A similar thesis is discussed in Lavoie and Stockhammer (2013) who then discuss the role of inequality in the 2007 financial crisis and put forward a wage-led strategy to stimulate economic growth instead of the dangerous debt-led growth that took place before the crisis.

To sum up, financialisation, labour flexibility and the weakening of trade unions, plus the retrenchment of the welfare state are the most important factors in my analysis (at least from an empirical point of view) explaining the explosion of income inequality over the past two decades. The econometric analysis of the book uses data from thirty-four OECD countries from 1990 to 2013 and clearly and robustly suggests all these factors are at play.

Globalisation and inequality

Globalisation and financialisation took place almost simultaneously in advanced economies. Financialisation is defined in several ways by scholars from the political sciences, sociology and economics. Most of these definitions, however, converge towards the identification of the financialisation process in a political economy phenomenon where a growing dominance of capital financial systems occur over bank-based financial systems (Krippner, 2005), or more broadly, the increasing role of financial motives, financial markets, financial actors and financial institutions in the operation of domestic and international economies (Epstein, 2005: pp. 3–4). This process culminated, according to the Bank for International Settlements, in a daily volume of foreign exchange transactions of about $2 trillion in 2006, just before the financial crash of the summer 2007. This is more or less equivalent to the GDP of France. In contrast, in 1989, this volume was about $500 billion per day (BIS, 2013).

Figure 2.1 is the simplest representation of this kind of globalisation. In particular, a first big wave of globalisation, identified purely according to the *intensive* definition, occurred after 1970 and may have been generated by a new international monetary system, the change in oil prices and the birth of the European Monetary System. However, this first wave of globalisation was unstable, and the process of intensification declined during the 1980s. Finally, the process of intensive globalisation, often accompanied by the extensive inclusion of more and more countries, steadily rejuvenated at the end of the 1980s when several institutional, geopolitical and technological changes occurred.

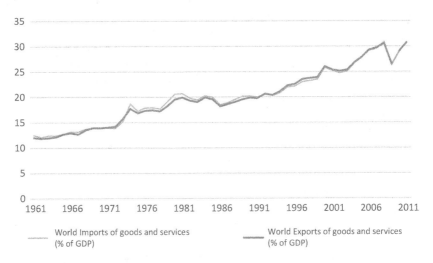

Figure 2.1 Globalisation in terms of trade intensification.
Source: The World Bank database.

Globalisation, or to be more precise, trade openness (defined as imports and exports as a percentage of GDP), was and is supported by the mainstream neoclassical approach.[2] Lewis (1980) and many other economists, such as Lucas (1993) and Bhagwati (2004), believe trade is the engine of economic growth. However, the experience of globalisation so far has shown that the performance of opened economies can vary dramatically (Rodrik, 1999; Rodrik *et al.*, 2004). Openness and integration in the world economy should be accompanied by appropriate institutions, state strategies and particularly by an important welfare state that supports internal cohesion and maintains external competitive advantages. In fact, according to Rodrik (1999), the best-performing countries are the ones that are integrated in the world economy with institutions capable of supporting the impact of globalisation on the domestic market and social cohesion. Countries with poor social institutions, weak conflict management institutions (which means poor welfare states) and strong social cleavages suffer external shocks and do not perform well in the world economy.

The current financial and economic crisis, which started in the US in 2007, suggests Rodrik's argument still holds true:

> The world market is a source of disruption and upheaval as much as it is an opportunity for profit and economic growth. Without the complementary institutions at home – in the areas of governance, judiciary, civil liberties, social insurance, and education, one gets too much of the former and too little of the latter.
>
> (Rodrik, 1999: 96)

For Lucas (1993), international trade stimulates economic growth through a process of structural change and capital accumulation, as in the case of Ireland, where according to Walsh and Whelan (2000), a structural change had already taken place during the 1970s and created conditions that allowed the Irish economy to grow considerably in the 1990s and later in the 2000s. Capital accumulation is determined by "learning by doing" and "learning by schooling" in a process of knowledge and innovation spillovers. A country that protects its goods made with intensive skilled work from international competition by raising tariffs on them will see a domestic increase in the price of those goods. Skilled workers' wages will increase and research and development (R&D) will become more expensive. Consequently, investments in R&D will decrease, and growth will be negatively affected. On the contrary, removing tariffs on those goods will cause a reduction in their price, a reduction in the cost of R&D, and thus an increase in investments in R&D, with positive effects on growth (Lucas, 1993).

This argument, however, does not take into consideration the inequality and uneven development caused by trade liberalisation and intensification via wage differentials. Increased capital flows are expected to raise income inequality in advanced industrial economies because capital outflows from capital-rich countries to less developed countries (LDCs) reduce domestic investment and lower the productive capability and demands for labour in these economies (Ha, 2008; Tsebelis, 2002). Since a reduction in total capital in the production process increases the marginal productivity of capital and reduces the marginal effect of labour, capital outflows increase the income of capital relative to labour, thus exacerbating income inequality. In particular, because foreign direct investment (FDI) outflows from advanced industrial economies tend to be concentrated in industries with low-skilled labour in the home country (Lee, 1996), rapidly rising FDI outflows often reduce the demand for low-skilled labour and increase income gaps in industrialised countries. In fact, several studies find that FDI outflows is associated with expanded income inequality in industrialised countries (Leamer, 1996; McKeown, 1999; Wood, 1994).

Empirically, it is interesting to observe the expansion of FDI, which experienced a strong increase in the 1990s due to the liberalisation of capital markets, followed by a collapse at the beginning of the 2000s due to the global uncertainty caused by the international events of September 11, 2001. A further and bigger increase in FDI flows can be observed immediately after and up to the financial crash of 2007, reaching a peak in 2006–07. The current crisis, marked by financial instability and depression, caused a further squeeze in FDI, although it remains at a substantially higher level than at the beginning of the 1990s.

With the rise of outsourcing practices and FDI outflows, globalisation has improved the position of capital with respect to labour. Firms' decisions to move capital and production across countries has distributional effects: the position of low-skilled workers in industrial countries is worsened by a combination of globalisation and new technology. The first increases the bargaining power of

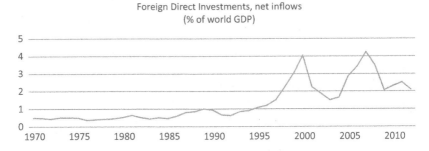

Figure 2.2 FDI in the world economy.
Source: The World Bank database.

capital against labour, with the consequence of easing capital owners' procurement of tax reductions and welfare retrenchment (Chusseau and Dumont, 2012). States are willing to embark on tax competition among themselves in order to keep investments and production at home. The second has a direct and negative impact on unskilled labour and income distribution without welfare support and social institutions (Tisdell and Svizzero, 2003).

In this context, wage shares in the richest countries have declined dramatically, as Figures 2.3a and 2.3b suggest, with negative consequences on aggregate demand and on income distribution.

Figure 2.3a Wage share in G7 countries plus Australia.
Source: Own elaboration on the ILO (2013).

Figure 2.3b Wage share in selected OECD countries.
Source: Own elaboration on the ILO (2013).

The new macroeconomic consensus of the last two to three decades is strictly linked to, if not completely correspondent with, the Washington Consensus doctrine, which called for the implementation of some institutional forms that better suit the globalisation process, such as the financialisation of the economy and the introduction of labour flexibility in the economy (see Tridico, 2012).[3] Acemoglu (2011) argues that the policies implemented over the last two decades in particular were more closely aligned with the preferences of a minority of high-income voters. Instead of redistributive policies favouring low- and middle-income constituents, politicians implemented financial deregulation policies favouring a small group of influential high-income earners (many of whom worked in, or directly benefited from, the financial sector).

To sum up, inequality has increased in most advanced and emerging economies over the last two decades – an era of growing interconnectedness of the world economy – as many studies have already shown (Atkinson, 1999; Galbraith, 2012; Piketty, 2014; Milanovic, 2016), and a simple look at Gini coefficients across countries exposes this trend (see Figure 2.4). In the next section, I examine the main factors underpinning this development and then I put forward a model, which tries to explain the determinants of income inequality.

Financialisation, labour market institutions and inequality

Financialisation and labour flexibility are two institutional forms of the neo-liberal paradigm, which were functional to the increase of inequality. Labour flexibility has increased in most advanced economies in the last two decades. However, some countries, such as Austria, Belgium, France and Germany have

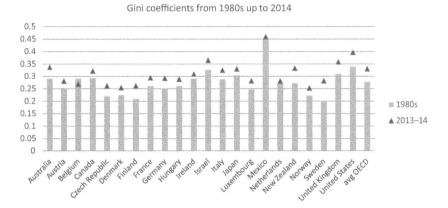

Figure 2.4 Income inequality evolution in OECD countries.
Source: OECD.

retained more rigid labour markets. Other economies, such as Denmark, Sweden, Finland and the Netherlands, introduced higher levels of flexibility along with higher levels of security (OECD, 2013). Countries such as the US, the UK and Ireland increased (or maintained) their already very flexible labour markets. Finally, Mediterranean countries such as Italy, Spain and Greece and most of the former communist economies in Europe combined very hybrid situations (of neoliberal and corporative elements) with an increased level of labour flexibility.

The political and economic roots of the financialisation process, which brought about a new financial-led growth regime, were established first in the US. Many other economies followed the American example of a financial-led regime of accumulation, which used flexible labour and compressed wages in order to increase firms' competitiveness (Tridico, 2012). Shareholders sought higher dividends because they invested their own capital in firms, taking on a higher level of risk. Since the economic growth of advanced economies under financial capitalism has not been higher than under previous phases as Figure 2.5 shows,[4] it follows that wages should be compressed in order for shareholders to obtain higher dividends. In fact, wages have not increased following the increases in productivity, and profits continue to soar.

Similarly, Lin and Tomaskovic-Devey (2011) argue that the increasing reliance by firms on earnings realized through financial channels generated surplus from production, strengthening owners' and elite workers' negotiating power relative to other workers. This resulted in the exclusion of most of the workers from revenue and therefore in the increase of inequality.

In light of the financial developments and financial innovation, labour flexibility and wage contraction were functional to obtaining this result (higher dividends for shareholders), at least in the short run. As far as financialisation is concerned, Figure 2.6 shows the expansion of financialisation among OECD economies over

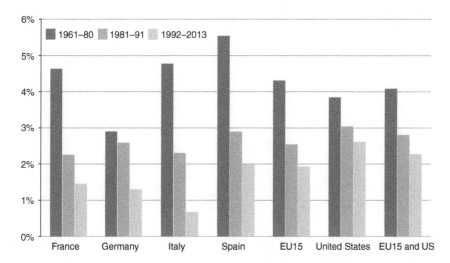

Figure 2.5 Average GDP growth in the EU15 and the US, 1961–2013.
Source: The World Bank database.

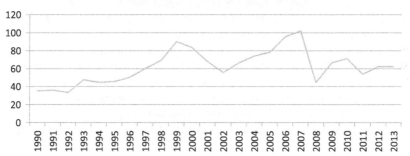

Figure 2.6 Financialisation.
Source: The World Bank database.

the past two decades. The variable here is the World Bank's "Market capitalization of listed [domestic] companies" as a percentage of GDP.[5] One can observe an important increase in the 1990s, driven probably by the "dot-com bubble"; the fall after September 11, in 2001; another consistent increase with a bubble, which reached its peak in 2006 driven by the housing sector; and finally the crash of 2007–08 and the following stabilisation after 2012 to a level that is almost double the average value of 1990 (more than 60 per cent of GDP versus less than 40 per cent).

More specifically, the highest level of financialisation is found in Anglo-Saxon economies (particularly the US, the UK, Australia and Canada, which have

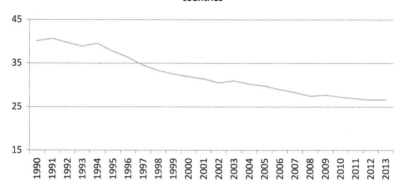

Figure 2.7 The decline of trade unions density.
Source: Own elaboration on OECD data.

enormous values of financialisation – between 100 and 150 per cent of GDP), while the lowest levels of financialisation are in continental Europe, with the notable exception of Switzerland.

The US promoted neo-liberalism as a main ideological paradigm for globalisation and financialisation through global, multi, and bilateral measures under pressure from all the major international financial institutions, multinational corporations, and Wall Street institutions (Epstein, 2005).[6]

As Feenstra (1998, p. 46) observes, the impact of globalisation on changing the bargaining position of labour and capital has far-reaching consequences. The decline in union power, particularly within trade-oriented industries, may well account for a portion of the increased wage inequality in the United States and in other countries (Borjas and Ramey, 1995; Gordon, 2012).

Of particular interest seems the case of the US where the inverse relation is clear, throughout most of the twentieth century, between trade unions membership and inequality. Gordon (2012) argues that between the New Deal, which granted among other important things, also workers basic collective bargaining rights, and the end of 1960s "labor unions both sustained prosperity, and ensured that it was shared". Since the 1970s and in particular during the Reagan administration, "unions came under attack—in the workplace, in the courts, and in public policy. As a result, union membership has fallen and income inequality has worsened—reaching levels not seen since the 1920s" (Gordon, 2012).

The decline in unionisation rates has contributed to the weakening of labour market institutions such as labour protection against firing and hiring, the level and duration of unemployment benefits with the introduction of constraints concerning eligibility and the reduction in most cases of their length and amount, the minimum wage, etc. In the appendix, one can find a list of ten labour market indicators (the eight in Table A1, plus EPL and TU density in Table A2). Out of them,

Figure 2.8 Unionisation and share of income to the top 10 per cent.
Source: Reproduced from Gordon, 2012.

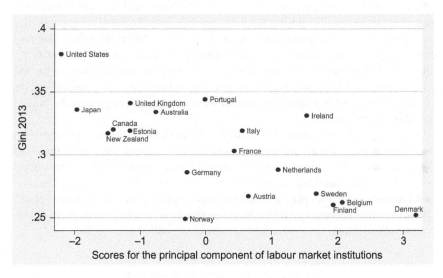

Figure 2.9 Inequality and labour market indicators.
Source: Own elaboration on OECD data.

Note: data concerning the set of ten labour market institutions used to create the score on the horizontal axe are available only for a limited number (19) of advanced countries (see Tables A1 and A2 in appendix).

a factor analysis was carried out in order to establish the most important elements explaining variation among the variables. This resulted in a principal component that, when scattered in a plot against the inequality index (Gini in 2013) produces Figure 2.9. This figure displays a clear correlation between the two: the higher the score of the principal component (more protection in the labour market), the lower the Gini level, and vice versa.[7]

The OECD's Employment Protection Legislation (EPL) indicator is probably one of the most important labour market indicators, as far as it is able to capture labour market flexibility, which represents a crucial variable in our analysis and whose evolution represents one of the most important changes in labour market in the last two decades in many advanced economies. Moreover, EPL, in the principal component analysis represented above, has the highest value of the component loading. It measures the general level of worker protection in the labour market and consequently the level of labour flexibility (it varies between 0 for very low protection and 6 for very high protection). In essence, it shows the level of protection offered by national legislation with respect to regular employment, temporary employment and collective dismissal – in other words, regulation that allows employers to fire and hire workers at will (OECD, 2004). Figure 2.10 shows the evolution of the average level of EPL among OECD countries from 1990 to 2013. Its decline clearly underlines an increase in labour flexibility.

As already noted by Hall and Soskice (2001) and by Storm and Naasteepad (2012), complementarities between labour flexibility and financialisation are strong in advanced economies. As I discuss in Chapters 3 and 4, in particular with respect to the financial crisis, an important correlation between these two complementary institutional forms of neoliberalism is evident. Labour flexibility allows for the reduction of firms' labour costs and thus wage savings at the expense of wage earners – that is, consumers, who in turn are pushed towards credit consumption. In such a situation, inequality increases, and aggregate demand is unstable and restricted.

As it was argued elsewhere (Tridico, 2012), the rise of inequality generated an increased demand for credit, which translated into a credit expansion provided for by accommodating monetary policies and financial deregulation. One should take notice of the particular path of Scandinavian countries (especially Sweden and Finland), which display a relatively high degree of financialisation yet are able to contain inequality (which nevertheless is increasing) with their strong welfare states (along with other labour market institutions).

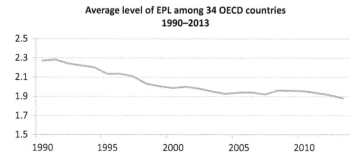

Figure 2.10 Labour market flexibility.
Source: Own elaboration on OECD data.

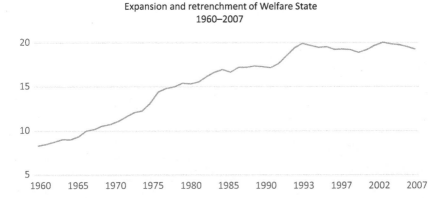

Figure 2.11 The welfare states since 1960 (public social expenditure, % of GDP).
Source: Own elaboration on OECD data.

Finally, our series of correlations and relationships suggest that what contributes to the increase or decrease of inequality seems to be the choice of the socioeconomic model that each country built during the decades after the Second World War. More specifically, what is most relevant is the set of policies that each country is currently able to implement in order to cope with the challenges of globalisation both in terms of income distribution and competitiveness (Rodrik, 1999). These include in particular social protection against unemployment and low wages, welfare programs against poverty, health and education policies, social policy for housing, and so forth. As Table A3 in the appendix shows, there seems to be a clear relationship between inequality and welfare expenditures in the sense that countries that spend more on welfare generally have a lower level of inequality. Between 1960 and 1990, welfare states emerged in most OECD countries, and high GDP share was spent for social expenditure. However, after 1990, several countries – not all – started to retrench welfare states and this had consequences on inequality as well.

Only countries that managed to keep relatively high levels of welfare spending (along with the other variables discussed) have managed to keep low levels of inequality, as my model in the next section shows.

The model: inequality determinants

The model that I put forward in this section takes into consideration the analysis and the relations discussed previously. The objective is to identify the determinants of income inequality over the last two decades in rich countries, or OECD countries.[8] We have observed that inequality increases in the past two decades or more, according to Gini coefficient and other inequality indicators such as the 90\10 ratio and the 90\50 ratio, as Figure 2.12 below indicates.

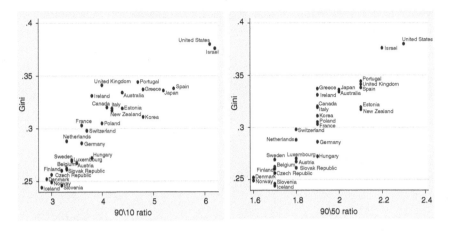

Figure 2.12 Correlation between Gini and other ratios, 2012.
Source: Own elaboration on OECD data.

Note: the 90/10 ratio is the ratio of the upper bound value of the ninth decile (i.e. the 10 per cent of people with highest income) to that of the upper bound value of the first decile. The 90/50 ratio is the ratio of the upper bound value of the ninth decile to the median income.

In my model, I preferred to use the Gini coefficient since it has a wider coverage in terms of years and countries than other ratios. My model is represented by the following equation:

$$Ineq = \alpha + \beta_1\, F - \beta_2\, EPL - \beta_3\, TU - \beta_4\, S + \varepsilon$$

where the dependent variable is inequality (Ineq) and the independent variables are financialisation (F); labour flexibility, indicated as LF, or as (the reduction of) EPL (Employment Protection Legislation); trade union density (TU); and public social spending (S). I use panel data for thirty-four OECD countries from 1990 to 2013, for a total of 816 observations.

The regression results are very interesting and confirm my hypothesis. I use a GLS model with a random effect to establish the relation, verified through the Hausman test against the fixed effect. The GLS Model (I) produces very robust results, according to which inequality increases when financialisation increases (i.e. the level of market capitalization as defined previously), when labour flexibility increases (i.e. the Employment Protection Legislation decreases), when trade unions are weaker (i.e. TU density declines), and when the level of public social spending decreases. All coefficients are statistically significant at least within 5 per cent level.

Thus, we can consider the following output (RE GLS model I):

$$Gini = 0.35 + 0.00005*F_{ij} - 0.004*EPL_{ij} - 0.0006*TU_{ij} - 0.0008*S_{ij}$$

where i = country, and j = year

Table 2.1 Regression results for inequality (Gini, 1990–2013)

Number of obs = 816; Number of groups = 34
Panel = 1990–2013

| Var | Random-effects (RE) GLS regression | | Fixed Effect regression | RE GLS regression | RE GLS regression | RE GLS regression | RE GLS regression | RE GLS regression |
	Model I	Model II (with control var)	Model III (with control var)	Model IV (without Luxemb and Iceland)	Model V (without Lux, Icel and Switzerland)	Model VI (Dummy for new rich countries)	Model VII (Dummy emerging countries)	Model VIII (1-y lag for Gini)
	Coeff.	Coeff.	Coeff.	Coeff.	Coeff.	Coeff.	Coeff.	Coeff.
Financialisation(F)	0.0000502 (–0.000019)	0.0000459 (–0.0000214)	0.0000451 (–0.000021)	0.0000531 (0.0000227)	0.0000628 (0.000025)	0.0000522 (0.0000189)	0.00005 (0.000023)	0.0000408 (0.0000221)
P>|z|	0.008**	0.032**	0.032**	0.019**	0.012**	0.006*	0.008	0.065
EPL (LF)	–0.004088 (–0.002127)	–0.0051814 (–0.0024638)	–0.0061798 (–0.0025251)	–0.0049253 (0.0024945)	–0.0051193 (0.0025129)	–0.0041828 (0.0021216)	–0.00448 (0.002121)	–0.0051295 (0.002553)
P>|z|	0.050**	0.035**	0.015**	0.048**	0.042**	0.049**	0.034**	0.045
TU density (TU)	–0.000573 (–0.000138)	–0.0005768 (–0.0001975)	–0.0004044 (–0.0002232)	–0.0008203 (0.0001766)	–0.0006967 (0.0001789)	–0.0005229 (0.0001407)	–0.000525 (0.000144)	–0.0007712 (0.0001892)
P>|z|	0.000*	0.003*	0.070***	0.000*	0.000*	0.000*	0.000*	0.000
Social spending (S)	–0.000829 (–0.000232)	–0.0010213 (–0.0003015)	–0.0007598 (–0.000301)	–0.0010029 (0.0002914)	–0.0009635 (0.0002935)	–0.0007807 (0.0002331)	–0.000771 (0.000235)	–0.0010285 (0.000291)
P>|z|	0.000*	0.001*	0.012**	0.001*	0.001*	0.001*	0.001*	0.000
Unemployment		0.0000153 (–0.0002661)	–0.0000472 (–0.0002632)	0.0000732 (0.0002762)	0.0001127 (0.0002771)			–0.0002249 (0.0002709)
P>|z|		0.954	0.858	0.791	0.684			0.406
FDI in		0.0000543 (–0.0000604)	0.0000384 (–0.000059)	–0.0000671 (0.000137)	0.0000529 (0.0000618)			–9.64e–06 (0.00006)
P>|z|		0.369	0.515	0.624	0.392			0.872

(Continued)

Number of obs = 816; Number of groups = 34
Panel = 1990–2013

	Random-effects (RE) GLS regression		Fixed Effect regression	RE GLS regression	RE GLS regression	RE GLS regression	RE GLS regression	RE GLS regression
	Model I	Model II (with control var)	Model III (with control var)	Model IV (without Luxemb and Iceland)	Model V (without Lux, Icel and Switzerland)	Model VI (Dummy for new rich countries)	Model VII (Dummy emerging countries)	Model VIII (1-y lag for Gini)
Import		-0.0001758 (-0.0001385)	2.92E-06 (-0.0001501)	-0.0001564 (0.0001351)	-0.000129 (0.0001301)			-0.0001419 (0.0001311)
P>|z|		0.204	0.984	0.247	0.322			0.279
Econ. Growth		0.0001935 (-0.0002315)	0.0001312 (-0.0002276)	0.000145 (0.0002396)	0.0001286 (0.0002348)			-0.0000147 (0.0002314)
P>|z|		0.403	0.565	0.545	0.584			0.949
Tertiary education level		-0.0001815 (-0.0003467)	0.0001228 (-0.000372)	0.000071 (0.0002659)	0.0001565 (0.0002778)			0.0000898 (0.0002688)
P>|z|		0.6	0.741	0.790	0.573			0.738
Time dummies (years 1990–2013)	YES	YES	YES	YES	YES	YES	YES	YES
Dummy for new rich (emerging + CEEC)						0.0382947 (0.019007) 0.044**		

	(1)	(2)	(3)	(4)	(5)	(6)	(7)
Dummy for emerging countries							0.0820868
							(0.029235)
							0.005*
Constant	0.3530048	−0.2291932	0.2456811	0.3681528	0.361551	0.3401881	0.3437974
	(−0.012458)	(−0.4890413)	(−0.5126353)	(0.0155447)	(0.0166885)	(0.013997)	(0.01288)
P>|z|	0.000*	0.639	0.632	0.000*	0.000*	0.000*	0.000*
	R-sq =	**R-sq =**	**R-sq =**	**R-sq =**	**R-sq =**	**R-sq =**	**R-sq =**
	0.2437	**0.3167**	**0.1447**	**0.2899**	**0.2708**	**0.3661**	**0.2696**
	Wald	Wald		Wald	Wald	Wald	Wald
	chi2(4)=	chi 2(10)=		chi2(9) =	chi2(9) =	chi2(5) =	chi2(9) =
	32.55	40.36		45.34	41.14	36.55	41.18
	Prob >	Prob >	Prob >	Prob >	Prob >	Prob >	Prob >
	chi2 =	chi2 =	F = 0.0009	chi2 =	chi2 =	chi2 =	chi2 =
	0.0000	0.0000		0.0000	0.0000	0.0000	0.0000

Hausman Test (RE vs FE):

b (RE) = consistent under Ho and Ha; obtained from xtreg

B (FE) = inconsistent under Ha, efficient under Ho; obtained from xtreg

Test: Ho: difference in coefficients not systematic

chi2(4) = (b-B)'[(V_b-V_B)^(-1)](b-B) = 3.50   Prob>chi2 = 0.4783

* indicates significance level at 1%; ** significance level at 5%; *** significance level at 10%.
Robust standard errors in parentheses. Source: Own elaboration.

The economic importance of this model is considerable. Take for instance two emblematic cases (very different, a sort of poles apart): US with a Gini = 37%, and Germany with a Gini = 27%. The model tells us how much of the variation in Ginis is explained by variations in F (and other independent variables). For US, F = 119%, and 44% for Germany. That is a difference of 75%; 75% × β_1 = 75% × 0.0000502 = 0.0375, which is about one-third of the difference in inequality between the US and Germany. The rest of the difference in inequality (the others two-thirds) can be explained by the other three relevant variables of the model: EPL (labour flexibility), TU (trade union density) and S (social spending), with this last variable having the most important role. Similar explanations can be drawn for all countries of the sample.

In Model II, I include some relevant control variables such as the unemployment rate, import (as a percentage of GDP), FDI inflow (as a percentage of GDP), economic growth and tertiary education level, plus the years (as time dummies). All these variables are used for the same span time covered by the panel (i.e. 1990–2013). As Table 2.2 suggests, adding these variables to the initial model does affect the results (they are all statistically insignificant), since the coefficients for these variables of interest (F, EPL, TU and S) stay approximately the same. This means that higher unemployment rates do not affect inequality levels, so long as the welfare state of that country is able to compensate the unemployed. Moreover, the other two control variables suggest that an open economy with more unskilled labour is not condemned to increased inequality if this economy has a stronger welfare state, powerful trade unions, a more rigid labour market and social institutions which mitigate the negative effects of globalisation and of technology. This seems to be the case, for instance, of the very competitive Scandinavian and continental European economies, which are also countries where inequality is low.

Model III shows also the results of the fixed effect regression, which however are not confirmed by the Hausman test performed. Economically, this has an important meaning: fixed effect is usually preferred when, it is assumed, variation of the dependent variables are due to structural (fixed) policies/institutions/factors that do not change much in short time. However, in my model, the time span of my panel (1990–2013) is long enough to allow for changes in policies/institutions/factors, which in a shorter time could be more or less fixed. Hence, random effect is a favoured option not only because it is consistent against the fixed effect according to Hausman test but also because it is a more reasonable option from an economic point of view. Inequality changed very much in the last two to three decades, and this has to do with policies and institutions (such as labour market flexibility and social spending) implemented in the last two to three decades, which vary consistently among countries and during this time span, so that cannot be considered fixed.

Models IV and V check the robustness of the findings and the sensitivity of the analysis to possible outliers, such as Luxemburg, which has a very high level of financialisation ratio (149 per cent), more than double the OECD average (62 per cent), despite the fact that its population is only about 350,000 people, and Iceland (about 300,000 inhabitants). Model IV shows that results do not change when Luxemburg and Iceland are dropped from the panel. Hence, findings are robust. In model V also Switzerland was dropped from the panel, having the highest level of financialisation (187 per cent). As well in this case, results do not change, hence the main conclusions of model I still apply.

The sample considered in the book includes, as I said before, all thirty-four OECD countries. While all these countries have in common the commitment towards market economy, as it is stated in the OECD mission,[9] they are relatively different in terms of GDP level, productivity, social performance (like inequality, employment) and policies. In particular, we have from one side initial (or older) members of OECD such as old European Union member states, plus the US, Canada, Japan, Australia, New Zealand, and to some extent Israel. From another side, we have new OECD members, which are new members of EU such as Poland, Czech Republic, Hungary, Slovakia, Slovenia and Estonia (i.e. Central and Eastern European Countries, CEEC), and few emerging economies such as Mexico, Chile and Turkey. CEEC and emerging countries, which joined OECD in the 1990s and 2000s, have similar levels of GDP per capita, and to some extent also similar levels of development. Moreover, Chile, Mexico and Turkey have also much higher inequality level than the rest of the OECD countries. For this reason, I considered, in model VI and VII, dummy variables which try to take into consideration these similarities among homogeneous groups of countries.

In model VI a dummy variable is considered for so-called new rich countries (i.e. CEEC), and the model has the expected results – i.e. inequality on average is 3 per cent higher in new rich countries than in older (initial) OECD members. This result is strengthened when the three emerging countries only are considered in model VII; in this case, inequality on average is 8 per cent higher than the rest of OECD countries. This is not surprising, and although financialisation in emerging economies may play a minor role with respect to advanced economies, the general model is confirmed since both CEEC and emerging countries have similar tendencies to the ones of advanced economies.[10]

A further robustness check is carried out with model VIII which includes a lag of one year for the dependent variable (Gini coefficient) in order to overcome possible auto-correlation problems in error terms. Also in this case results are very robust, and the model confirms the previous results: although lagged, the dependent variable seems to be caused by the same independent variables (F, EPL, TU, S). The control variables included, as usual, do not have any impact on inequality; and the dummies for new rich and for emerging countries, when included, produce the same results as in model VI and model VII (this is the case also when we exclude possible outliers and small countries such as Luxembourg, Iceland and Switzerland). Finally, the Hausman test for these models also confirms the appropriateness of the random effect. Hence, model I, which is our main specification, is confirmed.

As for other diagnostic issues, the correlation matrix in the appendix (Table A3) shows that there is a relatively small (imperfect) multicollinearity between F and EPL (−0.38), between TU and SocSpend (0.45), and between EPL and

SocSpend (–0.10). However, the multicollinearity test carried out in Table A4 in the appendix, the VIF test (*variance inflation factor*) excludes systematic multicollinearity among the explanatory variables: all the VIF values are much below 10, and the tolerance level (1/VIF=0.1) under which multicollinearity may take place, is overcome by all the independent variables used in the regressions (Drukker, 2003). Hence, multicollinearity is not biasing the estimated coefficients.

In Table A5 in the appendix, the Levin–Lin–Chu test was used to verify whether the panel data contains unit roots or is stationary. The null hypothesis tested, which I rejected with a level of significance below 1 per cent, is that the series contains a unit root, and the alternative hypothesis is that the series is stationary (Levin–Lin–Chu, 2002). Last but not least, the residual normality test (see Kernel test in Figure A2) confirms a symmetric and unimodal distribution.

To conclude, the econometric analysis confirms my hypothesis: the shift towards the financialisation of the economy, with a pressure on labour (and wage share) through increased labour flexibility, the decline of trade unions' power (accelerated by the globalisation process) and the retrenchment of public social spending (allowed for by global tax competition and efficiency thesis approaches) brought about an increase of income inequality in many advanced economies in the last two to three decades.

Notes

1 This approach follows the "efficiency thesis".
2 Interestingly enough, the IMF has recently backtracked with regards to capital market liberalization, arguing that opening capital markets in developing economies could increase economic instability if an appropriate regulatory environment is not put in place, IMF (2014).
3 It has to be said that in the last years, in particular after the 2007 financial crash, the Washington Consensus along with other mainstream policies evolved, and the main advocates of those policies started to acknowledge failures and mistakes (IMF, 2014).
4 Figure 2.5 shows that GDP growth during Fordism (which is usually identified by the period before 1980) is higher than growth during both the transition period (which is usually identified by the period during the 1980s, in particular the decade 1981–91) and post-Fordism (or the period of globalisation and financialisation), which is identified by the last period from 1992 until today. For more details on the periodization of Fordism and post-Fordism, see Jessop (2002).
5 Since financialisation refers to the rise of financial claims and incomes with respect to the real sector, one of the best variables able to capture it is the "Market capitalisation" (also known as capital market value), which is the share price multiplied by the number of shares listed in each stock exchange. A similar definition of financialisation is used also in Nölke and Vliegenthart (2009), in Engelen *et al.* (2010), and in van der Zwan (2014). Stock market capitalisation (SMK) is one of the major sources of business finance in most advanced economies. Hence, it makes sense to refer to it as a proxy for financialisation. Obviously also inward FDI are sources of business finance but of less magnitude than SMK. In the regression model, I used both variables, and the significant variable remains SMK.
6 Interestingly enough, financialisation also took place in Scandinavian economies. This is consistent with the results of Engelen *et al.* (2010) and van der Zwan (2014), who show that financialisation takes place everywhere, including in countries with

strong welfare states. However, here, the high level of social expenditure is able to contain inequality (which is nevertheless increasing in Scandinavian countries, too). The highest percentage of financialisation in terms of GDP is Switzerland, while, in terms of absolute value, the US is the most financialised market, followed by the UK.

7 Butcher *et al.* (2012) and Autor *et al.* (2015) obtained a similar result and found that minimum wages have little effect on employment but do have impacts on wage inequality in particular in the UK and in the US during the 1990s and 2000s.

8 OECD in the last two decades expanded from around twenty countries (the previous EU15 plus Norway, Switzerland, Iceland, North America, Australia, New Zealand, Japan, and Korea) to thirty-four countries, which include also Chile, Mexico, Turkey and several other Central and Eastern European Countries (CEEC), new EU member states. These latecomers are not typical rich countries, in particular Mexico and Turkey; however, GDP per capita in Mexico and Turkey is not much below the one in CEEC (in particular if you consider GDP per capita in the 1990s, or the average GDP per capita of our timespan – i.e. 1990–2013). Hence, excluding Mexico, Turkey (and possibly Chile) without excluding CEEC would not be fair. In order to gain in terms of representativeness, I include all the thirty-four countries, including countries that are not typical rich countries but have common tendencies and trajectories towards rich countries. Moreover, all these countries share the most important feature for OECD, being "functioning market economies", and some of the features of the market economies (such as labour flexibility, trade union, welfare, and financialisation) are crucial in my analysis to identify the determinants of the rise of inequality in OECD.

9 "The common thread of our work is a shared commitment to market economies backed by democratic institutions and focused on the wellbeing of all citizens" www. oecd.org/about/.

10 I preferred to keep these countries in the sample (emerging countries and CEEC) rather than just drop them all, because although differences in levels are important with respect to older OECD members, tendencies are very similar. Dummies variables, however, for emerging countries and CEEC take into account for differences with older OECD members and help to better calibrate the model.

3 Welfare capitalism versus financial capitalism during globalisation

Introduction

In this chapter, I investigate whether the welfare state is a barrier to economic growth, as neoliberal economists argue, or on the contrary, whether it can enhance economic efficiency along with socioeconomic development and reducing inequality. In examining this question, the chapter proposes a new classification of socioeconomic models and its consequences. The new classification is the division between the welfare capitalism and the financial capitalism. In the countries that belong to the first category, welfare states not only contribute to reduce inequality but also foster economic growth. On the contrary, the countries in the second category have higher inequality, and during the current economic crisis, they also exhibit worse economic performance. In other words, in this analysis, the welfare state does not appear to be a drain on economic performance and competitiveness or as a barrier to economic efficiency. On the contrary, the most generous of welfare capitalism states are also the most efficient and successful economies.

The chapter explores whether "the efficiency thesis" concerning the relation between welfare states and globalisation is functional for economic growth or, alternatively, whether "the compensation thesis" produces better results in terms of economic growth. The current economic crisis (2007–13) in particular was a test for many advanced economies to determine whether the socioeconomic model that those countries built in the last several decades was able to cope with the challenges of globalisation. My hypothesis is that the efficiency thesis, according to which globalisation needs to be accompanied by the retrenchment of welfare states in order for firms to be competitive, does not cause economic growth. The tests are conducted in a sample of thirty-nine countries made up of OECD and EU members. On the contrary, the econometric exercises indicate that the "compensation thesis" (i.e. regulated globalisation and an expanded welfare state) is better able to produce higher economic growth.

The chapter uses a comparative method and shows that the economic performance of the most generous welfare states, measured with a so-called performance index (PI) that combines GDP growth and labour market performances (employment growth and unemployment levels) since the 2007 global financial crisis, has been considerably better. During the crisis, the spending attitudes of governments varied consistently, although some general patters can be characterized: initially governments spent public money to save banks and financial institutions, then some Keynesian programs of public stimuli were implemented, and finally, after 2010/2011 austerity policies were introduced as Vis *et al.* (2011) argued. The PI is built simply by aggregating GDP and labour market performance in the following way: "g" (average GDP growth in 2007–13) + "n" (average employment growth in 2007–13) – "U" (unemployment rate, average 2007–13) as explained in the section "Welfare models and economic performance" on p. 88.

The new classification of socioeconomic models put forward in this chapter proves to be more consistent with respect to the evolution of welfare models in the age of globalisation, and it is an improvement with respect to the important classification made by Esping-Anderson (1990) when the globalisation impact on welfare was not yet very clear.[1] The evolution of welfare states, particularly the evolution that occurred during globalisation, leads us toward a new classification of only two socioeconomic models among advanced economies that are quite polarized to each other: the financial capitalism regime versus the welfare capitalism regime. In general, countries that rely more on the financial nexus, having higher levels of financialisation in the economy, as measured by the market capitalisation index shown in Figure I.3, fall into the financial capitalism category. However, my analysis suggests that financialisation alone does not guarantee for a country to fall in the category of financial capitalism. Other features are needed for a country to be included in this model: countries of this model have also relatively lower levels of welfare spending and a higher level of inequality, along with a more flexible labour market and a lower wage share over the GDP. Countries that rely more on the welfare nexus, having higher levels of welfare spending, lower level of inequality, lower levels of market capitalisation index (financialisation), and a labour market not very flexible with a higher wage share over GDP, fall clearly into the welfare capitalism category. In this analysis, the financial capitalism category embeds the Anglo-Saxon and Mediterranean groups, while the welfare capitalism category embeds the Scandinavian and the Continental groups. Another important result of my empirical analysis shows that countries that are winners in the process of globalisation are also countries that did not embrace *tout court* financialisation along with globalisation and managed not to retrench welfare states. The persistency and/or the expansion of the welfare state found to be in place in Scandinavian and in Continental European models functioned under the condition of globalisation to produce better performance during the years of the crisis (2007–13). As the empirical evidence suggests, investing in social dimensions is the best policy option not only because it allows them to reduce or to keep lower inequality levels but also because it produces better performance in terms of GDP growth and labour market performance (employment growth and unemployment).

Welfare regimes and capitalist systems: a brief literature overview

The standard classification of socioeconomic models widely used is the one proposed by Esping-Andersen (1990) according to whom welfare models can be divided into three groups: Liberal, Continental and Scandinavian models.[2] This classification, although methodologically still very relevant, was based on data from before 1990. Therefore, Hay and Wincott (2012) proposed a new one that takes into consideration the evolution of these models in the last two decades. They extended this classification to five models: the three models used by Esping-Andersen plus the Mediterranean group and the Central and Eastern European Countries (CEEC) group, claiming that a strong difference can be observed among these groups in general patterns. The peculiarity of a 'Southern Model' emerged already in the debate in the mid-1990s with distinct features (Ferrera, 1996), while the CEEC model (or perhaps is better to say the CEEC group) reflects more the transformation from planned economies to market economies occurred after the Fall of Berlin Wall in 1989 in Central and Eastern European Countries (Tridico, 2011a). Moreover, since 1990, welfare patterns are diverging even more with the Scandinavian model, which seems to clearly have increased welfare in order to cope with the challenge of globalisation (following the so-called "compensation thesis"); the continental model, which maintained stable or increased slightly the level of welfare spending in the same period; and the other three groups – the Anglo-Saxon, the Mediterranean and the CEEC – which converge among themselves in the sense that they reduced the level of welfare spending clearly following a so-called "efficiency thesis" during the last two decades of globalisation as I show later in this chapter.

Generally speaking, countries can also be classified according to their type of economic system, which can be characterized by particular institutional forms and macroeconomic factors like domestic competition, role of the state, international trade and openness, monetary forms, etc. Following this approach, Amoroso (2003) and Jessop (2002) identified four types of economic systems; the Anglo-Saxon model (or competitive capitalism), the Corporative model (Corporative capitalism), the Dirigiste model, and the Social-Democratic model. To these models, Chonj-Ju, (2004) among others (i.e. Yeager, 2004; Qian, 2003; etc.), added the current model of the Socialist Markets, represented in particular by China and Vietnam.[3]

Bruno Amable (2003) narrated a similar story in his book *The Diversity of Modern Capitalism*, proposing five different ideal types of capitalism, taking into consideration five institutional forms (product market competition, wage-labour nexus, financial sector, social protection, and education). He combined the Dirigiste and the Corporative models (forming a Continental European model) and added two new models (the Asian model and the South European model). The Amable (2003) classification is (1) the market-based economy (the US and the British economies are the closest to this), (2) continental European capitalism (led by Germany and France), (3) the Social-Democratic economies (the Scandinavian economies), (4) South European capitalism, and (5) Asian capitalism.

Certainly, the continental Europe models in particular the German, the French, and the Scandinavian model, have much in common and share similar features, particularly within the social dimensions and to some extent also in the financial sector (Sapir, 2005) despite the fact that still many differences exist among those models.

Table 3.1 summarizes the main characteristics of these socioeconomic models, and, in parentheses, lists the notable adherents to the model. The table combines the work of the authors cited above.

In parallel to the classification of welfare models, a theory of varieties of capitalism (VoC) emerged, in particular since the work of Hall and Soskice (2001), which sees the welfare state and capitalism as complements and not adversaries. This theory distinguishes between only two types of capitalist systems: the liberal market economies (LME) and the coordinated market economies (CME). VoC identifies model from the production point of view (firms). The main independent variable that distinguishes LMEs and CMEs are the kind of labour skills firms demand. When firms demand general skills and low education, it is in the interest of the firms to have a high degree of commodification of labour because regulations, minimum wages, employment protection, etc. will change the market equilibrium to the disadvantage of the firm, as it is the case in LMEs (Caramani, 2008 p. 554). When firms demand high skilled and educated labour, it is beneficial for the economy to have high social spending. This guarantees some degree of insurance against losing jobs, which makes the workers more willing to educate themselves and which is beneficial for the company (as is the case in CMEs).

Thus the CMEs have no incentive to unravel the welfare state and become a LME because they have a comparative institutional advantage over LMEs regarding skilled workers. This kind of classification is and can be criticized especially for its simplicity. First and foremost, it does not take into account the role of the family or market in providing welfare – for instance, the fact that the US has a low public social spending does not alter the fact that public and private social expenditure as percentage of GDP is similar to most of the CME countries (Caramani, 2008 p. 560). So in the US, people are also encouraged to educate because by educating they have higher levels of social security (assuming they get a job at some point in their life and thereby are able to buy unemployment insurance). Moreover, the division between LMEs favouring unskilled workers, whereas CMEs favour quality workers, is not always exactly finding empirical evidences (in theory, CME firms benefit from a high degree of employment protection while LMEs push for more labour flexibility and less protection) (Hancké *et al.*, 2007; Andersen, 2007).

For these reasons, I am going to adopt a more traditional socioeconomic approach to classify capitalist systems, which identifies models on a wider perspective, rooted in multi-dimensions and social dimensions, such as social spending, inequality, finance, decommodification, social rights, labour relations,

Table 3.1 Socioeconomic models and their main characteristics

Characteristics Models (leader country)	Competition	Economic regulation	Main economic actors	Relationship between public and private actors	International economic relation	Taxation	Finance
Anglo-Saxon model (US, UK, Ireland)	Promotes free competition	Deregulation; withdrawal of the state from the economy	Firms, corporations, markets	Residual public sector; market-oriented	Global competition	Low taxes, no or little progressive rate	Deregulation and full liberalization; financing for both consumption and investments
Corporative model (Germany)	Balances cooperation and competition	Decentralised	Tripartite structures (business clubs, trade unions, government)	Public-private partnerships	Protection of strategic sectors in an open economy	High taxation to finance welfare state	Developed finance for investment; extensive credit for small firms; limited finance and credit for consumption
Dirigiste model (France)	State control; regulated competition	National accumulation and regulation strategy	Private and public sectors	Public-private partnerships under state guide	Protectionism	High taxes and collective recourses	financial regulation, transparency and protection of savings; higher taxes on financial corporations
Social-Democratic model (Scandinavian countries)	State-controlled liberalisation and competition	Knowledge and innovation as an economic guide for regulation	Public and private firms, ethical corporations	Public-private partnership in order to achieve social cohesion	National actors; moderate free competition; an open economy	High wages; career perspective; high and progressive tax rates	

Sources: Adapted from the classifications of Jessop (2002), Amoroso (2003), Amable (2003), and Chonji-Ju (2004).

and employment regimes, and not only on social spending dimensions like other studies in the field (Bonoli, 1997). Yet the outcome of the classification will be simple and, contrary to other similar classifications (Arts and Gelissen, 2002), will allow for an unambiguous and consistent taxonomy. Finally, my new classification considers the challenges that both globalisation and financialisation posed on welfare states, taking into account the consequences of these processes.

3.3 Welfare and inequality in the age of globalisation: an empirical analysis

Globalisation has been one of the most debated topics in at least the last two decades by scientists of different disciplines such as economics, politics, sociology, business, anthropology, engineering and transport studies and environmental studies, among others. In fact, the emergence of globalisation is widely relevant to the subject of human lives from different perspectives concerning incomes, wealth, consumption habits, production, institution, governance, infrastructures, transports, and technology, among others. However, globalisation is still a generic term, which, in most definitions, is identified as a process of the *intensification* of, for instance, trade, capital mobility, finance, and labour. By contrast, authors such as Hay and Wincott (2012) disagree with such a definition of globalisation and would rather define globalisation as a process not only of the intensification of those flows but also of *extensive* increase at a planetary level of trade, capital and labour mobility, and technological exchange, among others (Held *et al.*, 1999). Because evidence of this second type of definition of globalisation is missing and not all countries in the globe are part of the globalisation process (quite the opposite; globalisation interests a limited yet increasing number of countries), they conclude that it would be more appropriate to speak about regionalisation rather than globalisation. For instance, trade, capital and labour mobility particularly increased in the European Union (Europeanisation), among advanced and emerging economies (trans-regionalism), or among North American countries (with regional agreements such as NAFTA), etc. Hence, the interpretation of globalisation remains quite controversial and remains an ongoing and evolutionary process. Figure 3.1 attempts to show the asymmetry of globalisation or essentially the intensification of the process in primarily advanced economies during 1980–2006 (i.e. until the eve of the financial crash in 2007), which is considered the period during which globalisation intensified tremendously.

Nonetheless, while is true that globalisation interests more advanced[4] (and increasingly more emerging economies, typically BRIC countries) and less poor economies, it is objectively impossible to deny the intensification of this process and the increase in the number of countries involved in the global economy in the last two decades.

Globalisation poses several challenges to national economies and governments. One of the most important is the consequence on inequality, both within countries and between countries, and its impact on welfare state

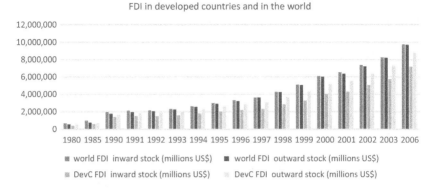

Figure 3.1 Capital mobility in terms of FDI.
Source: The World Bank database.

sustainability (Hay and Wincott, 2012). I will focus on inequality within countries and on the impact of globalisation on the sustainability of national welfare states.

In this context, the debate is very lively, and it has produced two main interpretations of the problem. The first one states that globalisation reduces the share of welfare states because it constitutes a cost for firms. Higher levels of welfare states produce higher income tax levels, social costs and contributions, which reduce profit prospective and increase costs for firms. Firms would be hence pushed to go abroad unless government retrenched welfare state spending and reduced taxes. Hence, in order to maintain higher levels of investments, firms and employment in the country, the welfare state needs to be reduced under the process of globalisation. This thesis, known as "the efficiency thesis", was developed within the neoclassical (or neoliberal) paradigm, and it argues that globalisation has forced (or should force) states to retrench social welfare in order to achieve a market-friendly environment and attract increasingly mobile international capital and competitiveness (Blackmon, 2006; Castells, 2004; Allan & Scruggs, 2004).

The efficiency thesis is contrasted by "the compensation thesis", according to which market openness pressured governments to expand welfare expenditures in order to compensate for the domestic "losers" of the globalisation process (Brady *et al.*, 2005; Rodrik, 1998; Swank, 2002). In a way, it can also be argued following the compensation argument that welfare expansion would allow states to further pursue globalisation. An extensive interpretation would then see welfare expansion not as a result but as a condition of globalisation so that in order to continue (or to start) with the process of globalisation, policymakers must expand social safety nets. Empirical evidence concerning the relation between globalisation (intensification) and welfare (expansion/retrenchment) is often found to be inconsistent and mixed.

However, it is true that globalisation favoured by outsourcing and FDIs out-flows has increased the position of capital relative to labour in higher-income countries, and trade unions lost bargaining power. In this context, wage shares decline dramatically, as Figure 3.2 suggests. The figure reports the average data aggregate by groups of countries. Anglo-Saxon economies (later included in the neoliberal competitive market economy model) and Mediterranean economies suffered the most from the restructuring process that occurred since the 1980s and intensified during the 1990s and 2000s.

This argument was already very clear to Adam Smith in his book *Inquiry into the Nature and Causes of the Wealth of Nations*, published in 1776, as the following passage, which helps to understand the tensions between globalisation and welfare, suggests:

> The proprietor of stock is properly a citizen of the world, and is not necessarily attached to any particular country. He would be apt to abandon the country in which he is exposed to a vexatious inquisition, in order to be assessed a burdensome tax, and would remove his stock to some country where he could either carry on his business or enjoy his fortune at his ease. A tax that tended to drive away stock from a particular country, would so far tend to dry up every source of revenue, both to the sovereign and to the society. Not only the profits of stock, but the rent of land and the wages of labour, would necessarily be more or less diminished by its removal.
>
> (Smith, 1776 [1976]: 848–49)

Inequality during globalisation increased in different magnitudes among countries and their models, as Figure 3.3 shows. The following figure, displaying Gini coefficient by socioeconomic models, tries to capture these differences.

This suggests a prominent role played by the welfare in compensating market inequality – i.e. income inequality after taxes and transfers (Piketty, 2014;

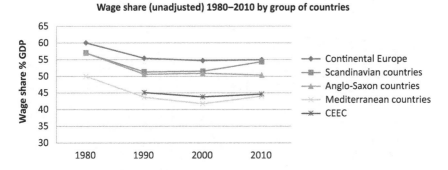

Figure 3.2 Wage share in advanced economies.
Source: Own elaboration on the ILO database.

Note: The unadjusted wage share is calculated as total labour compensation of employees divided by value added and does not consider self-employment.

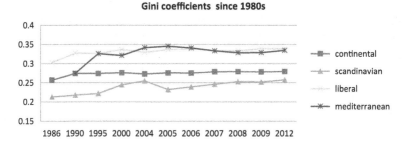

Figure 3.3 Inequality by welfare models.

Source: OECD database.

Note: Because of the lack of historical data, it is not possible to reconstruct the variables for the CEEC group.

Tridico, 2010; Galbraith, 2012). In fact, it is not surprising that countries that reduced less market inequality (calculated as a difference between Gini coefficients before taxes and transfers and Gini coefficients after), are the United States, Canada, New Zealand, and Australia. While at the opposite spectrum, with the higher levels of reduced market inequality, one can find Scandinavian and continental European countries, as Figure 3.4 indicates.

Most of the advanced economies in the last two decades introduced more flexibility in the labour market with the objective to stimulate business, increase start-up and create positive dynamics in the economy. Markets became more "aggressive" and market inequality increased. Governments focused on supply-side policies and so-called structural reforms. Labour was compressed and continuously adjusted

Figure 3.4 Market inequality and its reduction.

Source: OECD 2016, online database.

to supply needs. Globalisation and market integration pushed for export-led strategies, even in relatively big countries such as Italy, France, and Germany. The results were twofold. From one side, workers' purchasing power decreased; and from another side, global demand (at least in advanced economies) compressed. These reforms were, however, functional to the financialisation process, because, as we argued before, shareholder principle ("downsize and distribute") and finance managers' short-term objectives need labour flexibility and labour compression. In fact, the highest level of financialisation is found to be in the Anglo-Saxon group (and also in the Scandinavian group), which are also groups where labour flexibility is the highest (EPL is the lowest) as the correlation scatter plot in Figure 3.5 shows (however, the Scandinavian group embraced a model of so-called flexicurity where the highest level of labour flexibility compensated by the highest level of welfare expenditure and labour policy expenditure).

When labour flexibility increases, inequality increases unless more welfare spending occurs. In fact, it is not surprising to notice an inverse relationship between inequality and the EPL index (labour flexibility): the lower the EPL (higher flexibility), the higher the inequality. Continental European countries have a higher EPL (lower flexibility) and lower inequality, while Anglo-Saxon and Mediterranean countries generally show the opposite values of higher inequality and lower EPL (higher flexibility;[5] see also Tridico, 2013). Hence, a parallel trend of these variables occurs: when financialisation increases, one notices both increased flexibility and inequality.

However, what determines whether inequality increases or decreases under the condition of globalisation seems to be the pattern of the socioeconomic model

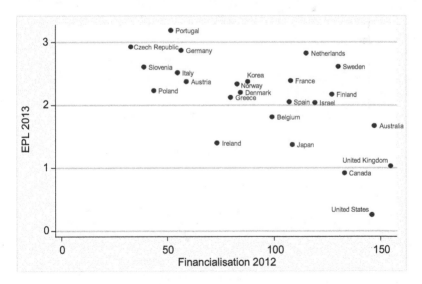

Figure 3.5 Correlation scatter plot between financialisation and labour flexibility (EPL).
Source: Own elaboration on the OECD and World Bank database.

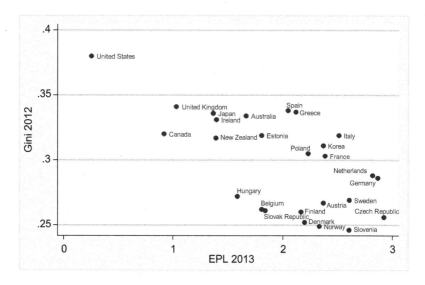

Figure 3.6 Correlation scatter plot between inequality and EPL.
Source: Own elaboration on the OECD and World Bank database.

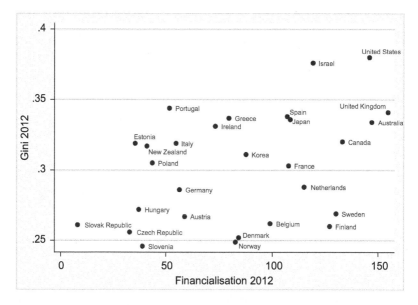

Figure 3.7 Correlation scatter plot between financialisation and inequality in 2012.
Source: Own elaboration on the OECD and World Bank database.

that each country built during the decades after the Second World War. More specifically, what is most relevant is the set of policies that each country is currently able to implement in order to cope with the challenges of globalisation, both in terms of income distribution and competitiveness (Rodrik, 2004). In particular, the institutions and the conflict management policies that countries put in place during the last two decades, social protection against unemployment and lower wages, social expenditures against poverty, public expenditures and programs on health and disease, social policy for housing, and so forth. In this context, our contribution is relevant. A proxy of these patterns can be offered by the relationship among OECD countries – which are considered the most advanced market economies between inequality and welfare expenditures. As Figure 3.8 shows, a clear relationship exists between inequality and welfare expenditures in the sense that countries that spend more on welfare have a generally lower level of inequality.

After the Second World War, particularly since 1960, countries, especially those in Europe, invested increasing shares of their GDP on developing welfare states. This increasing trend continued until the beginning of the 1990s. After that, and particularly after the peak reached in 1993, governments started to retrench welfare states, and the percentage of welfare expenditures was lower at the eve of the financial crisis in 2007 than in 1993.

The efficiency thesis at first glance seems to provide an explanation here: advanced economies that embarked on globalisation had to reduce their welfare expenditures in order to satisfy firms' needs and requests and to increase their competitiveness. However, as I will show, this explanation is not appropriate to

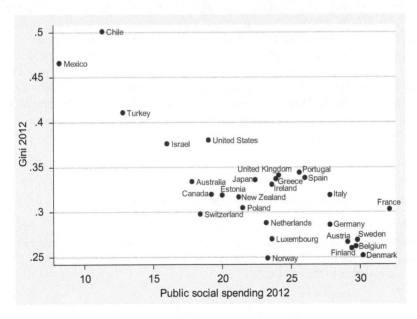

Figure 3.8 Gini coefficients and public social expenditure (% GDP) in 2010.
Source: Own elaboration on the OECD database and OECD (2012).

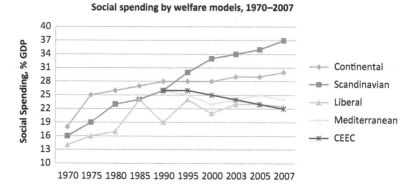

Figure 3.9 Welfare expenditure by models.

Source: Own elaboration on the OECD database.

Notes: Social spending (% of GDP) is the sum of "social benefits in-kind" and "social transfers other than in-kind" as defined as well before (OECD definition). Continental: Belgium, Germany, Luxembourg, the Netherlands, Austria; Scandinavian: Denmark, Finland, Sweden, Norway; Liberal: UK, Ireland, US, Australia, Canada, New Zealand; Mediterranean: Greece, Spain, Italy, Cyprus, Malta, Portugal; CEEC: Czech Republic, Estonia, Latvia, Lithuania, Poland, Slovenia, Slovak Republic, Romania and Bulgaria. Source: Own calculation on the OECD database. See also Adema and Ladaique (2009).

understand which countries in the end had actually better economic performance in terms of GDP dynamics and labour market performance. In particular, we will see that countries that reached a relatively higher level of welfare expenditures and where cuts did not occur or occurred relatively less had better economic performance during the crisis that started in 2007 and continued until today. On the contrary, countries that at the eve of the crisis were found to have poorer welfare states and cut welfare expenditures more profoundly during the 1990s and 2000s had worse economic performance in terms of GDP dynamics and labour market indicators (like employment growth and unemployment). These results will be shown in the following section.

The model: welfare state and economic performance

In order to test these hypotheses, particularly the consistency of the compensation thesis versus the efficiency thesis, a sample of thirty-nine advanced economies within the OECD and EU members was used.

The equation to test is as follows:

$$GDP = \alpha + \beta_1 \, SocialSub. + \beta_2 \, EducationExpendit. - \beta_3 \, Import + \beta_4 \, Export + \varepsilon$$

The model predicts that countries have higher income if they invest more in welfare (SocialSub.), invest more in Education (EducationExpendit.), import less and export more (var Import and Export); a term of error, ε is added to the equation.

The model uses longitudinal panel data of six years for the period between 2007 and 2012. These were the years where most of the advanced economies fell into economic crisis and stagnation. The results, presented in Table 3.2, confirm the predicted model of the above equation, according to which GDP per capita in 2012 is higher if countries invest more in welfare (as percentage of the

Table 3.2 Regression results

Regression model on a longitudinal panel Dep Var.: GDP per capita (Log Natural)		
Variable	*Coeff. (standard errors)*	*P-values*
Public social subsidies (% of GDP)	0.0085532 (0.0029786)	0.008
Education_Expend. (public), % of GDP	0.1323674 (0.0372624)	0.001
Import, % GDP	−0.02696 (0.0068556)	0.001
Export, % GDP	0.0223626 (0.0061447)	0.001
Investment (capital formation), % GDP	−0.0041776 (0.0034335)	0.234
FDI (out), % GDP	−0.0008266 (0.0005231)	0.126
FDI (in), % GDP	−0.000998 (0.0085615)	0.908
Constant	**10.34326 (0.7078016)**	**0.000**
Time dummies (Years 2007, 2008, 2009, 2010, 2011, 2012): YES		
R-sq (between) = 0.8097 sd(u_i + avg(e_i.)) = 0.1875238 Prob > F = 0.0000		
Number of obs = 240; Number of groups = 39 **Panel (2007–2008–2009–2010–2011–2012) Between-group effects (BE)**		

Hausman Test (BE vs FE):
b (BE) = consistent under Ho and Ha; obtained from xtreg
B (FE) = inconsistent under Ha, efficient under Ho; obtained from xtreg
Test: Ho: difference in coefficients not systematic
    chi2(12) = (b-B)'[(V_b-V_B)^(-1)](b-B) = 138.73 Prob>chi2 = 0.0000

Hausman Test (BE vs RE):
b (BE) = consistent under Ho and Ha; obtained from xtreg
B (RE) = inconsistent under Ha, efficient under Ho; obtained from xtreg
Test: Ho: difference in coefficients not systematic
    chi2(11) = (b-B)'[(V_b-V_B)^(-1)](b-B) = 97.00 Prob>chi2 = 0.0000

Note: the sample included OECD plus the EU members not part of the OECD. There are thirty-nine countries: Australia, Austria, Belgium, Bulgaria, Canada, Switzerland, Chile, Cyprus, Czech Republic, Germany, Denmark, Spain, Estonia, Finland, France, the United Kingdom, Greece, Croatia, Hungary, Ireland, Iceland, Israel, Italy, Japan South Korea, Lithuania, Luxembourg, Latvia, Malta, Netherlands, Norway, New Zealand, Poland, Portugal, Romania, Slovak Republic, Slovenia, Sweden, and the United States. Public social subsidies are subsidies, grants, and other social benefits including all unrequited, non-repayable transfers on current account to private and public enterprises; grants to foreign governments, international organisations, and other government units; and social security, social assistance benefits, and employer social benefits in-cash and in-kind (World Bank definition, see World Bank database).

social subsidies on GDP), in education (as percentage of education expenditures on GDP) and manage to import less and to export more (Import and Export as percentages of the GDP). All the data refer to the period 2007–12, for a total of 240 observations.

As Table 3.2 suggests, social subsidies and education expenditures – both with positive and significant coefficients – are functional to higher GDP. Positive coefficients and significance are noted for the variable Export (as a percentage of GDP), while a negative significant coefficient is noted for the variable Import (as a percentage of GDP). Hence, richer countries export and are more competitive than countries that import more instead. However, they also have a stronger welfare state. Moreover, other openness variables used as control variables, such as FDI (inward and outward) and Investments (as a percentage of GDP), are not significant. In this sense, the "compensation hypothesis" is confirmed: regulated globalisation and an expanded welfare state are better able to produce higher GDP per capita. In other words, countries that perform the best during this period (2007–12), results suggest, invested more in welfare state (social subsidies and public education expenditures) and adopted mercantilist policies, importing less and exporting more without being as open towards FDIs. These countries do not properly represent an orthodox model of liberal capitalist economy. On the contrary, they represent a corporative or social market economy model: in fact, most of these best-performing countries are Continental and Scandinavian European economies.[6]

In other words, from these results, it follows that richer countries are those that rely on a corporative socioeconomic model rather than on a liberal competitive model. This means that countries that managed to keep higher levels of public expenditure on the welfare state in the global economy are better off today.

The method used, a regression model on a longitudinal panel data, with a "between-group effects" is more relevant in this case, since I am mostly interested in the differences between groups of countries. Moreover, the Hausman test, which checks for the validity of the between effect (BE) against both the fixed effect (FE) and the random effect (RE), produces positive results in the sense that the hypothesis zero (Ho), of consistency of the BE, is accepted with the maximum level of significance, against the alternative hypothesis (Ha) of consistency of BE and RE.

Welfare models and economic performance

The long-term empirical analysis of welfare spending, and the evidence of economic data during the crisis (2007–13) confirm our hypotheses: countries that had better performance are those that managed not to retrench the welfare state under the process of globalisation and therefore reached the eve of the crisis in 2007 better equipped in terms of the welfare state, as the figures in this section show. Figure 3.10 reports performance using the so-called performance index (PI), which was used also in other studies (Tridico, 2013; 2014). The PI here is built simply by aggregating GDP and labour market performance in the following way:

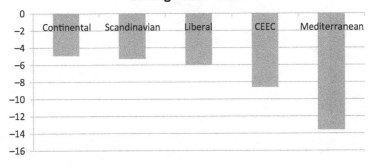

Figure 3.10 The performance index.
Source: Own elaboration on the WEO IMF, and OECD database.

the sum, of "g" (Average GDP growth in 2007–13), plus "n" (Average Employment growth in 2007–13), minus (–) U (Unemployment rate, average 2007–13).[7] Taking into consideration, as a PI, g, n and U contributes to avoid biases and to look at the economic performance from a broad perspective: in fact, some countries can have relatively better GDP dynamics but very bad employment performance or unemployment levels (and vice versa, good GDP performance and higher unemployment). The PI takes into account both aspects – labour market and GDP – hence it captures better the general economic performance. Moreover, to subtract U (the unemployment level, which is more a structural indicator) to g and n (which are variables which indicates changes, respectively of GDP and Employment) is a way to evaluate the performance of a country in a wider way. Finally, since we are going to use the PI for a group of countries only (and not to use it as an absolute measure for performances), which are to a large extent similar in terms of income and structure of the economy, the index remains a consistent method of comparison.

The compensation approach contributed to both maintain lower levels of inequality and to have better performance in terms of GDP and the labour market.

This emerges clearly in particular when we group countries in the respective model with simple calculations, and we account for the average values of inequality (Gini coefficients in 1990 and 2010) and welfare (social spending in 1990 and in 2010). Given all of that, several lessons can be learned.

First of all, it appears clear from Figure 3.11 that some countries that were rightly included by the Esping-Andersen (1990) classification in the continental model, such as Italy, can no longer be included in this model. On the contrary, Italy, along with Greece, Portugal and Spain, constitute a specific model, which has a pattern closer today to the liberal model rather than to the continental model. When data are available, the same pattern is also confirmed for Cyprus and Malta.

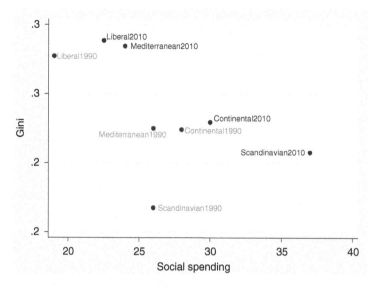

Figure 3.11 Inequality and social spending by welfare models in 1990 and in 2010.
Source: Own elaboration on the OECD database.

Note: Because of the lack of historical data, it is not possible to reconstruct variables for the CEEC group.

Disaggregate data about inequality and public social spending confirm this transformation. Figure 3.12 reports data for each country and shows that it is possible today to merge Mediterranean and Liberal countries from one side and Continental and Scandinavian countries from another side. To some extent, a problem remains as far as the financialisation index is concerned, in the sense that both the Mediterranean and the Scandinavian groups have middle values of this index; yet they are grouped in different models. However, when we consider and aggregate all the three relevant variables (financialisation, inequality, social spending) in a tri-dimensional graph as in Figure 3.13, rather than consider financialisation alone, we would obtain a more consistent convergence towards the two new categories identified.

1   There is a strong and steady correlation between welfare spending and inequality. Countries in the Scandinavian and Continental models maintain higher levels of social spending along with lower levels of inequality. On the contrary, the countries of the Liberal and Mediterranean models, which in the last two decades retrenched the welfare state or did not increase it, also experienced increasing inequality.

2   The evolutionary path of welfare models under the condition of globalisation presented a challenge for all countries involved in the process.

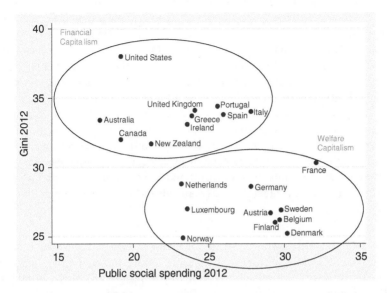

Figure 3.12 Financial and welfare capitalism.
Source: Own elaboration on OECD data.

Some countries, typically the Mediterranean countries, did not manage to increase welfare spending, and they ended up with both higher inequality levels and the worst performance in terms of GDP and labour market performance. The case of Scandinavian economies shows exactly the contrary: the challenges and the threats to income distribution and competitiveness of globalisation could be better coped with by increasing welfare spending.

3 Countries that are winners in the process of globalisation are also countries that did not embrace *tout court* financialisation along with globalisation and managed not to retrench welfare states. The persistency and/or the expansion of the welfare state found to be in place in Scandinavian and in Continental European models functioned under the condition of globalisation to produce better performance during the years of the crisis (2007–13). As the econometric results suggest, investing in social dimensions (such as public education expenditures and social subsidies) is the best policy option not only because it allows us to reduce or to keep lower inequality levels but also because it produces better performance in terms of GDP growth and labour market performance (employment growth and unemployment). Hence, from the trilemma (globalisation, welfare and financialisation), it is better to adopt globalisation and welfare because any other solution would contribute to poorer socioeconomic performance.

4   Last but not least, the evolution of welfare states, particularly the evolution that occurred during globalisation, leads us toward a new classification of only two socioeconomic models among advanced economies that are quite polarized to each other: the financial capitalism regime versus the welfare capitalism regime. Countries that rely more on the financial nexus, having higher levels of financialisation in the economy, as measured by the market capitalisation index shown in Figure 3.12, fall clearly into the financial capitalism category. These countries have also relatively lower levels of welfare spending. Countries that rely more on the welfare nexus, having higher levels of welfare spending and lower levels of market capitalisation index, fall clearly into the welfare capitalism category. The financial capitalism category clearly embeds the Liberal and Mediterranean groups, while the welfare capitalism category clearly embeds the Scandinavian and the Continental groups.

Figure 3.13 illustrates well this type of classification with a clear polarisation between the two categories, which also suggests the end of "The Three Worlds of Welfare Capitalism" described by Esping-Andersen. Countries of the Continental and Scandinavian models are aggregated in the welfare capitalism type, sharing higher levels of social spending, lower levels of inequality (indicated in brackets with the average Gini coefficient), and from middle (the Scandinavian group) to very low levels (the continental group) of financialisation. On the contrary, the Liberal and the Mediterranean models are aggregated in the financial capitalism type, sharing lower levels of social spending, higher levels of inequality (indicated in brackets with the average Gini coefficient) and from very high (the Liberal group) to middle levels of financialisation. In terms of performance, the welfare capitalism regime proved to be superior to the financial capitalism regime not only as far as inequality is concerned but also in terms of economic performance (GDP and labour market).

Table 3.3 Welfare capitalism versus financial capitalism

		Welfare spending (% GDP)	
		high	low
Financialisation (market capitalisation index, % GDP)	high		Liberal model
	middle	Scandinavian model	Mediterranean model
	low	Continental model	

Source: Own elaboration.

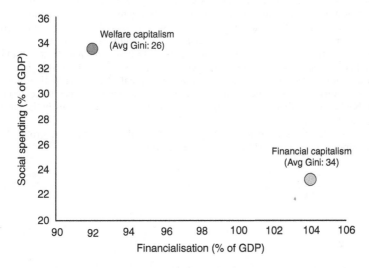

Figure 3.13 Poles apart: welfare capitalism and financial capitalism (data 2010).
Source: Own elaboration.

Notes

1 In general, in this analysis, I am interested in the "old OECD countries" – that is, more or less the old European Union (EU15, and Norway), plus Anglo-Saxon countries (the US, Canada, New Zealand, Australia), twenty countries in total. This is also the sample used originally by Esping-Andersen, and it is the sample on which I build my new classification. These are also the countries for which exist longer series and more reliable data. However, sometimes I have figures and data where other countries (such as new OECD countries like Mexico, Chile and Turkey, and new EU member states from Central and Eastern Europe) appear. However, this does not alter the final results.

2 Esping-Andersen, Gøsta (1990) ranks welfare models mainly according to the level of social spending, to the level of (de)commodification of welfare and to degree of extension of welfare among citizens.

3 China and Vietnam represent "Socialist Markets" and seem to be the only two countries that embrace such a model today. This represents an evolution and is the result of a reform process, which started first in China in 1978 and intensified during the 1990s (Yeager, 2004). This process transitioned China and Vietnam from planned economies to "Socialist Market" economies, characterized by forms of property rights that allow both private and government investment, without complete liberalization, privatization and political pluralism; integration (though modest) into the world economy; and government control and monitoring of domestic financial markets.

4 Advanced economies mostly correspond to OECD countries, termed in Figure 3.1 as DevC (Developed Countries).

5 Scandinavian countries, protected by their particular flexicurity model, have relatively low EPL but lower inequality.

6 You can obtain similar results if you consider as dependent variables in a cross-section regression the cumulative rate of growth (instead of the per capita GDP in 2012) that

countries experienced during the last years, when the crisis occurred (2007–12). It is clear again in this context that countries that implemented unconventional policies managed to get better results in terms of growth. In fact, the cross-section regression shows that countries that performed better implemented their own way of globalisation that is more regulated, with higher levels of tax on trade, and always with higher levels of welfare expenditures and education expenditures. The results suggest that these countries followed mercantilist policies typical of the corporative model pursued in Germany (and other countries such as Switzerland, Austria, Luxembourg and the Netherlands), then reaching higher levels of imports and surplus in the balance of payment.

7 This calculation is done for each country. Then the countries are grouped in the correspondent model, and the average values are calculated.

Part II

Financialisation and financial crisis

Policies and empirical evidences

4 The foundation of the financial crisis

Inequality and labour flexibility

Introduction

The financial crisis that started in 2007 in the US is considered the consequence of the financial capitalism model characterized by uneven development and inequality and driven by credit consumption and finance, as described in the first part of the book. Hence, the financial crash was not the cause for inequality, but it is the other way around: the crash was caused by the worsening of income distribution, which first of all weakened aggregate demand and caused structural problems in the functioning of the economic system. This argument will be explored in this chapter, whose objective is to articulate how the 2007–09 financial crash and the following economic crisis are rooted in the uneven income distribution and inequality caused by the current financial-led model of growth.

As we discussed in the first part of this book, the process of financialisation, which took place in the 1980s in the united States and then in the European Union was coupled with labour flexibility, wage moderation and soaring of profits in the financial sector. The flexibility agenda of the labour market and the end of wage increases, along with the contraction of indirect wages (i.e. public social expenditure) diminished workers' purchasing power. This was partly compensated with increased borrowing opportunities and the boom of credit consumption, all of which helped workers to maintain unstable consumption capacity. However, in the long term, unstable consumption patterns derived from precarious job creation, job instability, and poor wages have weakened aggregate demand. Hence, labour market issues such as flexibility, uneven income distribution, poor wages, and the financial crisis are two sides of the same coin. Both have a direct impact on the real economic crisis and the current global imbalances.

The economic crisis that started in the financial sector in 2007 had a negative and strong impact on the US and European economies, causing decreases in output and employment levels. This was the largest financial crisis since the Great Depression of 1929 and several arguments regarding the financial collapse have already been put forward (Obstfeld and Rogoff, 2009; Krugman, 2008; Skidelsky, 2009; Whelan, 2010, Semmler *et al.*, 2010; IMF, 2009a; Bini Smaghi, 2008; Allen, 2009; Caballero *et al.*, 2008; Fitoussi and Saraceno, 2010; etc.). These competing arguments offer differing analysis of both the origins of the crisis and the recovery policies implemented in its wake. Some economists argue that the origin of the crisis can be found mainly in the interaction between the financial bubble and the cheap money and loose monetary policies, which allowed for the money glut in the economy (Taylor, 2009). The consequences of this interaction were the breakdown of the financial sector followed by the crisis in the real economy (Greenspan, 2007). The opposing view finds that the main explanation is the saving glut, on the global level, which drove increased saving in China and East Asia while spurring extra spending in the US and other Western economies (Skidelsky, 2009). This caused huge imbalances in the current accounts of nations, specifically surpluses in Asia (mainly China) and deficits in the West (mainly in the US). Finally, a third group finds the structural roots of the financial crisis in the unfavorable income distribution and in the decline of the wage share over the GDP which has weakened consumption and the effective demand (Barba and Pivetti, 2009; Fitoussi and Saraceno, 2010).

From these different explanations, different causations and policy consequences are derived. I will show that along with the process of financialisation, income inequality increased and labour flexibility improved, both in the US and in the EU with negative consequences on aggregate demand and GDP dynamics.

Conflicting explanations of the crisis: a review

The starting point for an economic analysis of the current crisis should be with an understanding that the origin of the crisis is internal. The financial crisis originates in the heart of financial and global capitalism; it is an endogenous crisis that stemmed from a failure of the institutions tasked with regulating its mechanisms (Posner, 2009). It is the first crisis of the finance-led growth regime over the past two decades. No external influences, such as wars, oil shocks, natural disasters, or global pandemics were at fault, as is sometimes found with past economic crises. Therefore, the remedies to the current crisis have to be founded on the reinvention of the system, in creating a new form of governance according to which the marketplace would operate (EuroMemorandum, 2010). Since this is a global crisis, it can also be considered a crisis of globalisation. In other words, it can be considered a consequence of globalisation and financialisation which proliferated during the past two decades (Rochon and Rossi, 2010; Tropeano, 2010; Pitelis, 2010; Arestis and Pelagidis, 2010; Sawyer, 2010).

This is the first global crisis endured by capitalism since World War II. The blame, therefore, has been spread generously. In the US, neo-liberals argue that everyone is to blame starting with the profit-driven bankers, continuing to all of the institutions that played a part, and of course, to China, whose low exchange rate caused a deficit in the US (Mundell, 2009). However, the market has changed little and big financial institutions still exert the lion's share of the power. The alternative view, rooted in both Keynesian (Skidelsky, 2009) and neo-Marxian thought (Wolff, 2010), blames the neo-liberal global order and the internal and external imbalances that this financial regime of accumulation has created. In general, the explanations of the crisis can be divided in three groups. The first of which explains the slump of 2008–09, which resulted due to an excess of money ("money glut"; Taylor, 2009). A second group claims the excess of global saving ("saving glut") as a main explanation for the crisis (Skidelsky, 2009). A third group identifies structural problems in the economic system as the main drivers of the current crisis (Fitoussi and Saraceno, 2010).

Going into more detail of the first group, Cooper (2007), Caballero *et al.* (2008), and Mendoza *et al.* (2007) argue that global imbalances are a benign and temporary phenomena caused by a propensity to save by citizens of nations with emerging economies (where financial markets are less developed), and a propensity to consume in advanced economies (with more developed financial markets and financial availability). They argue that if people save more in Asia, this would be offset by more consumption in the West, and the equilibrium would sooner or later be reached (Mendoza *et al.*, 2007).

Greenspan (2005) and Bernanke (2005) argued that the causes of the American foreign deficit, and therefore its cures, were primarily external to the US.[1] This view assumes that perfect capitalist markets in countries like the US are able to take on ever-increasing leverage without risk. Alan Greenspan, as the chairman of the US Federal Reserve Board (Fed), was the main force behind American monetary policies between 1987 and 2006 and fundamentally created the monetary regime that the current financial system requires. According to the monetarist view, Greenspan is said to have kept money too cheap for too long, at least in the first part of the 2000s (Greenspan, 2007). Loose monetary policies accommodate the asset bubble, in particular the housing sector (Bernanke, 2005; D'Apice and Ferri, 2009). High prices required more liquidity and the Federal Reserve allowed for this. At the same time, a low interest rate stimulated more and more households to buy homes, and the housing sector enjoyed high prices and high profits. By means of securitization and "financial innovation", the financial market was able to insulate itself from risk. Private mortgages were available for everybody from middle-income to no-income borrowers. A new target group of borrowers was addressed, the so called NINJA (No Income, No Job and No Asset) class. This lending approach had been favoured since the Clinton administration, which encouraged the politically and economically marginalized to buy their own homes, instead of putting into place public housing programs similar to those found in several European countries.

However, according to the saving glut argument, Greenspan's loose monetary policies and the Bush administration's budget deficit were facilitators of the crisis and of the imbalances, not the causes (Skidelsky, 2009; Lowenstein, 2009). More in detail, in this second group, some commentators like Posner (2009), Dunaway (2009), and Skidelsky (2009) argue that global macroeconomic imbalances are the underlying cause of the crisis, the very root of it. Some others like Obtsfeld and Rogoff (2009) and Bini Smaghi (2008) find global imbalances to be co-determinants of the crisis. As they cannot be a source of economic recovery, loose monetary policies could not have been the main source of the crisis. On the contrary, public investments can be stabilizers of imbalances and provide the fiscal stimulus needed for recovery. Similarly, a lack of investment in the US, consequence of a very low rate of savings, was the main source of the imbalance. According to this argument (known also as the global imbalances argument), the external surplus run by China and other Asian economies underlies the excess of savings over investments. Following the famous *paradox of thrift*,[2] these saving excesses reverse in the US economy as an imbalance of aggregate supply over aggregate demand, but not as an increase in induced investment, which would be able to offset the saving glut. Hence, the excess savings brought about an excess of production compared to demand. However, this excess was compensated by the consumption credit boom, which kept the aggregate demand artificially high for a very long period. Economic growth in the US over the last fifteen years was mainly driven by consumption and not by demand for new investments, particularly after the dot-com bubble burst in 2001 (Skidelsky, 2009). According to Obstefedl and Rogoff (2009), the dot-com crash, along with its negative effects on investment demand, caused a saving glut, which policy-makers in the US reacted to with loose monetary policies, creating cheap money and low long-term interest rates. As a result, house and commodity prices increased. At the same time, home buyers and consumers were encouraged by financial instruments and the credit boom – both in the housing sector and in the commodity market. This allowed the US to enjoy a decade of economy growth, carried by consumption, within a framework of financialisation and imbalances.

As Bini Smaghi's (2008: 4) stated: "[E]xternal imbalances are often a reflection, and even a prediction, of internal imbalances. [E]conomic policies ... should not ignore external imbalances and just assume that they will sort themselves out." The essential truth of Keynes's ideas is that even the most productive economy can fail if consumers and or investors spend too little. At the global level, it applies to the current crisis as follows: Asia, especially China, saves too much (and consumes too little), while the US saves and invests too little. Furthermore, at the policy level, the Keynesian theory states that sound money and balanced budgets are not always wisdom (Krugman, 2008; Arestis and Pelagidis, 2010).

Along with the global imbalances argument, some of the more heterodox contributions, such as Barba and Pivetti (2009), Fitoussi and Saraceno (2010), Fitoussi and Stiglitz (2009), Brancaccio and Fontana (2011), identify structural problems in the economic systems of advanced economies, in particular the US and the UK, which were badly affected by the crisis. These structural problems are deep causes of the recession and of the global disorder. They refer to the income distribution bias and to the inequality that caused lack of consumption and effective demand in the economies. I will develop this third argument which, in my view, is the very foundation of the crisis, in strong correlation with the process of financialisation, which took place some thirty years ago. In brief, my argument is that the aggregate demand, which was not sustained by appropriate wage increases, and by productive investments, was artificially boosted through the channels of financialisation and credit to sustain consumption.

The meltdown[3]

The background of the crisis is the increase of household debt in advanced economies (like the US) and the bubble in the housing sector created by low interest rates. This is coupled with global imbalances which occur when a saving glut in Asia is not compensated by increased investments in the US and other developed economies. Price bubbles, both in the housing and in the commodity sectors, emerged as the twin Figures 4.1 and 4.2 show.

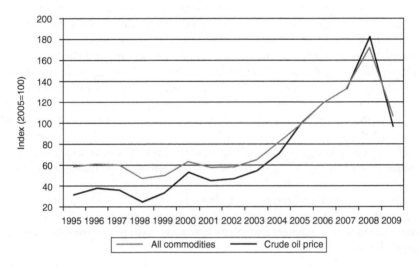

Figure 4.1 Global commodity prices.
Source: World Bank.

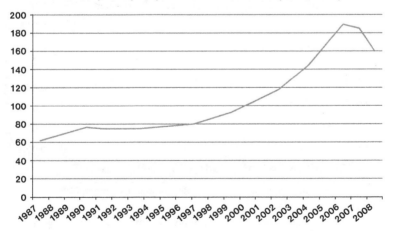

Figure 4.2 Home price indices.[5]
Source: Standard & Poor's.

Prices in the US housing sector rose almost 200 per cent since 1997. The situation in other countries is even worse; in Ireland, the increase in housing prices over the same period is about 300 per cent and about 225 per cent in the UK and Spain. In Australia, Norway, Sweden, France, Denmark, Italy, Canada and the Netherlands, housing prices increased around 200 per cent.[4]

The loosening of monetary policies and the resulting cheap money favoured the financial bubble, according to the following well-known causation chain: $\uparrow M/p$, $\uparrow Dshare$, $\uparrow Pshare$, $\downarrow i$.[6] Nevertheless, the fall of interest rates (i) was not followed by an increase of investments, according to a classical "Keynesian effect". On the contrary, high asset capitalisation allowed only for portfolio movements and financial investments. In contrast, the financial sector, supported by general enthusiasm and an excess of liquidity, manufactured a revolution; inventing financial instruments and financial packages for everybody, promising high returns to all. Financial innovation allowed for an impressive variety of instruments, securitization, derivatives, and speculative funds such as collateralized debt obligations (CDO), mortgage-backed securities (MBS), mortgage-backed bonds (MBB), credit default swaps (CDS), asset-backed securities (ABS), hedge funds, and futures.[7] The result was an explosion in the availability of financing, in particular mortgage financing (Lowenstein, 2010), as Figure 4.3 shows.

Financial institutions and banks, in order to protect themselves against NINJA and other weak borrowers, securitized mortgages with financial tools, which were traded with customers and others banks and institutions in order to spread the high risk.

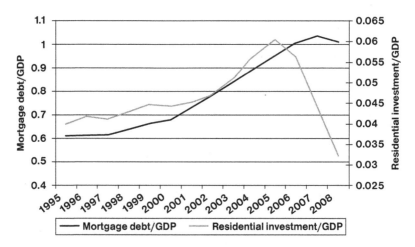

Figure 4.3 US mortgage debt and residential investment.
Source: US Federal Reserve System.

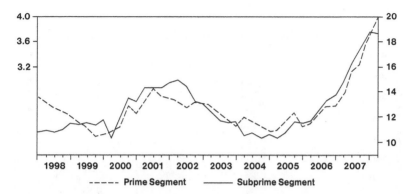

Figure 4.4 Percentage mortgage delinquencies.[8]
Source: US Mortgage Banking Ass.[9]
Note: Prime Segment left axe. Subprime Segment right axe.

Obviously, high-risk investments were associated with high returns and vice versa. Customers could choose from a menu, as if they were in a casino. The camouflaging of toxic assets and securities, along with collusion with the Credit Rating Agencies (CRA), completed the picture.

Perverse incentive schemes within financial institutions and extra bonuses for managers and brokers contributed to excessive risk taking. Increasing risky trades made fortunes for financial intermediaries, who were rewarded according to the short-term expansion generated by these risky activities, rather than the long-term profitability of investments. Benchmarks became the delivery of exceedingly high expected quarterly earnings in terms of dividends and share prices for investors. This hugely increased financial pressure generated manias and reinvigorated the bubble. But banks are not casinos, and a crisis could potentially, and actually did, emerge when only a small fraction of mortgage holders declared default, causing a so-called *default correlation*. As a matter of fact, these defaults actually caused the value of the most risky instruments to fall to zero. In turn, investors in the securities tools (MBS, CDO, ABS, etc.) demanded now, with higher levels of risk, higher compensatory interests, paid again by mortgage owners, causing further defaults. The fact that these instruments were spread out across the world only increased the level of panic, because nobody actually could know precisely where the toxic assets were. Paraphrasing Kindelberger (2005), panic follows mania. As a result, the American housing bubble burst. Banks started to worry seriously and drastically limited the levels at which they were willing to lend to each other, causing a huge increase in the intra-bank rate of lending, therefore worsening the position of many creditors. This caused even more default correlation because an increasing number of borrowers could not repay their debts. Simultaneously, a crisis of solvency (for borrowers) and a crisis of liquidity (for banks) emerged at the end of 2007 and beginning of 2008 (Chorafas, 2009).

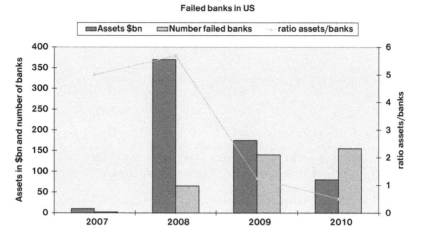

Figure 4.5 Bank failures in the US, 2007–10.
Source: Federal Deposit Insurance Corporation.

Despite the initial political consensus over the protection of big bank defaults (*too big to fail*), Figure 4.5 shows that at the beginning of the crisis, the first banks to fail were limited to the big ones, while later, in 2009 and 2010, the small ones failed as a consequence of correlation defaults (Goldstein and Veron, 2010).

The CRA started to revise their ratings of CDO, MBS, ABS and the like downwards. Consequentially, banks adjusted their risk upwards. The already highly leveraged financial institutions and the banking system were in worse trouble than before. They tried to raise fresh capitals by looking for funding from sovereign funds and state intervention as they now faced serious solvency and liquidity problems.

Now, not only individuals (borrowers, mortgage owners) but also banks started to declare default. In the UK, the Northern Rock Bank default was clearly the symptom of a liquidity problem. In the US, the unexpected default of the Lehman Brothers in September 2008 indicated that the crisis would be very big and could extend to the real market, since Lehman's shares were spread widely throughout the financial world and investor confidence would now be close to zero.

Western central banks, the Fed, the Bank of England and the European Central Bank (ECB) in particular acted immediately, providing liquidity and lowering the interest rate in stages. The Fed provided $200 billion in the first quarter of 2008 and another $700 billion in the second quarter of 2009. During the same period, the interest rate was lowered from 5 per cent to 0.25 per cent. The ECB, although traditionally more prudent with money supply and more focused on targeting low inflation and price stability than the Fed, followed the same line, although with some delay and at lower paces, by providing massive liquidity and lowering interest rates.

The crisis showed what was already known: securitization – i.e. the process of spreading the individual risk of sup-prime mortgage in many tranches – posed a danger to the market. Faulty guarantees by credit rating agencies such as Moody's[10] showed that the financial system was entirely built upon a conflict of interests[11] between controller and controlled societies. CRAs make profits advising firms whose products they are going to assess. Moody's has been awarding improper Triple-A ratings to many of the investment banks and insurance societies which went bankrupt in the fall of 2008, such as Lehman Brothers,[12] or were bailed out or saved by the government, such as Fannie Mae, Freddie Mac,[13] Bear-Stearns, Merrill Lynch, AIG, Goldman Sachs, Morgan Stanley, and Washington Mutual.[14] Trust collapsed immediately, matching the rate at which big financial colossuses were going into bankruptcy. The lack of transparency in the financial market and mystery surrounding complex financial tools, combined with corruption and manager greed completed this recipe for disaster. Similar stories, although on a smaller scale, can be told regarding European banks and financial institutions, saved by their governments as the market fell (Frangakis, 2010).

The failure and corruption of the very guarantors of the market economy, the CRAs, is just an example of how little real competition and transparency there is in the capital markets. There is a troupe of 150 rating and vigilante enterprises in the world. However, the majority of securities analyses are made by just two CRAs: Moody's and Standard and Poor's, which account for 80 per cent of the market. Thirteen per cent is controlled by Fitch. The remaining market share, approximately 7 per cent, is split amongst the rest (147 enterprises).

The labour market and the crisis under the financial-led growth model

The saving glut in the US and in other European and advanced economies is the background in which the current crisis emerged. The labour market is in fact a complementary pillar of this systemic crisis. The impact of the financial crisis on the labour market including the persistent and deep impact of the crisis on the real economy has been explored by many authors (Choudhry *et al.*, 2009; European Commission, 2009; IMF, 2009b; ILO, 2010).

The argument that I want to put forward is that the institutional and structural changes that occurred in the labour market and in the economy over the last twenty years in Europe and over the past thirty years in the US was functional to the financialisation process and have culminated in the current economic crisis. These changes allowed for labour flexibility, wage moderation and ultimately inequality and profit soar in the financial sector. All this occurred with the demise of the Keynesian policies.

First, the neoliberal approach requires a higher degree of labour flexibility because, in the current post-Fordist era, with the massive shift from the industrial sector to the service sector, technology and innovation bring about rapid

Table 4.1 Financial-led model of accumulation

	Wage-labour nexus	Form of competition	Monetary regime	State/ society relation	International regime	Coherence of the growth regime	Typical case
Financial-led model	Employment flexibility, profit soar, poor wages, and unstable pension funds	Mainly on financial markets, but trends towards oligopoly	Accommodate emergence of financial bubbles	Under scrutiny of financial markets.	Trends towards global finance	Risk of systemic instability	US and UK

structural changes, which demand quick responses from firms. Therefore, labour should adjust to the firms' needs. The financial sector in particular, because of its peculiarities, requires a very flexible workforce and fast adjustments. The financial sector asked for and obtained deregulation in the early 1980s, at all levels, first in the UK and the US and later in Europe. In turn, this has brought about more labour flexibility (Petit, 2009; Boyer, 2000). The rest of the economy then followed the financial-led regime of accumulation, with flexible labour and compressed wages. Shareholders want higher dividends because they invested their own capital in firms, taking on a higher level of risk. Since the economic growth and productivity of advanced economies in the post-Fordist market has not been much higher than in the Fordist market, it follows that wages should be compressed in order for shareholders to obtain higher dividends. Labour flexibility and wage contraction is a means to obtain this result.

As we have shown before, the market capitalization increased among all the countries, in particular the US, UK, Switzerland, Australia, and Canada. The highest percentage of financialisation, in terms of GDP, belongs to Switzerland. However, in terms of absolute value, the US is the most financialised market, followed by the UK. The trend of hyper-financialisation spread around the world, first to Europe and then to emerging markets. Wall Street argued that financialisation is beneficial to facilitate innovation and economic growth, despite a paucity of evidences supporting the claim. Quite the opposite is true, as clear evidence exists of a correlation between financialisation and inequality (showed in Chapter 3), manifesting in the compressed wage share (Petit, 2009; Basili *et al.*, 2006).

A clear and concise story is emerging from these relationships. Stopping short of suggesting causality, there is a positive correlation between the level of market financialisation and inequality. Anglo-Saxon countries have traditionally higher levels of financialisation and inequality. In contrast, Scandinavian countries and continental Europe, typically more equitable regarding income distribution, are also less financialised. The most interesting case is the US when compared with Denmark, which seem poles apart.

An exception is represented by the Mediterranean countries, which traditionally have less effective states, with bad distribution policies, and an informal economic sector that contributes to an increase in inequality (higher for instance than Australia and Canada and to some extent the UK). Moreover, lower employment rates, in Mediterranean countries, contribute to make the economy more uneven and the aggregate demand more unstablee.

Interestingly enough, while income inequality increased in the US dramatically in the last thirty years, consumption inequality did not increase, because borrowing opportunities allowed for workers to consume using credit channels. In fact, income inequality is more marked than consumption inequality. As shown in Figure A3 in the appendix, consumption inequality, thanks to finance, increased only 6 per cent, despite the fact that, during the same period (1980–2005), income inequality increased 23 per cent. This process, in particular in the US, brought about a soar of profits and a dramatic increase in the finance compensation with respect to the rest of the economy (as it was already shown with Figure A1 in the appendix). On the other hand, this consumption was needed by the economy because otherwise the saving glut in Asia and the low-income capacity of domestic workers would leave firms with un-bought goods and services and this would create aggregate demand unbalances. Thanks to financial innovation and cheap money, workers could now afford to buy cheap goods from China, as well as expensive houses, luxury cars, and other durable goods at home. Such a model of consumption is however unstable, as the financial crash of 2007 showed.

In the financial sector, short-term results and stakeholder dividends are favoured over long-term results and productivity. The ratio between manager's compensation and average wages of blue-collar workers increased steadily in the 1980s and in the 1990s. At the beginning of the last bubble, in 2003, it was 1 to 369, and at the eve of the financial crisis, in 2007, it skyrocketed to 521 thanks to bonus and compensation which do not find a proper justification (see Figures A4 and A5 in the appendix).

Before the current crisis, the new financial-led model had already been fully explained, along with its weaknesses and instabilities. Interestingly enough, Boyer (2000) argued in 2000 that under the new financial-led regime of accumulation, the fundamental role, which had belonged to the wage-labour nexus under Fordism, belonged now instead to finance. The wage nexus, on the contrary, has been relegated to a secondary role and simply adjusts to the needs of the financial system. It is easy to show, using the Boyer model of the mechanisms of the financial-led system (Boyer, 2000: 117), that one does not need to claim greed and opacity to explain the current crisis. These are just complementary problems that emerged in the financial sector. The figure shows that instability emerges from the model by itself.

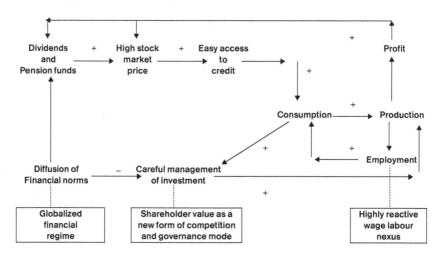

Figure 4.6 The mechanism of finance-led growth and its institutions.
Source: Boyer, 2000.

There are three major weaknesses seen in this model:

1 The careful management of investments (affected by shareholders), which
  means a low (real) investment rate and a high tendency towards speculative
  financial investments, which do not guarantee stable accumulation and sustained aggregate demand.
2 The highly reactive wage labour nexus, which in substance means labour
  flexibility, allows for wage compression, precarious job security and further
  reduction of aggregate demand.
3 The easy access to credit, which is necessary to finance consumption in
  order to artificially increase an otherwise low aggregate demand. It is
  a paradox for the neoliberal approach, which advocates the financial-
  led model of accumulation, to notice that from one side consumption is
  considered crucial (even when financed by cheap credit), and from another side neoliberal policies do not allow for proper wages to sustain
  consumption.

It is astonishing to notice how well the forecasts of Boyer in 2000 antici-
pated the current crisis, as the following text from the conclusion of his paper
shows:

> Contrary to a widely diffused belief, the main source of major financial cri-
> ses may not be NICs that suffer from bad financial and banking supervision
> and weak surveillance from international organizations. From 1997 to 1999,

all actors on financial markets have clearly perceived this NICs risk and, accordingly, raised their risk premium, while public authorities have undertaken ambitious reforms in order to assess more correctly the financial risks and tried to develop instruments in order to reduce such risk. Thus, a major lesson of the model is that the major current risks seem to be observed in the US. The more extended the impact of finance over corporate governance, household behaviour, labour-market management and economic policy, the more likely is an equity-based regime to cross the zone of structural stability. The next act of the financial drama may well start on Wall Street!

(Boyer, 2000: 142)

The foundation of the crisis: wage inequality, low productivity and flexibility

In this section, I will explore the very foundation of the current economic crisis. In particular, I assert that the crucial problem in the US is the issue of stagnating wages, with productivity growth, which allowed for a profit soar, an issue which has been present since the 1970s (see Figure 1.4 in Chapter 1). In Europe the increase of labour flexibility which was introduced since the 1990s was functional to a profit soar. Certainly in Europe, the situation is more variegated and differentiated than the US and the difference between a neoliberal and Anglo-Saxon model and a European social model is not always easy to trace. However, on average, wage share over GDP in the US is lower than the EU15, and it fell more rapidly in the US than in Europe. More in detail, countries like the UK still have a higher wage share than the US and some EU countries, since its initial levels were much higher because in the past, the UK's trade unions played an important role in defending labour. Nevertheless, flexibility and stagnant wages simultaneously contributed to the new finance-led model of accumulation as well as to the financial crisis of today. Both these phenomena are interconnected with the issue of extreme financialisation, which is necessary in order to sustain consumption. Flexibility, precarious and unstable jobs and poor wages encourage the increased demand for credit to finance consumption (see Figure A6 in the appendix). The US case is very well described by Wolff (2010), who claims that US wages today are stuck at the 1973 levels. After 150 years of growth, during the US boom and the realisation of the American dream from 1830 to 1970, productivity increased spectacularly with industrialisation; consequentially wages increased, immigration filled the continuous labour supply shortage and GDP reached high levels. Consumerism was just a natural development of that process. The Great Depression, which lasted about a decade, was the only bad experience during that century and a half, albeit one of dramatic proportions. After 1973, wages stagnated. Although productivity in the US continued to grow after that, productivity gains, a crucial pillar of Fordism, were no longer shared (Aglietta, 1979). Wage inequality increased dramatically as the Gini coefficient shows, passing from around 28 per cent in the mid-1970s to 40 per cent in the mid-2000s (OECD, 2010). The end of the labour supply shortage, the international competition, and the massive outsourcing of investments completed the picture. Consumerism, a natural and institutionalised mindset in American culture, did not stop either (Ivanova, 2010a). However, in order to continue, it had to use financing and credit to replace lost wages: consumption credit for cars and durable goods, multiple mortgages for houses, loans for colleges, etc. (see data in the appendix). Moreover, even with stagnant wages, American consumers could still enjoy higher purchasing power with respect to international prices, since productivity kept increasing and therefore real prices of imports decreased. The following data, from the US Department of Labour (Bureau of Labour statistics), confirm such an analysis.

Productivity between 1973 and 2007 increased 83 per cent, while hourly wages increased only 3 per cent. It is obvious that inequality increased in this scenario. Since during the same period consumption increased, too (25 per cent between 1996 and 2006),[15] one must assume that the increase was supported by financing and credit (see Figure A6 in the appendix). The winners in this scenario in the US are in the upper part of the income distribution (see Figure A7 in the appendix): corporate managers, shareholders, and capital gains recipients who benefited most from the productivity improvements in the economy (Wolff, 2010; see Figures A1, A4 and A5 in the appendix).

In Europe a similar story can be told. However, two details are different, with respect to the US economy:

1   Productivity in Europe did not grow as much as in the US, particularly since the 1980s[16] (see Figure A8 in the appendix).
2   Wages, on the contrary, kept growing after 1973, although at a lower rate than between 1947 and 1973. Since the 1990s, however, in Europe as well, real wages ceased to increase.

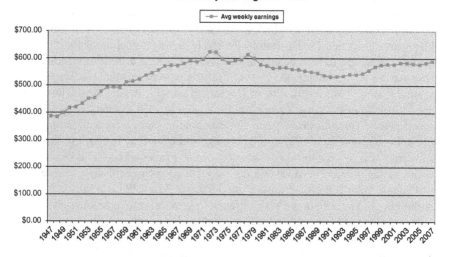

Figure 4.7 Real wage, non-supervisor workers (in 2007 US$).
Source: US Department of Labour, Bureau of Labour statistics.

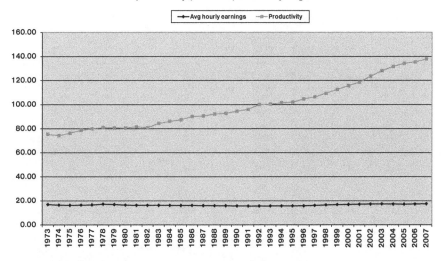

Figure 4.8 US economy, non-agricultural sector (in 2007 US$).
Source: US Department of Labour, Bureau of Labour statistics.

Hence, in the EU, we find an economy with lower productivity than the US and modestly growing wages until the 1990s. However, one should keep in mind that the EU is an economic entity with strong variation within its borders, and, one can observe, an entity experiencing growth in the productivity of some countries (like France and Germany) and decreasing productivity in others (like Spain and Italy). Nevertheless, a general trend of stagnant productivity in the EU, when compared to the US economy, as Figure 4.9 shows.

While in the US economy, which has always had a flexible labour market, the pressure of the financial-growth model stifled the growth of wages; in the EU, the pressure was on the governments to allow for, politically and financially, more labour flexibility (Wolfson, 1994). Both phenomena, labour flexibility and financialisation, contributed to a profit soar. A third actor, operating between firms and trade unions, has always had a strong role in Europe (including the UK): the state. Cost savings for firms were possible at the expenses of the state, which guarantees social support and financial subsidies to workers (Sapir, 2005; Nickell, 1997).

In the EU, because trade unions, traditionally, defended better wages, inequality did not increase as much and, to some extent, wages continued to increase until the mid-1990s. However, labour flexibility increased after the mid-1990s; the EU agenda of "flexicurity" in the labour market and the Lisbon Strategy confirm this (European Commission, 2003). More flexibility has been introduced, and the EU promises more security will be given to workers by the states in exchange. This relieves firms and gives them more power to determine wages, achieve profits, and evaluate working conditions in the face of

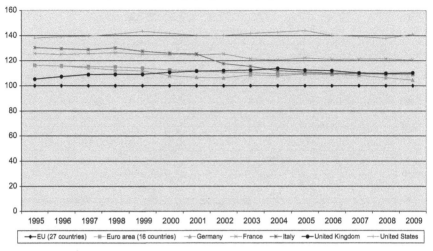

Figure 4.9 Labour productivity in the EU and US.
Source: Eurostat.

trade unions. The pressure then is on the state, which, in order to guarantee social cohesion, increases social expenditures (Leon and Realfonzo, 2008; European Commission, 2009).

Labour flexibility, however, gives European workers the same anxieties and precarious situations of workers in the United States (EFILWC, 2006; Dymarsky, 2008). Unstable income earners need help from credit and financing, as in the US. Hence, in the EU as in the US, demand for financing for consumption developed, too, albeit a bit later and in smaller proportions than in US. The numbers may be different, but the trends are similar (see data in the appendix). As Figure 4.10 shows, there are bad interactions in the current economic systems of the EU and of the US, which are characterized by a finance-led accumulation regime. Such interactions affect labour, finance, consumption, and investments, allowing for the creation of bubbles and their subsequent bursting, hence financial instability and economic crisis. Such an extreme financial-led growth model, which does not distribute productivity gains, compresses wages, increases inequality and labour flexibility, and which requires financing and credit to sustain consumption, lacks substantially productive investments and is subject to recurrent bubbles and dangerous price increases in the commodity market, with negative effects on the purchasing power of consumers. Therefore, it is not a sustainable model in the long term, and the current crisis testifies to the instability of such a system and the need for a radical change to it.

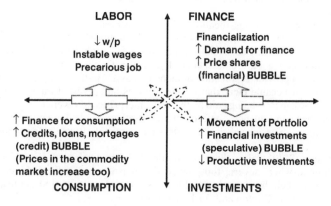

Figure 4.10 Interactions and bubbles within the finance-led growth model.
Source: Own elaboration.

Notes

1 Bernanke's view in 2005 was quite different from today's, during the crisis (Obstfeld and Rogoff, 2009). He now argues that it is impossible to understand this crisis without references to the global imbalances in trade and capital flows that began in the latter half of the 1990s (Bernanke, 2009). However, he is to blame for the huge dollar soar in summer–fall 2008 (Mundell, 2009). Against the euro, the dollar soared to $1.60 in July 2008, and this had bad consequence for the US current account.

2 The paradox of thrift: if everyone one wants to save more, firms will sell less and output will fall until the induced investment increases.

3 With the word "meltdown", financial analysts and economists are referring to the financial crisis that arose in the mortgage market after a sharp increase in mortgage foreclosures, mainly subprime, collapsed numerous mortgage lenders and hedge funds. The meltdown spilled over into the global credit market as risk premiums increased rapidly and capital liquidity was reduced. The sharp increase in foreclosures and the problems in the subprime mortgage market were largely blamed on loose lending practices, low interest rates, a housing bubble and excessive risk taking by lenders and investors.

4 Consistent with the story of surplus countries, which we will narrate later, house prices were stable or even fell in Germany, Switzerland and Japan.

5 The S&P/Case-Shiller Home Price Indices are the leading measures for the US residential housing market, tracking changes in the value of residential real estate both nationally as well as in twenty metropolitan regions.

6 M/p is the real quantity of money; Dshare is the demand for shares; Pshare is the price of shares, i is the interest rate.

7 Maurice Hank and Lewis Ranieri are the two financial gurus considered to be the main inventors and financial innovators among Wall Street people. Hank (AIG founder) conducted a vast business with CDS, generating huge profits and personal revenues before the failure of AIG. Ranieri (elected as one of the greatest innovators of the past seventy-five years by Businessweek, together with Bill Gates and Steve Jobs) is considered the father of MBS and MBB in the 1980s. His idea of disconnecting borrowers and lenders through securitization was one of the main factors leading to the financial meltdown.

8 That is a mortgage for which the borrower has failed to make payments as required in the loan documents.

9 Sub-prime includes a classification of lending to borrowers with a tarnished or limited credit history. Sub-prime loans carry more credit risk, and, as such, carry higher interest rates as well. Occasionally some borrowers might be classified as sub-prime despite having a good credit history. The reason for this is because the borrowers decided to not provide verification of income or assets in the loan application process.

10 After 2001, it became clear that rating agencies had a vested interest in providing positive assessments, being paid by the very enterprises they were rating (Petit, 2009). This had bad consequences: before Lehman Brothers crashed, many others in the US and in Europe experienced similar ends: Commerzbank, Parmalat, and Enron among them.

11 Lowenstein (2010) claims that this conflict of interest arises also in the US federal government, where several top jobs at the Treasury and in the Cabinet of the US President are held by alumni of Goldman Sachs and other Wall Street firms, in particular during the Clinton and Bush administrations.

12 Hank Paulsen (Secretary of US Treasury) decided to bail out Bear-Stearns and allowed Lehman Brothers to fail.

13 Fannie Mae was created in 1938 as a Federal National Mortgage Association in response to the massive foreclosures as a result of the Depression. Fannie Mae was then privatized between 1968 and 1970 but was taken over by the Federal Housing Finance Agency (FHFA) on September 6, 2008, due to its huge losses. www.fanniemae.com. Freddie Mac is a Federal Home Loan Mortgage Corporation and was created as part of the Emergency Finance Act in 1970. Similarly to Fannie Mae, Freddie Mac was privatized in 1989 and also taken over by the FHFA on September 6, 2008. www.freddiemac.com.

14 People like Maurice Hank, founder of AIG, the biggest insurance firm in the world, are among the ones to blame for the 2007–08 crisis, along with Alan Greenspan and Ben Bernanke at the Fed, Bill Clinton and George Bush (as political leaders and US Presidents), Hank Paulsen (Secretary of US Treasury) and Lewis Ranieri (the bond trader who turned home loans into tradable securities). No rational or socially grounded explanation can be found for the decision of Paulsen, who decided to save AIG and not to save Lehman. Of course the crisis is not, in our view, a consequence of individual behavior. They just symbolize the main institutions which, within such a financial-led growth system, are bearer of responsibilities for the collapse. It follows then that, in my view, the solution to the crisis is not only the substitution of those people but also the change of the institutions.

15 US Census Bureau.

16 Given the fact that EU economies were poorer than the US, the level of productivity in the US has always been higher. However, productivity changes were higher in EU for a long time. This was the case until the 1980s. After that and in particular after 1996 also the changes along with the levels of labour productivity were higher in US.

5 Varieties of capitalism, regulations and responses to the financial crisis

The European social model versus the US model

Introduction

The 2007 financial crisis has caused worldwide losses amounting to about €5 trillion, according to estimates by the International Monetary Fund. Just to give an idea, that is a bit less than the GDP of Japan, twice the GDP of the UK, or three times the GDP of India (IMF, 2009a). It has driven the global recession we are currently struggling against, causing mass unemployment, high social costs and enormous levels of public debt in many countries.

Some kind of limited Keynesian policies and fiscal stimuli were implemented both in Europe and the US between 2007 and 2009.[1] Along with these approaches, a great number of bank rescue packages were implemented. However, after the Greek economic crisis in May 2010, governmental policies shifted towards austerity measures, balanced budgets; and as a result, the consensus that had allowed for partial recovery, monetary liquidity, and the bailout of banks and financial institutions almost dissipated. Fiscal stimuli are no longer unanimously accepted, and the main concerns of industrialised nations became sovereign debt crises, budget sustainability, and public spending cuts.

The objective of this chapter is to show how the European Union, which employs different varieties of capitalism, and the US, which operates based on a competitive capitalist model, are coping with the current economic crisis. Although the EU is fragmented and needs to work towards better and deeper integration among member states, the main features of the European social model (ESM) allowed for lessens the social costs in the initial phase of the crisis (2007–10). However, Europe, although in an initial better position than the US, was not able to strength its social model and started instead to dismantle it through austerity policies, which did not help to recover and worsened social costs (2010–15). In this chapter, I develop a new index: the synthetic vulnerability index (SVI), which shows that the US position, initially, was worse than the Eurozone position in terms of social costs. Nevertheless, current financial reforms, both in the US and EU seem to be insufficient and the fiscal austerity measures in Europe seem to be moving the European economies in the wrong direction.

Instead, I argue, new levels of government involvement is required in order to keep aggregate demand stable, make full employment possible, and create a transparent financial sector, serving the real economy and encouraging productive investments.

Welfare states, varieties of capitalism and transformations in the age of post-Fordism

In this section, I will discuss briefly the growth regime during the Fordist period. Economic systems of the Fordist regime, in particularly in Western Europe, enjoyed high stability, accumulation, productivity, and economic growth. The basic mechanisms of the Fordist model of accumulation are described in Figure A9 in the appendix.

The prevailing model of development during the Fordist era had three characteristics: first, the Taylorist form of labour organisation, organised around a semi-skilled workforce within a framework of particular industrial relations; second, the regime of accumulation, which allowed for a sharing of the benefits of productivity gains between workers and firm owners; third, the Keynesian Welfare State, which on one hand provided unemployment benefits, allowing people excluded from the Fordist organisation to consume, and, on the other supported a high level of aggregate demand. In Europe, this model had different executions but similar results in term of GDP performance and social outcomes. Each European country had its own style of development and built a model of capitalism specific to its needs (Gillingham, 2003).

After the demise of Fordism, an unstable new regime of accumulation emerged (Jessop, 2002; Boyer and Saillard, 2002). From the production point of view, it is characterized by high market financialisation, a so-called flexible accumulation regime, and markedly uneven development, with micro-electric, Internet, advanced technology, the Knowledge Based Economy driving further cycles of accumulation (Peck and Tickell, 2003; Jessop, 2002).

The shape of regulation during post-Fordism changed dramatically to allow for financialisation (Lipietz, 1992). As Petit (2003: 20) pointed out, with the transition to post-Fordism, institutions are evolving and, in particular, the institutional forms of competition tend to prevail in the emerging regime. On this argument, Boyer (2005) says that in the "hierarchy of the institutional forms", the one leading the way in the advanced economies during the transition period seems to be the finance sector (2005: 4), which shapes all other institutions (2005: 18).[2]

Moreover, at the political level, the transition to post-Fordism seems to be assisted by a neo-conservatism ruling class. Hence, a comparison with the previous pre-1920s Fordist era seems legitimate, when the neoliberal model of development was based on an extensive accumulation regime (Aglietta, 1979) with a pressure on labour costs, without government playing a significant role in the economy, without a productivity sharing compromise, and without the Keynesian Welfare State (Basso, 1998). Such a process of finacialisation was coupled with both an increase of inequality and a decline in the wage shares over the GDP. Biased income distribution and inequality is one of the main factors that gives instability to the current financial-led growth regime, since aggregate demand is weak and economic growth remains under its real and stable potential path. In general, financialisation represents a most incoherent set of experiments that cannot be considered a growth regime at all, and its literature try to impose a coherence to a model that is absent in reality (Engelen *et al.*, 2008; Wolfson, 2003).

The result of Reaganomics and Tacherism, in particular in social terms, was uneven development (Peck and Tickell, 1992), with regions and countries divided between financial services and technology-oriented ones, and increasing trends in inequalities and income disparities, in particular in the US and the UK, the countries which were keener towards financialisation.

A similar transition towards post-Fordism, although less severe than in the US and the UK, is exhibited by other continental European countries, such as Germany, France, Italy, and Spain (Jessop, 2002), where severe fiscal and monetary policies, along with industrial restructuring, generated precarious jobs and higher inequality in particular since the 1990s (Fitoussi, 1992).

These are the roots of the current financial-led unstable model of accumulation, and they put in place the mechanisms that helped spur the current crisis. In particular, when the wage-nexus was compressed and labour became extremely flexible, the investment dimension was neglected and replaced by speculative financial investments driven by shareholders' interests, and consumption needs to be sustained by fragile financialisation and risky financial tools. Failures of the financial-led model of accumulation are evident today because of the crisis but can be traced to the relatively poor performance of most of the advanced economies during the post-Fordist era, in terms of productivity and GDP growth (see Figure 2.5 in Chapter 2). Petit (2009) refers to the period between 1997 and 2007 as a lost decade of financialised capitalism in terms of productivity gains and growth. Liberalisation of finance and globalisation did not bring more innovation, since new investments, in which technological progress is usually embedded, lacked substance.

The ESM ensured better economic performance in Europe during the Fordist era of accumulation with respect to the US. It was able to deliver better GDP performance for an extended period of time, at least until the end of the 1970s (see Figure 2.5). After that, the process of financialisation, with all its contradictions and instabilities, began and a finance-led growth regime took over; the old Fordist regime went into crisis. According to the Regulation School, the reasons for that have to be found in the lower productivity performance, in the poor labour organisation, in the internationalisation of problems through pressure on labour costs, and in the resulting decrease in the demand. These are supply-side causes, national and international ones, and exogenous to the core of Fordist economic doctrine (Lipietz, 1992; Jessop, 2002; Boyer and Saillard, 2002).

Under the Fordist model of development, the EU, or more accurately the Eurozone, was able to outpace the US in social and economic benchmarking areas such as inequality, poverty, public education, and life expectancy, thanks to a large public program of social expenditures (as Table A6 and Figure A10 in the appendix display). The US, on the contrary, saw slightly faster GDP growth since the 1980s in comparison to the EU, in particular during the past two decades of financial-isation, but a concerning drop of important social indicators (inequality and poverty). This, however, does not identify a trade-off between efficiency and equity, at least for two reasons. First, the EU was also growing over the past twenty years (albeit at lower rates than the US economy), not simply maintain-ing its social indicators. Second, the current financial crisis affected the US very badly in particular, putting into doubt the US model and its vaunted efficiency (Posner, 2009; Wolff, 2010). For these reasons, I argue that the ESM, which was in force in Europe until the 1990s, would be able to produce not only better social performance but also more efficient and sustainable economic development in the long run than the US model.

The ESM, however, started to be dismantled in the last two decades in many European countries. The Maastricht treaty in 1992, which set the criteria for the convergence by the future Eurozone members to the Euro area, was the start-ing point of this dismantling process (Preece, 2009). Severe limits to debt and to deficit, in a period of relatively lower economic growth in Europe were the main tools that allowed for welfare retrenchment. Competitiveness strategies, export-led approaches, and capital attraction policies were followed in most European countries with negative consequences on labour costs, progressivity of tax systems, and welfare states.

The secular stagnation, of which we spoke earlier, was also possible because the structural reforms, the austerity programs, and the deflationary policies com-pressed the component of indirect wage (public expenditure and welfare) and weakened the aggregate demand and the dynamics of GDP since 1992–93 at least. The current euro crisis has to find here its origins and therefore also its remedies. The change of the European social model, operated through the Maastricht Treaty, and its criteria, and the others subsequent tougher constraints imposed by the Fiscal compact (see Chapter 6) in particular during the crisis, deepened the crisis and contributed to dismantle further the European social model, with negative consequences on inequality and poverty in many EU countries.

Maastricht was accompanied also by a lack of solidarity in Europe between economically stronger and weaker countries, which did not allow for important redistribution policies among member states, as it would be necessary. The dis-cussion about a European public debt and an EU budget (beyond the current 1 per cent of EU GDP), which would help to compensate uneven development and asymmetric shocks, and to stabilise aggregate demand, was always rejected by richer members of Northern Europe, and never really in the agenda (Peet and La Guardia, 2014). As a consequence of all of that, southern European members, which already had higher debt and lower income, worsened their position. In particular, the competitive strategies, the constrains of Maastricht criteria and the EU competition policies, which did not allow for state aids, disadvantaged southern regions in Europe, which became weaker and increased their gaps with respect to northern regions.

With the beginning of the crisis in 2007, or at least since 2010, Maastricht ideas were followed by further restrictive measures, austerity policies and an even more severe approach against EU solidarity and redistribution. These measures not only worsened the situation from a social point of view; they put in dangerous situation the very essence of the process of the European integration from a political point of view. Disaffections and untrusty feelings increased almost everywhere in Europe among European citizens who suffered strong social costs, such as higher unemployment rates, poverty, inequality and lower level of welfare states and living standards. In this situation, political discontent increased, "populism" and anti–European Union feelings disseminated among European parties and movements which organized exit referendum (such as in the UK in June 2016 where the support for "leave the EU" won with 52 per cent of votes) or threaten to organise in the future (in France, in Denmark, in Hungary, in Greece, in Italy, etc.).

In light of this, the Esping-Andersen (1990) classification of three worlds of capitalism seems to have been overcome by the last two decades of welfare evolutions. Globalisation and technological changes also participated to this transformation (Hay and Wincott, 2012). Europe in particular has been facing a deep transformation in social and economic terms, and the European member states (MS) today diverge with respect to models of welfare systems. A single European social model does not seem to be an easy objective. European member states remain very independent in social affairs. Therefore, a common socio-economic model for the EU is very difficult to reach. Since the EU is a construction of several nation-states already with their own socioeconomic development model, it is difficult if not impossible to combine them within a single model suitable for all EU member states. In order to overcome this difficulty, EU proposed, in the past years, through the European Employment Strategy first in 1997 then transformed in the Lisbon Strategy in 2010 and renewed with the Europe 2020 strategy, an ambiguous project based not on the convergence of different socioeconomic dimensions such as health system, pension system, tax system, education, etc. but on "objectives" to be reached by each MS according to its national tools, such as the level of employment, the level of R&D, etc. However, the common key of these national tools is the path of the labour relations, which are converging, among MS, towards a similar form (i.e. the flexibility of labour). Such a form of labour relations would be on the basis of an emerging socio-economic model in Europe more market oriented and with neoliberal features. The ambiguity, in this process, is crucial in order to overcome trade union and social forces opposition.

After the 1980s, all the European member states have progressively moved towards a more distinct market-driven economy with similar features (Hemerijck *et al.*, 2006). The core idea of that project was to enhance market mechanisms in order to free the economy from the incumbent state. The Keynesian policy paradigm was considered unable to solve the crisis started at the end of the 1960s. Moreover, it was considered inefficient and very expensive in terms of governmental budget, domestic debt and inflation. Hence, following the "Reaganomics recipe",

European states started to restructure their economic systems. The dominant policy paradigm was the monetarist one, supported by the (anti-Keynesian) Milton Freedman, awarded with the Nobel Prize.[3] This neoclassical paradigm aimed at anti-inflation targets and domestic debt reduction, because high debt and high inflation rates would curb economic performance. The rules became "adjust, stabilize and privatize" the economies. "Structural Adjustments programs" were often uncritically implemented (Stiglitz, 1998) throughout liberalisation of prices and sectors, privatization of State assets, and deregulation – i.e. the withdrawal of the state from the economy.[4]

In the European post-Fordist context, driven by the knowledge economy, several paths could emerge because path dependencies at national levels can play a role, and European decisions in terms of policies and development strategies can be affected by single states, which could be leaders of dominant positions. Theoretically, four or five European models can be described in EU as shown by Bob Jessop (2002: 262–5) who distinguishes four "ideal types" of contemporary state. Each of them seems to be led by an EU leader country and seems to aggregate other MS with similar features (see Table 3.1 in Chapter 3).

Although Europe has a variety of welfare states, the different social systems still have some important characteristics, in particular when compared with the US and the rest of the world. However, the majority of EU countries, pushed by national and European policies and institutions, seem evolving towards a neoliberal model, although several pressures and resistances exist within the national political arena. In particular Italy, Spain, Portugal and Greece representing already a not yet specified "Mediterranean model" are evolving towards a model characterised by a lower level of social protection expenditure on the GDP and by flexible labour relations. Several EU countries, which in the past adopted a continental or Scandinavian model are today changing for a more liberal model. An example is Denmark, which seems to be oriented towards a rather undefined "flexicurity" model, which combines elements of British liberalism and social elements of Scandinavian origins (Amoroso, 2003). To this picture, one should add the New Member States (NMS) of Central Europe, which do not have a clear and consistent model and share characteristic of several models.[5]

Jessop (2002: 263) describes, abstractly, the *neocommunitarianism* model, which would be "a challenge to the logic of capital accumulation in the economy, its extension to other spheres of social life and the struggle to establish bourgeois hegemony over society as a whole". In this model, the role of social economy and social cohesion is stressed and the need for fair new labour relations. Unlike the previous models, this model does not seem to have a leader country. This model could be an alternative scenario to the incumbent neoliberal model in Europe.

Varieties of responses to the financial crisis in the US and EU

The 2007 financial and economic crisis produced painful outcomes in the labour market and society in general, both in the US and in Europe. In short, it caused a global recession, mass unemployment, high social costs, and enormous public debts in many countries (see Figure A11 in the appendix). Here, I analyse the responses to the crisis put forward by the US and EU. The US made its response in line with its Competitive Market Economy (CME) model, the EU within the framework of a traditional European social model at least until 2010. The latter, however, tends to represent more specifically a Eurozone model (with the exception of Ireland) rather than an EU model since the UK position[6] more often resembles US regulation (see Table A7 in the appendix).

In general, regarding the financial overhaul, the EU (except UK and Ireland) relies more on the existing institutional governance structures of non-market coordination, while the US, UK and Ireland rely more on the presumed efficiency of financial markets. It is very interesting to see how, at the April 2009 G20 meeting in London, the different types of socioeconomic models and their strategies for recovery were clearly divided: the Franco-German axe, supported by Sarkozy and Merkel, called for all-encompassing state regulation and financial restrictions on hedge funds and tax havens. The Anglo-Saxon strategy, backed by Brown and Obama, aimed mostly at reaching a consensus in order to provide monetary liquidity to the financial system.

The G20 summit, since its first meeting in Washington, DC, in November of 2008, has created conditions to change the global financial structures. However, progress has thus far been made only at very superficial levels, such as tax haven limitations and calling for limitations on executive compensation. An interesting step towards a more democratic and global system of financial governance seems to be the creation of a Financial Stability Board (FSB), which should enhance coordination and improve macro and micro prudential supervision.[7] The FSB was established to address vulnerabilities and to develop and implement strong regulatory, supervisory, and other policies in the interest of financial stability. It includes all G20 major economies, the IMF, WB, the Bank for International Settlements (BIS), and the European Commission. The Secretary of the US Treasury Tim Geithner has described it as a fourth pillar in the architecture of global economic governance, along with IMF, World Bank, and WTO. That said, within the EU, many differences exist. These differences can be classified in the following ways:

- Differences between Eurozone and non-Eurozone nations
- Differences between member states and the central position of the EU Commission
- And, above all, differences between the Eurozone (Germany and France in particular) and the UK, in particular in the light of the recent "Brexit" referendum (June 2016), of which the consequences are not yet clear

Tensions and contradictions exist within the EU in general, and this is affecting the final outcomes of financial regulation. Compromises, carve-outs, and generic language weaken the new EU regulation (Wahl, 2010).

US regulation (the "Frank-Dodd Act")

In July 2010, the US adopted a financial reform package, despite the strong opposition of Republicans and Wall Street lobbyists.[8] A lot of compromises and carve-outs weakened the original proposal of the White House and Secretary of Treasury Tim Geithner. The important elements of the US reforms can be synthesized into the following ten points:

1   They include new requirements for higher capital and liquidity standards for corporations and banks.
2   The famous "Volcker Rule" comes into play, which eliminates the dangerous coexistence between investment and commercial banks.
3   Under the Volcker Rule, banks are limited in engaging in proprietary trading.
4   Banks must hold enough capital in reserve to reflect their off-balance sheet, cope with crisis, and avoid illiquidity.
5   A new insolvency regime is introduced, not only for firms but also for banks, and it gives more regulatory and supervisory power to the Treasury.
6   Trade in derivatives is strictly regulated and centralized within a third party clearing authority.
7   Financial firms and hedge funds managers are required to submit swaps to a third authority to back their operations.
8   A new supervision was introduced for Credit Rating Agencies (CRA). The supervisor has the right to examine rating agency operations, data, and methodologies. They can be eliminated from a CRA book if they are shown to have been providing bad ratings for a long time, and, most importantly, they are prohibited from advising an issuer and rating that issuer's securities in order to reduce/eliminate conflict of interests.
9   US households and consumers, as well as investors, are better protected under the new laws, with a special agency (Consumer Financial Protection Agency).
10 The Fed has stronger supervision and oversight, with the creation of a Financial Stability Oversight Council that monitors Wall Street's largest firms and financial institutions.

After the US Frank-Dodd Act, a new supervisory architecture system will be in place, with a major role for the Fed and a stronger advisory role for the Treasury. A *Council of Regulators* is set up to coordinate supervision with the Fed. The Fed wields more prudential supervision over large firms and has an oversight role to play along with other US authorities. This supervision and oversight can be summarized at macro and micro levels. However, the problem remains at an operational level, because vigilance, supervision and oversight have to be implemented through the creation of about twenty new authorities.[9]

At the micro level: prudential supervision in the US

Banks are now required to hold more capital and liquidity than before. Large hedge funds have to register with the Securities and Exchange Commission

(SEC)[10] and are regulated by it. Under the Volcker Rule, although this was curtailed by Senate with respect to the initial Obama proposal, proprietary trading is limited. This refers to trading stocks, bonds, currencies, commodities, their derivatives, or other financial instruments with the bank's own capital rather than that of its customers. In general, proprietary trading is considered to be riskier and is associated with more volatile profits (Conzelman *et al.*, 2010: 4). Moreover, the Volcker Rule introduces the separation between commercial and investment banks.[11] Banks are also required not to bet against their own clients. Commercial banks can no longer make speculative bets for their own profits. Banks will be allowed to invest in private equity and hedge funds but at a level limited to 3 per cent of their capital. At the same time, a new Consumer Financial Protection Agency, housed in the Fed, was set up to provide consumers with services related to mortgage brokers, debt collectors and credit counsellors. New federal banking regulators have been created, also. At the top of this regulatory and supervision hierarchy sits the Fed, which monitors commercial banks and large firms while the SEC monitors the securities market and the Commodity Futures Trading Commission (CFTC) monitors futures. Insurance is monitored at the state level

At the macro level: prudential supervision in the US

The Fed is empowered as a systemic regulator in its role of market vigilance and monitoring financial institutions at the macro level. The new Council of Regulators chaired by the Secretary of Treasury advises the Fed on systemic risks. It has been created as a new insolvency regime for bank and non-bank firm bankruptcies, with special and extended powers of the Treasury. The new financial architecture was reinforced by the introduction of the newly created Financial Stability Oversight Council, which should reduce the deficit in the US for financial institutions and large firms in particular (Conzelman *et al.*, 2010), thanks in part to the new role of the Fed. The Fed will lead the oversight of large financial institutions whose failures could threaten the financial system. At the same time, the Fed's relationship with banks is controlled directly by the US Congress and the Government Accountability Office (GAO). The GAO can audit the following: (1) emergency loans made by the Fed (including the ones made after the 2007 financial crisis); (2) the Fed's low-cost loans to banks; and (3) the Fed's buying and selling of securities to implement interest-rate policy (Conzelman *et al.*, 2010).

EU regulation and responses

The immediate EU responses to the crisis managed by the European Central Bank (ECB) were delayed in comparison to the Fed's reaction, which put immediately huge monetary liquidity back into in the system and lowered the interest rates (from 5.25 per cent to 2 per cent in 2008 and to 0.25 per cent in 2010). The ECB did the same but in a more passive way and with some delay. Moreover, monetary quantitative easing was less consistent and the interest rate was lowered at a slower pace.[12] By contrast, the inadequate response of the ECB was followed by a stronger EU regulatory approach to the crisis. This was mainly the result of the recommendations made by the De Larosière Report (2009),[13] which were adopted by following EU directives and regulations, and by a declaration of support from the EU Commission (2009), the European Council (2009), and the ECOFIN meeting on June 9, 2009. However, as I mentioned above, the EU regulation is weakened by the fragmentation among the EU member states and their different national regulations of financial markets.

At the micro level: prudential supervision in the EU

The new EU regulations for financial supervision of banks, insurance, and securities created the European System of Financial Supervisors (ESFS), with three functional authorities and regulatory powers over banks, insurance, and securities: the European Banking Authority (EBA), the European Insurance and Occupational Pensions (EIOP), and the European Securities Markets Authority (ESMA).[14] This is a compromise between the UK and the EU commission, plus the France-Germany position. The former did not want to give the EU strong supervisory power. The latter pushed for a stronger role for EU in the financial supervision. The result is a system of oversight, which, at the operational level, remains the responsibility of nations. The role of the EBA, EIOP, and ESMA is to promote cooperation, financial harmony, a common culture of supervision, and common technical standards for monitoring and control.[15]

The harshest legislation the EU is introducing concerns OTC derivatives (EU, 2010a), securitizations such as Credit Default Swaps[16] and all kind of Alternative Investment Funds (AIF) like hedge funds, private equity funds, real estate funds, commodity funds, and infrastructure funds (EU, 2009c). The EU has realised that there is much speculative activity among those funds that need to be regulated. The biggest hedge fund was a fraud (Madoff's fund),[17] and many AIF activities rely on opaque Ponzi schemes. Most OTC derivatives operate wildly in off-shore financial havens across the world, avoiding regulation protections for investors, as EU Commissioner Barnier reported.[18] Only 10 per cent of derivatives traded are standardized and traded on a stock exchange; the remaining 90 per cent are traded Over the Counter (OTC) – i.e. bilaterally and without control or supervision. At the end of 2009, the volume of OCT trade was around $614 trillion (ten times global GDP of the world; BIS, 2010).

At the macro level: prudential supervision in the EU

The newly created European Systemic Risk Board (ESRB) will be at the centre of the new system in the EU, although only with advisory functions.[19] European Central Banks play a major role within this board, helping to define, identify and prioritize all macro-financial risks. Macro-financial stability may need to be pursued through different means from the ECB's price stability objectives (Smaghi, 2009). This is a possible area of tension between the two institutions, and that is why the ECB, which prioritizes price stability, wants to maintain the leading role.[20] The ESRB deals essentially with macro prudential supervision and reports to ECOFIN. It is also allowed to make warnings and recommendations directly to EU national governments.

Tensions, vulnerabilities and differences among the US and EU

The regulatory overhauls passed after the crisis, both in the US and the EU, are different. The differences are just consequences of different perspectives on the crisis, which in turn underlines the different models in which the crisis simultaneously occurred: the ESM and the CME. These differences will likely bring about a new phase of post-financial crisis relations between the US and EU. In fact, the post-financial crisis phase brought about both new and old disagreements between the EU and US. These disagreements reflect the basic differences between the economic systems of the EU and US. Varieties of capitalism and the different styles of market economy are issues that have already been explored in literature, as I mentioned earlier. This affects national problem solving and global answers to the crisis. Institutions are put in place by countries according to each one's own model of capitalism. Hence, finance and financial regulation is an institutional form that reflects a nation's individual economic model.

Tensions and differences between the EU and the US

The most important disagreement, both within the EU and on a global level, concerns a financial transaction tax (FTT). This is an old issue: the first to advance a proposal for a financial activity tax was James Tobin (1978). Now the issue has a twofold significance. First of all, the FTT would serve to finance the huge costs of this crisis. Since the financial sector bears much of the responsibility for this crisis, it is only fair, the advocates of the FTT say, that it pays for the societal costs. The expenditures of governments on stimulus programs to counter the crisis in the real economy were around 3.5 per cent of global GDP. Along with the government money that went to rescuing banks, the total cost is €3.5 trillion at the global level (IMF, 2009a). Second, as in the original opinion of Tobin, it would regulate financial markets, limit speculation, and reduce short-term and electronic financial activities, which have little to do with investment and saving operations. The FTT is discussed mostly in the EU, in particular among Eurozone nations, with Germany and France the principal supporters. The UK, the US, and Canada strongly object it and the G20 Pittsburgh meeting has already rejected it. Bank lobbies are strongly against the FTT, too. The Obama administration sees a potential compromise in a sort of Bank Levy, which would have a more modest impact on tax collection ($14 to $19 billion in estimated revenues, against $738 billion in revenues from the FTT).[21] However, in the US, many Congress members, in particular after the mid-term election of November 2010 was won by the Republicans, are strongly against a Bank Levy as well. An interesting proposal comes from the IMF, the Financial Activities Tax (FAT), which would tax the profits and remunerations of banks only (IMF, 2009a).

A controversial issue remains over the Basel agreements. On the eve of the financial crisis, the EU had just adopted (in 2006) Basel II, a set of rules regulating the capital requirements of banks, which were very flexible and favourable so that banks would agree to them. The new Basel agreement reached after the crisis (Basel III), in September of 2010, increases banks capital requirements, limits their liabilities and leverage ratios, and requires higher liquidity standards to meet customers' needs. Moreover, banks are required to fulfil the primary role in the game of securitization; holding higher shares of the securities in the credit risk products. Most importantly, a new definition of "capital" is introduced, according to which equity capital and disclosed reserves only (i.e. liquid and own bank assets) are considered. This improves the quality and consistency of capital and of leverage. However, while the EU will immediately adopt Basel III as it is suggested in an EU Parliament Proposal of 2010 (EU, 2010b), the US and UK are still devoted to a more flexible definition of capital and continue to refer to Basel II for guidance on most capital requirements. Moreover, the EU (with the exception of the UK) would support even higher standards, with capital requirements set at or near 10 per cent.

Finally, another controversial issue is over Alternative Investment Funds (AIF). The EU recognises that risks associated with AIF have been underestimated and are not sufficiently addressed by current rules. Many activities of large AIF, particularly those employing high levels of leverage, have greatly contributed to the current financial instability of the UE. Toxic assets related to AIF were implicated in the commodity price bubbles that developed in late 2007.[22] The new legislation tries to regulate not only AIF, but most importantly, AIF managers (AIFM) whose activities in their off-shore headquarters, on behalf of AIM, often avoid regulation. The new EU regulation on these matters is a good step forward (Wahn, 2010). However, the issue of AIF regulation in the EU is very complicated, in particular because of the UK opposition, in line with the US position, which prefers to keep looser regulations and protect British interests: at the London stock exchange, 80 per cent of all hedge funds in the world operate, and the AIF's lobby is very strong. They do not like the idea of stricter supervision, disclosure of strategies, leverage limits, higher costs, or lower risks, which mean lower profits. Since the operational supervisors of the new authorities created by the EU remain at the national level, implementation can be difficult.

Another issue of discordance within the EU, in particular between Germany and the UK, is the case of CDs. New EU regulations impose stricter supervision and introduce the right to ban short selling and the trade of CDs temporarily when it realizes that there is a speculation. Uncovered or "naked" short selling is banned (European Council, 2010). Such measures would have limited the severity of the Greek crisis in the spring of 2010. The ESMA is the newly elected vigilance institution for that. Furthermore, requirements of transparency and information are required at the stock exchange where CDs are traded, and individual traders have to disclose their short positions over these assets.[23]

The synthetic vulnerability index

These disagreements are crucial to the definition of new global financial governance and show how deep the differences are between the EU and the US and UK (and Anglo-Saxon countries in general; Semmler and Young, 2010). Beyond these differences, and despite the attempts to reform the financial sector, finance and the economy at large still remain vulnerable, both in the EU and the US. This is due to a combination of four indicators that were in dangerously vulnerable positions: government deficits, unemployment, current account deficits (CA), and slow recovery. The average of these four variables was calculated with the synthetic vulnerability index (SVI)[24] in Figure 5.1, for the Eurozone and the US. From the SVI, the position of the US appeared to be consistently weaker than that of the Eurozone (and in 2010 is −4.8 against −3.975) due in particular to higher government deficits and negative CA balance. Similarly in 2011. Moreover, the bilateral position of the EU-US, in terms of import-export merchandise and CA, showed a better position for the EU, in a constant surplus versus the US (see Figures A12 and A13 in the appendix).

Besides that, another indicator supports the idea that the US was more vulnerable than the Eurozone and in particular indicates that the US faces higher social costs. That is the recent evolution of the labour market indicators of employment and unemployment. Despite a lower recession in the US as compared to the Eurozone (−2.6 per cent against −4.1 per cent), in the US, the labour market was seriously affected by an unemployment rate that went from 4.6 per cent to 9.8 per cent (+5.2) and employment rate that fell from 72 per cent to 64.5 per cent (−7.5) in 2010 (see Figure A14 in the appendix). Moreover, in the US, official

US economy: synthetic vulnerability index

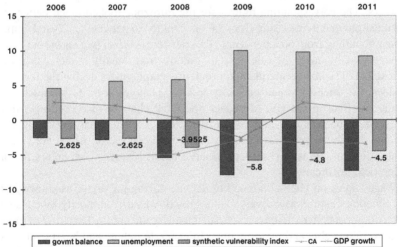

Figure 5.1a US synthetic vulnerability index.

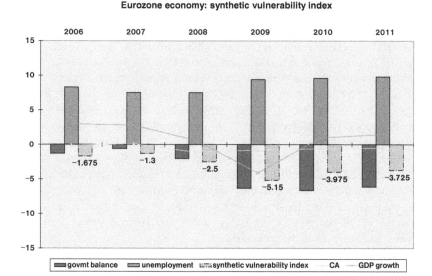

Figure 5.1b EU synthetic vulnerability index.
Source: Own elaboration on IMF, 2010 World Economic Outlook (online database).

unemployment seemed to be very much underestimated (Feng and Hu, 2010). Many workers get a part-time job while they would like a full-time job. Many of them have precarious and unstable jobs. Around 15 per cent of employees were in a position that can be called "semi-employment" rather than standard employment, and this has very bad effects on purchasing power and consumption.[25] Poverty and social exclusion is increasing consistently among semi-employed workers. The corresponding figures for the Eurozone looked much better, with the unemployment rate rising from 8.6 per cent to 9.6 per cent (+1.2) and employment rate falling from 66.2 per cent to 65.7 per cent (–0.5%) (see Figure A15 in the appendix). Obviously the role of trade unions, traditionally stronger in Europe (Nickell, 1997), has been crucial in protecting employment during the recession; besides, the unemployment elasticity to GDP changes seem to be much lower in the EU than in the US. Moreover, the GDP changes (and recovery) in the US seem to be seriously affected by structural problems that negatively shape income distribution and favours mostly the financial sector, which are continuously compensated with short-term finance bonus biases (which do not find any theoretical justification).

Wage shares on GDP continued to decline during the crisis, as shown in the introduction chapter. Moreover, such a growth was driven mostly by consumption components, which in turn was sustained by the credit. This kind of growth is uneven, unstable and more inclined to generate bubble and burst cycles. It is far from what the International Monetary Fund and the World Bank define as "high-quality growth" (HQG). In particular, the IMF defines HQG as "growth

that is sustainable brings lasting gains in employment and living standards, reduce poverty and inequality (IMF, 1995: 286). Finally, given the relatively lower
percentage of US public expenditure directed towards unemployment policies
(0.49 per cent of GDP against the 2.8 per cent of GDP countries on the Eurozone spent), the human cost of unemployment is much higher in the US than
the Eurozone (see Figure A16 in the appendix). All of this should confirm the
argument that the ESM (roughly the Eurozone) was better able to cope with this
crisis, allowing fewer social costs and creating better social performance than
seen in the US.

However, what instead happened was a slower recovery in Europe after 2010
and a faster recovery in the US. In Europe, and in particular in the Eurozone, after the Greek crisis, austerity became a dominant policy approach. The structural
European problems emerged. The EU faces a major issue, which the US does not
have – that is, the Euro situation and the contradiction of the European Monetary
Union (EMU) – having a common monetary policy, without (1) a central budged,
(2) a common fiscal policy and, (3) a de-facto, no labour mobility within the
Eurozone. Quite the opposite, the US dollar, the federal budget and a labour mobility within the US are the main strengths of American economy vis-à-vis the EMU.
The European common currency paradoxically, but perhaps not surprisingly, has
divided the EU between core and periphery. This division could be accepted and
somehow managed, however it needs to be backed by political decisions that introduce wider common fiscal policies and a central budget (a central budget of around
1 per cent of EU GDP as today, is unacceptably low). It follows that EU imbalances
should be treated as an internal issue, managed through Euro-Bonds redistribution
policies, ECB policy of buying member state bonds, and a permanent European
Fund such as the Financial Stability Facility, which could contribute to manage EU
aggregate demand and could work (if not the ECB) as a lender of last resort. In this
sense, the Tremonti-Junker proposal of issuing European Union Bonds (to which
we will come back in the next chapter) would go in the right direction.

From expansionary policies to austerity

In order to recover from the crisis, governments initially put in place fiscal
stimuli and bank rescue packages (see Tables A8 and A9 in the appendix). These
policies were supported by a great consensus among the policymakers, politicians, and academics who had begun to look at Keynesian policies in a favourable way. In the US under the Bush administration, the TARP (Troubled Asset
Relief Program) Act was launched in order to purchase "troubled" assets and
equity from financial institutions and to strengthen trust in the financial sector.
The Act allowed the Treasury to purchase illiquid, difficult-to-value assets from
banks and other financial institutions as a first reaction to the subprime mortgage
crisis, for a value of US$700 billion (or 2.3 per cent of US GDP).[26] Similar saving
plans were implemented in the UK.

It is, however, debatable whether the policies introduced in the US and the UK
over the period 2007–09 represent orthodox Keynesian policies at all. Certainly,

the UK case, much of this intervention involved direct and indirect handouts to banks with remarkably few strings attached on the assumption that this would enable the latter to rebuild their balances and encourage them to resume lending to the non-financial sector. In practice, much of this money appears to have leaked out to fund new rounds of speculative activity, whilst the promised 'trickle down' has proved limited.

The TARP was followed by Obama's fiscal stimulus, known as ARRA (American Recovering and Reinvestment Act), which entered onto the scene in February 2009 for a value of US$775 billion (or 2.7 per cent of US GDP). The stimulus aimed at promoting, in the Keynesian tradition, job creation, investment, and consumer spending during the recession (Romer and Bernestein, 2010). In the main EU countries, fiscal stimuli were implemented, too, for a total around US$300 billion (or 1.5 per cent of EU GDP; IMF, 2009b).

ARRA included federal tax incentives, expansion of unemployment benefits and other social welfare provisions, and domestic spending in education, healthcare, and infrastructure, including the energy sector, which aims to promote green jobs. Such a plan, Republicans and neoliberals argue, was not useful because employment did not increase. Supporters of the Obama stimulus plan argued that, without the plan, unemployment would be even higher and recession deeper and longer, as during the 1929 Great Depression (Bartlett, 2010). This argument seems to be convincing (Romer and Bernestein, 2010). However, I maintain that economic recovery will not come without further direct government packages intended to support public employment. In fact, with GDP recovery already in process, job creation does not seem to be occurring. At least it does not seem to be occurring at the necessary pace to recover 10 million jobs (Mishel *et al.*, 2010), which would be needed in order to reach the pre-crisis level of employment. Direct public employment would contribute immediately to a recovery from high unemployment. A great example supporting this is Roosevelt's New Deal, which created, before the US's involvement in World War II, around 11 million new jobs, enough to restore America to a pre-1929 level of employment (Wolff, 2010). In order to do this, however, a new policy paradigm and a different approach are needed in the US. Such an approach should favour a public culture and a deeper government involvement in the economy.

There are at least two reasons to favour this stimulus: first, the need to prevent further output declines and job destruction, and second, the evidence that easy access to cheap money was not successful. The Fed cut interest rates almost to zero, and one can envision clearly a well-known Keynesian liquidity trap, where monetary policies are ineffective. Many Keynesian economists argued that ARRA is a good step in the right direction, but they point out, critically, that it is far below what is needed to restore economic growth (Krugman, 2010; Zandi, 2010). Monetarist economists, on the contrary, worried that fiscal stimuli do not favour consumption multipliers because during recession individuals tend to save more and to postpone consumption (Taylor, 2010). Moreover, future debt needs to be repaid by taxpayers who are seeing future available income reduced (Giavazzi and Pagano, 1990; Cochrane, 2009).

While many economists agreed that a fiscal stimulus was needed under the recession conditions of the liquidity trap, others maintained that fiscal policy would not work because government debt would use up savings that would have otherwise gone to investments – what is known as a *crowding out* effect (Barro, 1989). However, counter-Keynesian arguments maintain that the negative effects of the crowding out are limited when investment has already stagnated (Romer and Bernstein, 2010).

The outcomes of these 2009 stimuli were quite positive: in the second quarter of 2010, Germany grew at an extraordinary rate of 8.8 per cent, and the UK at 4.8 per cent. Similar stories, although of less magnitude, occurred in other European economies. The US recovered, too, with 1.6 per cent growth for the same period.

Nevertheless, in Europe (as we will see better in the next chapter), after the spring of 2010, policy consensus switched towards austerity measures. Such austerity packages have gone hand in hand with a continued lifeline to the banks and financial institutions. Therefore, these austerity packages, one can argue, represent a larger transfer of resources to the financial sector, the costs being borne by society at large, with half-hearted attempts at regulation being combined with renewed speculation. There is a clear link between bank recapitalization and bond vigilantism: austerity is imposed both by cutbacks in government spending to pay for the bailouts and further austerity to fend off even the vaguest threat from bond vigilantes, whose access to funds in part depends on the bailouts.

Notes

1 The extent to which those policies reflected orthodox Keynesianism is, however, very questionable.
2 However, both, Petit (2003) and Boyer (2005) agree that in the Fordist era, the wage relation was the dominant institutional form and that is what made consistent economic growth possible.
3 At the same time, a change in the social norms and class relations, among European countries, occurred. Some values, such as equality, solidarity, and cooperation were substituted with competitive behaviour, meritocracy, egoism etc. (cf. Fitoussi, 2005). As well from that point of view new neoliberal policies were supported and socially justified.
4 This policy packet constitutes the core of the so-called neoliberal paradigm, which became internationally known as the "Washington Consensus". The phrase referred to a decalogue of policies advised by Washington-based international financial institutions (IMF and WB). However, after fifteen years, "this consensus has by now largely dissipated" (Rodrik, 2004: p. 1), but it has caused many economic and financial crises (Stiglitz, 1998).
5 In the case of NMS, the inconsistency of the national development model is even greater because of their transition from a planned economy towards a market economy. The market economy in these countries mainly approaches the neoliberal model (in Estonia, Lithuania, Latvia, Czech Republic, and Slovakia). It is closer to a neostatism/neocorporatism model in Hungary, Slovenia and, to some extent, Poland (Tridico, 2004).
6 For a detailed overview on the British position, see Turner Review (2009), a UK regulatory report named after Lord Turner, chairman of the United Kingdom's Financial Services Authority, who chaired the review's research group.

7 The FSB was established after the 2009 G20 summit in London as a successor to the Financial Stability Forum. The latter was founded by G7 countries in 1999 to promote international financial stability but has had little impact. The FSB is based in Basel, Switzerland. The first chairman of the board was Mario Draghi, then governor of the Bank of Italy.

8 The Dodd-Frank Wall Street Reform and Consumer Protection Act was named after the chairmen of the two congressional committees dealing with banking and was signed into law by President Obama on 21 July 2010.

9 See The Economist (2011).

10 A government commission created in 1934 by Congress to regulate the securities markets and protect investors. In addition to regulation and protection, it now also monitors corporate takeovers in the US. The SEC is composed of five commissioners appointed by the U.S. president and approved by the Senate. The statutes administered by the SEC are designed to promote full public disclosure and to protect the investing public against fraudulent and manipulative practices in the securities markets. Generally, most issues of securities offered in interstate commerce, through the mail or on the Internet must be registered with the SEC.

11 The coexistence was introduced by Clinton, who repealed the Glass-Steagal Act, which had ensured the complete separation between commercial banks, which accept deposits, and investment banks, which invest and take risk, prompting the era of super bank and primed the subprime pump. In 1998 sub-prime loans were just 5 per cent of all mortgage lending. In 2008 they were about 30 per cent.

12 Surprisingly enough, on July 2008, two months before the collapse of Lehmann, the ECB increased its interest rate to the high level of 4.5 per cent, even though the crisis had already reached European banks (British Institute Northern Rocks was nationalized in February of 2008, and the German IKB went bankrupt in July of 2007). Since the end of 2008, the interest rate was lowered to 2.5 per cent and then to 1 per cent, although still above the rate of 0.25 per cent set by the Fed.

13 The De Larosière Report, published in February 2009, is the result of the research of the High-Level group chaired by Jacques Larosière, commissioned by the European Commission.

14 See EU (2009b).

15 The opposition to the EU finance regulation of the UK Parliament's Treasury Committee was immediately clear, and in an internal paper it suggested to the UK government to use its veto in the EU Council against it if the initial EU text would not be modified (UK Treasury Committee, 2010: 5).

16 They are a kind of insurance against credit default but turned out to be speculative tools on the large scale, thanks to the mistaken evaluation of the CRA. During the financial crisis, the link between the initial credit and its securities derivatives was lost. Creditors could take more risks, because through CDS they could transfer the risk to somebody else. In the end, nobody knew how many CDS existed and where they were held. CDS were used massively to speculate against the Euro in the Greek crisis (Wahl, 2010).

17 Investors in Madoff's funds lost $60 billion. In 2009, he was sentenced to 150 years in prison for defrauding investors through a massive Ponzi scheme.

18 EU Observer, 16.09.2010, http://euobserver.com/19/30821.

19 The Steering Committee of the ESRB is composed of the seven European System of Central Banks (ESCB) members (including the president of the ECB), the three chairs of the European Supervisory Authorities, a member of the EU Commission, and the president of the Economic and Financial Committee. The General Board of ESRB comprises apart from the Steering Committee members all central bank governors of the EU 27.

20 The primary objective of the ESB is to maintain price stability. This is different from the mandate of the US central bank, as stated in its Statute: "Fed shall maintain long run growth of the monetary and credit aggregates commensurate with the economy's long run potential to increase production, so as to promote effectively the goals of maximum employment, stable prices, and moderate long-term interest rates." For the ECB instead, the goal of economic growth secondary to inflation: "Without prejudice to the objective of price stability, it shall support the general economic policies in the Union with a view to contributing to the achievement of the objectives of the Union as laid down in Article 3 of the Treaty on European Union" (Article 2 of ECB Statute).

21 The estimate is done with a FTT at 0.1 per cent and a medium reduction of the transaction volume per year (Schulmeister *et al.*, 2008).

22 In its proposal, the EU acknowledges that AIF are covered by a lack of transparency when building stakes in listed companies, conflicts of interest, and failures in fund governance, in particular with respect to remuneration, valuation and administration, market abuse, misalignment of incentives in management of portfolio companies, weakness in internal risk management, inadequate investor disclosures, pro-cyclical impact of herding and risk concentrations, and direct exposure of systemically important banks (EU, 2009c).

23 The German regulation is even stricter on short selling because it bans speculation on falling prices, not only temporarily and in case of threats to stability. The German position is heavily criticized by the UK, which would prefer limited bans or none at all.

24 The SVI is simply the arithmetic average of those four variables all having the same weight. Reasonably, I suppose that governments give the four issues the same importance and priorities. The lower, the worse. In regards to unemployment, which normally has a positive value, it was considered with the opposite sign in order to be consistent with the other variables.

25 Economic Policy Institute Research and ideas for shared Prosperity, Online database, www.epi.org/.

26 More than a Keynesian fiscal stimulus, TARP was an Act made in order to save, in a direct way, financial institutions. Several commentators and newspapers in the US criticized TARP for being a paradoxical representation of a sort of "financial socialism". A similar approach was followed in Europe (see Table A8 in the appendix).

6 Economic policies and growth strategies after the crisis

Different approaches in the US, Japan and the EU

Introduction

After the 2007 financial crisis, mass unemployment emerged in the US and in Europe (Krugman, 2008; Wolff, 2010). After a recession of the GDP in the European Union with an average of −4.2 per cent in 2009, many EU members states have still not recovered. In 2012, several European countries, particularly in the South and in the East of Europe, experienced a double dip in terms of GDP recession and unemployment, while in other European countries in the core of Europe, GDP is stagnating and the level of unemployment is not declining (Fitoussi and Stiglitz, 2009; Barba and Pivetti, 2009; Tridico, 2012). Besides that, other problems exist, such as low levels of consumption, bank liquidity problems, low levels of private investment, a lack of trust and negative expectations in the financial market and between banks and investors, as well as high public deficits and debts. Despite the variety of problems, the governments of member states and EU institutions (in particular the EU Commission and ECB) focused mostly on a single problem, as I will argue in this chapter: the sovereign debt of member states (Fitoussi and Saraceno, 2010).

In order to recover from the crisis, governments in Western economies, particularly the US and the EU, initially in 2007–09, put in place fiscal stimuli and bank rescue package (as we saw in the previous chapter). These policies were supported by a great consensus among the policymakers, politicians, and academicians who had begun to look at Keynesian policies in a favourable way. The objective of this chapter is to investigate how the United States (US) and Japan managed relatively better than Europe to emerge from the crisis, and why instead Europe or more appropriately, the Euro Area (EA) of the European Union (EU), did not. I will examine the main policies implemented by the main fiscal and monetary authorities in the US – i.e. the Federal Reserve (Fed), and the Federal Government; in Japan: the Bank of Japan (BoJ) and the Japanese Government (focusing in particular on the so-called "Abenomics"); and in Europe: the European Central Bank (ECB) and EA Member State Governments. I will try to understand how in the US and Japan these policies caused some recovery in terms of GDP growth and employment, while on the other hand, the same result could not be obtained in Europe.

The chapter will also propose a political agenda for the EA, which would favour economic recovery and sustainable development in the next decade (we refer to the Euro Area as a country, at least from an economic point of view, despite the strong weakness of this definition from a political point of view). In this context, the case of Japan (with the so-called "Abenomics"), along with the recovery strategy embarked in the US are better examples that Europe should follow.

Economic crisis and recovery strategies in advanced economies: an overview

The United States

As we saw in the previous chapter, the US's initial answer to the crisis was the TARP, a public financial programme for about US$700 billion (2.3 per cent of US GDP), which aimed at saving banks and financial institutions from bankruptcies and failures.

Monetary policies were simultaneously manipulated by Western central banks. A combination of actions by the Fed, the European Central Bank (ECB), the Bank of England and the Bank of Japan, provided a huge amount of liquidity to the private sector, and to the banking sector in particular, in order to avoid the crunch of the inter-lending among banks. The first injections came in the summer of 2007, with the leading role going to the Fed and the Bank of Japan. The ECB and the Bank of England reacted by releasing similar proportions of liquidity into their own financial markets. Moreover, the interest rate in the US had been reduced from 5.25 to 0.25 per cent. In Japan it used to be always at very low levels. Similar action was taken in the UK. In the Eurozone, given that the greatest priority of the ECB was to foster price stability, the interest rate was lowered to 2.5 per cent in 2009 and to 1 per cent in 2010 (Tropeano, 2010; Sawyer, 2010).

From a more traditional fiscal policy point of view, the TARP was followed, during Obama's first administration, by a fiscal stimulus programme called ARRA (as we discussed in the previous chapter) for a value of US$775 billion (2.7 per cent of US GDP). This stimulus was able to launch new productive investments and create jobs. To some extent, it represented a breakdown of the main economic consensus, which favoured spontaneous recovery – i.e. recovery driven by the market or, in the less conservative case, monetary policy (quantitative easing) over fiscal stimulus. In fact, economic recovery, in terms of GDP, was immediately guaranteed, with growth of around 2 per cent since 2010 (see Figure 6.1).

Japan

In Japan, the situation before the global economic crisis was very different than in the US or the EU. Japan's economy during the 1990s experienced a serious stagnation of GDP, which started after the burst of the housing bubble at the end of 1980s and the beginning of the 1990s. Deflation and lower growth characterized

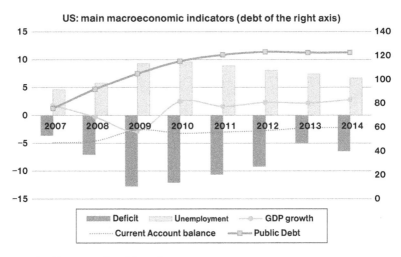

Figure 6.1 US: economic crisis and recovery.
Source: Own elaboration on Eurostat and IMF data.

Japan for almost two decades, and the consequences on the explosion of public debt were enormous: today, Japanese public debt is a bit less than 250 per cent of GDP. In 2008 and in 2009, during the global economic crisis, Japan's cumulative recession was about –6 per cent of GDP. However, since the end of the global crisis, and particularly after the 2011 recession caused mainly by the terrible Tsunami and earthquake, which destroyed the nuclear power plant in Fukushima, the Japanese economy seems to have embarked on a path of economic recovery clearly linked, according to many economists, to the so-called "Abenomics" (Irwin, 2013; The Economist, 2013a; IMF, 2013).

Abenomics refers to the economic policies implemented by Shinzō Abe, the Japanese prime minister since 2012. Abe was already prime minister in 2006–07, and also during these two years he tried to boost the Japanese economy with expansionary policies. His attempt to boost the Japanese economy with monetary expansion and fiscal stimuli, although less strategically organised since 2012, was able to produce economic growth of about 2 per cent a year. Abenomics is based on three pillars: fiscal stimulus, monetary quantitative easing and structural reforms. In other words, Abenomics *is a* program characterized by a "mix of reflation, government spending and a growth strategy", as *The Economist* (2013b) argued, aiming at raising the economy from two decades of suspended stagnation. Abenomics consists of monetary policy, fiscal policy, and economic growth strategies to encourage both public and private investments. Since 2012, Japanese policymakers have implemented a strategy that includes inflation targeting a 2 per cent annual rate, the correction of excessive yen appreciation, the setting of negative interest rates, huge quantitative easing, expansion of public investments, buying operations of treasury bonds by the Bank of Japan (BOJ), and the revision of the Bank of Japan Act, which impeded higher inflation

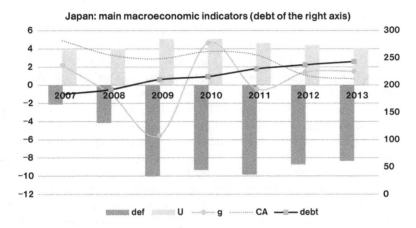

Figure 6.2 Japan: economic crisis and recovery.
Source: Own elaboration on Eurostat and IMF data.

targets. During 2013, the yen devalued 25 per cent over the US dollar, boosting exports and increasing the trade balance. However, after the 2011 nuclear disaster in Fukushima and the subsequent political decision to shut off all nuclear power in Japan, energy started to be heavily imported. This may have negative results in the long run with the yen continuously devalued. Nevertheless, the results of this program are positive so far: the economy started to grow; and deflation seems defeated, with a new target of 2 per cent, which both the Bank of Japan (BoJ) and the government seem to pursue simultaneously and co-ordinately.[1] Unemployment decreased further, reaching below 4 per cent in 2014 (Haidar and Hoshi, 2014; Wolf, 2013; Irwin, 2013).

The Euro Area

In the EU, the fiscal stimuli, implemented singularly by MS, mobilized around US$300 billion of resources (or 1.5 per cent of EU GDP; IMF, 2009). However, fiscal policies among member states are fragmented and often uncoordinated. Moreover, the EU is a supranational organisation with much less power than the US federation and little possibility of economies of scale. Nineteen countries adopted the euro so far (out of twenty-eight EU members) to which the ECB and the Maastricht criteria impose common monetary policies, fiscal constraints and harmonisation. Nine other countries maintain their own currency and sovereignty over their monetary policy, financial systems and fiscal policies.[2] This means that Europe has ten different currencies.[3] This represents a concrete difficulty in policy coordination. However, the biggest problem in this context relates to the fact that the UK is not part of the Eurozone (and probably, in the future, after the result of the exit referendum in June 2016, will not be part of the EU).[4] The UK is the second largest economy in the EU, and the British Pound is still an internationally important currency, with London as the biggest financial centre in Europe (Wahl, 2010). Market capitalisation in London is €1,962 trillion (2010 data), while Frankfurt and Paris have around €0.900 trillion each in market capitalisation (Eurostat, 2010). When national interests are on the table, EU members states, and in particular the UK, demonstrate a strong opposition to EU financial regulation and supranational power (UK Treasury Committee, 2010).

In 2009, Spain, which was one of the countries hit hardest by the crisis, put in place the biggest stimulus in Europe, favoured by a socialist government, of 3.7 per cent of GDP (see Table A9 in the appendix). This plan focused on €40 billion to support infrastructure investments and the automobile industry. France's plan was smaller, €26 billion, which includes a boost for the construction and automobile sectors; moreover, the government has promised €20 billion for small businesses and the construction industry. Germany's package includes generous amortization rules for companies and incentives for climate-friendly home renovation; the total package is expected to reach €82 billion, including private investments. Italy proposed a nominal stimulus for unemployment subsidies and firm support that amounted to only €9 billion. The UK has introduced a temporary reduction of the VAT rate from 17.5 per cent to 15 per cent. In addition, the government invested €31 billion on infrastructure.

The outcomes of these stimuli were quite positive: in the second quarter of 2010, Germany grew at an extraordinary rate of 8.8 per cent, and the UK at 4.8 per cent. Similar stories, although of less magnitude, occurred in other European economies.

Nevertheless, in the US and Japan, expansionary policies, quantitative easing, a continuous program of buying Treasury bonds, and lower interest rates continued to the present. In the EU, after the Greek crisis of spring 2010, governments turned

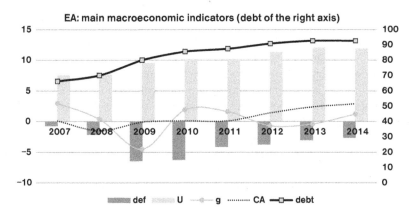

Figure 6.3 The Euro Area: economic crisis and recovery.
Source: Own elaboration on Eurostat and IMF data.

their interests, irrationally, toward budget cuts and policies of contraction (Arestis and Pelagidis, 2010). In the fall of 2010, the new Liberal-Conservative government in the UK implemented an austerity plan with cuts in public expenditures and a freezing of public employment wages and jobs for the next three years. Chancellor Merkel proposed similar restrictive plans in Germany, and other continental European countries prepared financial laws very much focused on restrictive fiscal measurements. The objective was to reduce deficits. This seemed more like a reaction to the Greek and Irish crises rather than a rational decision that would help economic recovery (Arestis and Pelagidis, 2010).

At the same time, the actions of the member states, particularly in the South of Europe, were, and still are, strongly limited by the tough rules of EU treaties such as the Maastricht Treaty and the Stability and Growth Pact, which were reinforced, as I will argue later, in the last three years. They became tighter in terms of austerity and public expenditure rules with the introduction of the so-called "Fiscal Compact", the "Six-pack", and the "Two-pack", which impede member states from implementing deficit policies if they have macroeconomic imbalances. This is a vicious circle that does not allow MS policymakers room for manoeuvers unless the treaties are violated or changed.

Quantitative easing in the US, Abenomics in Japan and austerity in Europe

Two major challenges emerged during the crisis: the rise of unemployment with growing public deficits and financial instability threatening economic development. In this context, Europe, and the Euro Area in particular, seems stuck in a stagnation trap, without private investments, and with policymakers refusing to increase public deficits and public investments, which would help the economic recovery. In fact, while the other major advanced economies managed, through expansionary policies to end the crisis, the Euro Area is very much worried about price stability. In 2014, the situation was very clear: Japan and the US are emerging from the crisis. They reduced unemployment and started economic recovery through expansionary policies, which are visible in both the increasing of the public spending, resulting in higher deficits, and the loosening of monetary policies, resulting in lower interest rates. Finally, deflation was defeated in Japan after twenty years and new targets of inflation rates deliberately met by the BoJ were reached above 2 per cent; similarly, in the US, there are no worries about inflation nor deflation. On the contrary, in the EA, the spectrum of inflation mostly spread by Germany, and the consequent more prudent monetary and fiscal policies operated by the ECB, lead instead toward the specular and major problem of deflation. In 2014, the risk of a deflation spiral is real, with the average price index close to zero, and in some countries, like Italy, below zero.

From Figure 6.4, there is evidence of a strong relation, of the Keynesian type, between deficit, debt, inflation and unemployment: Japan, followed by the US, is increasing public expenditure and it is getting the expected results, in terms of reducing unemployment and boosting economic growth;

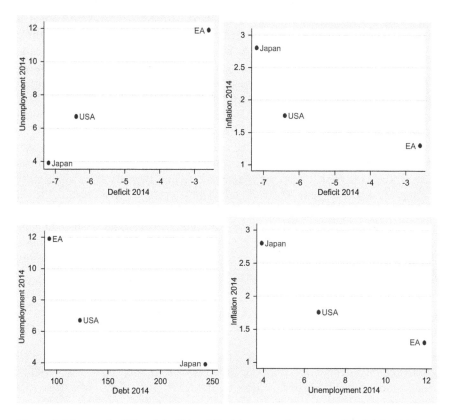

Figure 6.4 Japan, the US and the EA public debt, unemployment and deficit in 2014.
Source: Own elaboration on Eurostat and IMF data.

moreover, Japan managed, thanks mainly to the quantitative easing program and more generally to the "Abenomics" described above, to escape two decades of deflation and restore economic growth. On the contrary, the Euro Area prefers lower deficits and debt at the expenses of higher unemployment and stagnation. It is also possible to identify a clear Philips curve between (higher) inflation and (lower) unemployment among the countries analysed, which give hope to policymakers who are willing to reduce unemployment. As far as economic growth is concerned, we can observe the same results: the US, followed by Japan, is recovering in terms of economic growth, while the Euro Area is lagging behind.

Despite its well-known high public debt (around 240 per cent), the Japanese economy, as well as the US economy (which has a debt of 125 per cent of GDP today), did not avoid implementing fiscal expansionary policies in order to recover from recession after 2008/09, and to foster employment. Both the Central Bank in Japan and the Fed in the US cooperate with their governments, loosening monetary policies, decreasing the interest rates, pumping money into the systems and contributing to the accomplishment of better performances than in Europe.

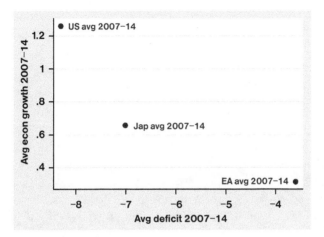

Figure 6.5 Japan, the US and the EA government deficit and economic growth in 2007–14: averages, (avg).

Source: Own elaboration on Eurostat and IMF data.

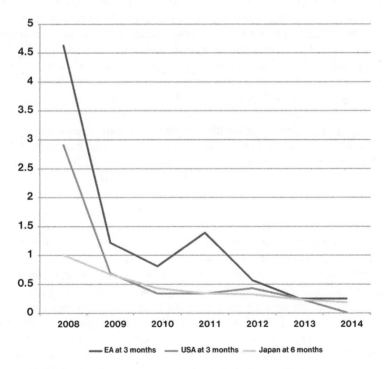

Figure 6.6 Money market (interest rates) in the EA, the US and Japan.

Source: Eurostat.

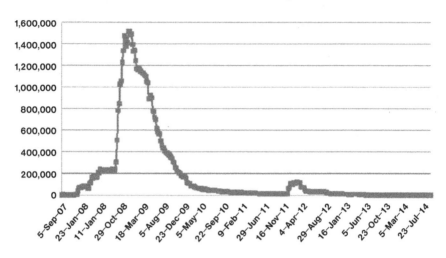

Figure 6.7 Fed quantitative easing.
Source: Fed balance sheet.

Of particular interest is the extraordinary monetary policy implemented by the Fed in the US called quantitative easing (i.e. the systematic introduction into the system of huge amounts of liquidity). With this strategy, the Federal Reserve responded aggressively to the financial crisis that emerged in the summer of 2007 from different angles; not only in the reduction of the target federal funds rate from more than 5 per cent in 2007 to effectively zero in 2014, but also in implementing a number of programs designed to support the liquidity of financial institutions and foster improved conditions in financial markets. Figure 6.7 shows the quantitative easing program with all the liquidity facilities used weekly to stimulate the economy (i.e. the Term Auction Facility, the Commercial Paper Funding Facility, the Central Bank Liquidity Swap, the Term Assed-backed Securities Loan Facility). These liquidities reached the extraordinary peak of US$1.5 trillion in the weeks of December 2008 and January 2009 and then declined towards lower levels in 2010, below US$100 billion weekly in 2010 and in 2011. However, at the end of 2011, the weekly liquidity increased again above US$100 billion weekly in 2010 and in 2011 and then decreased in 2013 and in 2014 to an average of US$3 billion weekly. In general, during the whole period since the beginning of the crisis in the summer of 2007 up to today, the Fed introduced into the system an amount of liquidity of around US$200 billion per week.

A similar aggressive monetary policy was followed in Japan in the framework of Abenomics. In Japan, quantitative easing took the form, mainly, of loans to financial institutions through long-term funds at a very low interest rate (the interest rate on loans is fixed at 0.1 per cent per annum for four years) and a vast program of buying, without prior limits, Japanese treasury bonds (Bank of Japan, 2014). Figure 6.8 shows these measures during the whole period from the beginning of the crisis until today. Liquidities increased in 2009 to US$370 billion of weekly funds being introduced into the system. However, the peak was

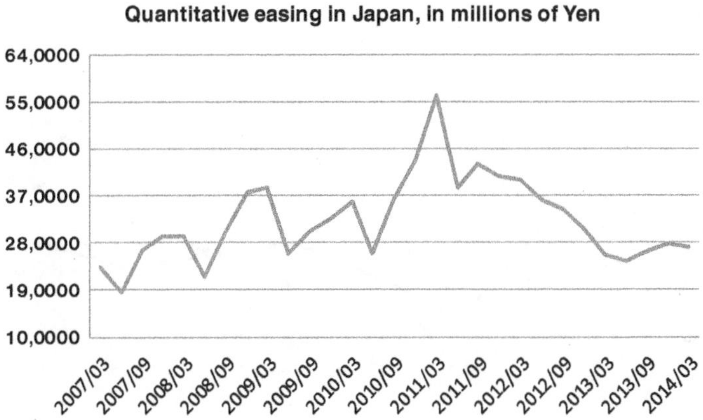

Quantitative easing in Japan, in millions of Yen

Figure 6.8 BoJ quantitative easing.
Source: Bank of Japan.

reached after the Fukushima disaster in 2011 and continued in 2012 during the second mandate of the premier Shinzō Abe at a similar speed and magnitude of the liquidities introduced by the Fed in the US.

Contrary to the Fed and to the BoJ, the EU, and in particular the Euro Area, and its monetary institutions kept relatively higher interest rates.[5] It put into the system less liquidity and did not put forth the main tools that the economy required, such as the issuing of Euro bonds and a program of buying member states' debts, particularly the ones in difficulty.

The cost of these actions, or more appropriately these inactions, is exemplified by Figure 6.9, particularly with respect to the US recovery, which in 2014 reached a GDP per capita higher than nearly 10 per cent of the one of 2007, the year when the crisis started. The EA, on the contrary, is still below its 2007 level. Japan is collocated in an intermediate position between the two countries, and its projections for growth are currently the same as the US. This gap, along with mass unemployment and deflation, which worsen indebted countries' situations even further, represents the cost of the EU failure in managing the current crisis.

At the same time, the EU moved toward tighter rules concerning austerity and public expenditure. Policies for austerity were imposed with new intergovernmental treaties. Several agreements were signed within the EA between 2011 and 2013. A so-called "Fiscal Compact" (more formally Treaty on Stability, Coordination and Governance, TSCG) was signed in 2001 and entered into force in January 2013. The TSCG commits countries that signed the treaty (all EU MS except the UK and Czech Republic) to amend national law to guarantee budget balance, newly defined as an "adjusted structural deficit"[6] below 0.5 per cent for a country with a debt above 60 per cent and below 1 per cent for countries with a debt below 60 per cent). To complement the TSCG, other rules were set to

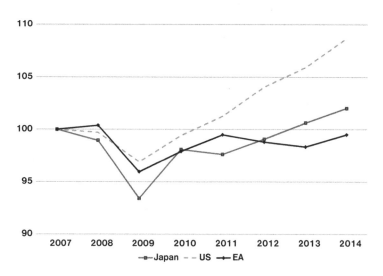

Figure 6.9 The cost of EA inaction. GDP in 2007=100.
Source: IMF World Economic Outlook, database summer 2014.

sync procedures (sanctions) against "excessive deficits": the so-called "Six-pack", "Two-pack", and "Euro plus". Collectively, these provisions and rules are known as the "European Semester". The six-pack refers to five regulations and a directive to control budget deficits and macroeconomic imbalances; the two-pack refers to the provision to monitor and if necessary to require change to national budget by the European Commission. These provisions are subject, if not respected, to European sanctions that can take the form of monetary sanctions (up to 0.2 per cent of MS GDP), freezing of European Structural Funds and reduction of the right to vote in the EU institutions (these are more stricter rules and more effective sanctions than the ones already stated in the Maastricht Treaty). Finally, the Euro Plus pact signed by six other EU countries beside the EA MS, concerns broader economic co-ordination.

Policies and results: the DDC index and the performance index

To synthesise the economic policies implemented and the results obtained by Japan, the US and the EA in the last years of the economic crisis, I introduce two indexes: the DDC index, which proxies the policies implemented during 2007–14, and the performance index (PI), which accounts for the performance obtained by Japan, the US and the EA in the same period.

The DDC (Deficit-Debt-Current Account) index is obtained through the algebraic sum of Government Deficit (+), Public Debt (+) and Current Account balance (−). The index is constructed in a way that shows that the higher

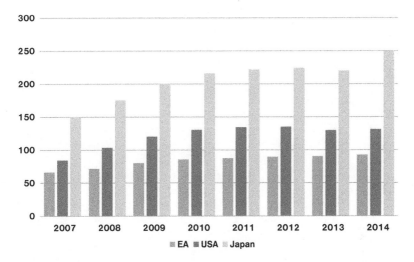

Figure 6.10 The DDC index.
Source: Own elaboration on Eurostat and IMF data.

the index, the "worse" it is for the country, at least in the orthodox view that considers deficit and debt necessarily negatively. In other words, according to this view, the higher the index, the weaker the position of the country and more vulnerable the economy is in the future. It follows that a higher index would be a worse option. Advocates of this view would argue that public spending is not a good option for recovering from the crisis. At the same time, the DDC index can be considered a proxy of macroeconomic policies or, more correctly, of macroeconomic policy preference. Thus, in Japan and the US, governments prefer to keep lower unemployment, boost economic growth and therefore are willing, more than in Europe, to increase deficits and debt. On the contrary, in the EA, austerity and fiscal constraints oblige the MS to implement tight fiscal policy and to reduce the deficit.

In the end, the results of these policies were higher unemployment and lower economic growth (or stagnation) in Europe, and recovery with economic and employment growth in Japan and in the US after 2010. The performance index (PI), shown in Figure 6.11, which is a combination of economic growth rates and unemployment rates, highlights these differences.[7]

In particular, policies between Europe and the US (and the rest of the world's advanced economies) started to diverge after the Greek crisis, which began in May 2010. This crisis showed how EU member states are much more concerned with national issues than EU integration during times of crisis (Frangakis, 2010) and showed the fragilities of the EU and the EA.[8] A lack of coordination and financial solidarity emerged dramatically, and the issue of European imbalances was wrongly regarded as a problem of laziness against effort; virtuous balance

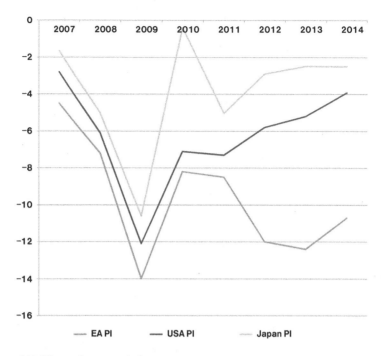

Figure 6.11 The performance index.
Source: Own elaboration on Eurostat and IMF data.

against poor discipline; Mediterranean corruption against Northern European integrity (Cesaratto, 2011). This does not help us to see the real problem behind the deficit-surplus issue within the EU, which is an imperfect single market.

A single market (with many imperfections) and a common currency within a non-Optimal Currency Area (OCA) at the very least needs labour coordination, budget centralisation, and fiscal policy harmonisation (Wray and Randall, 2010). In addition, the strong "internal devaluation" (i.e. wage moderation) that Germany carried out in the past ten years, along with other mercantilist policies and the cooperation of the ECB's strict monetary policies before Draghi took over in 2010, allowed German exports to increase dramatically (Cesaratto, 2011). Such policies were not really in the spirit of EU integration and solidarity. Consequentially, the EU situation today looks fragmented. On one side, Greece and the other Mediterranean countries suffer vis-à-vis the efficiency of Northern European firms. Free competition and the imperfect single market affected the domestic markets in those countries, which were lagging behind in terms of competitiveness and technology at the creation of the Eurozone and the single market. Moreover, the Maastricht criteria and stability pacts appreciated the euro and contributed to the declining foreign competitiveness of Southern European economies. On the other hand, the poorer economies in the EU cannot use monetary policies and exchange rate manipulation to gain competitiveness. They are unable to use state aid and firm subsidies, nor fiscal policies which are constrained by Maastricht criteria. Hence, markets have to regulate imbalances despite the fact that labour mobility, single markets, and budget centralization are strongly limited in the EU. It follows that surplus and deficit are the two malaises of the same problems: an imperfect single market and an imperfect currency union.

In the EU, Germany's surplus could not exist without Greece's deficit (and similar). Greece should accept, within the EU rules, the German market's super-competition, which is historically rooted and state supported, despite the fact that they cannot use policies to enhance their firms' competitive advantage. Unless these imbalances are covered by a central EU plan, it would not be convenient for Greece to accept European monetary union constraints.

A new strategy to overcome the European impasse of austerity without growth

The longevity of the current economic and financial crisis confirms that its na-ture is different from the one observed after the great depression in the 1930s. In Europe, because of the common currency shared by a number of EU member countries and differences in their economic competitiveness, currency devalua-tion is not a simple tool for recovery. Massive public interventions in the market at the beginning of the financial crisis were connected with huge increases to public deficits. If we add to these high levels of public debts, which in some European countries like Ireland, Portugal, Belgium, Italy and Greece are higher than 100 per cent of GDP, and in others like Spain, France, the UK and Germany are a bit less than 100 per cent of GDP, it is obvious that stimulating economic recovery by increasing public spending is not a simple solution.

Given these two major limitations existing in the EA concerning the impos-sibility for all MS to implement currency devaluation and the difficulty to im-plement expansionary policies in deficits, both caused by the existence of an imperfect EU single market and of a non-Optimal Currency Area (beside the strict rules of the treaties), a EU/EA strategy is required in order to solve the issue in a coordinated way. This strategy, which I will discuss at the end of this chapter, should go beyond austerity.

In fact, the experiences of implementing austerity measures in the EA, which can reduce the public deficit in the short term, are negative. They are accompa-nied by increases in unemployment and the decline of GDP, which can also lead to political destabilisation, weakening social cohesion and to further increases of public debt instead of a reduction of it. The consequences of cuts in public spending can therefore cause more negative impacts on economic growth and essentially increase budgetary problems.

The creation of the European Stability Mechanism[9] (ESM) along with the Outright Monetary Transactions (OMT) program proved to be very effective in solving the European crisis and saving the Euro currency in 2012; much more than any other austerity program implemented before and after this date in the EU. These two institutions, with all the limitations that they have, show what should be the most appropriate road to follow in the EU to fill the missing spots and to fix the flaws of the European Economic Monetary Governance.[10] However, the problem with the ESM and the OMT is that they are not guaranteed by treaties as EU institutions: the ESM is an intergovernmental organisation financed mostly by the richest MS (Germany, France, Italy), created in an emergency circumstance, and it is not clear yet whether this will be a permanent fund or it will disappear (because of lack of funds from MS) after the crisis. Moreover, the ESM is not a fund that acts on regular basis as a lender of last resort buying government bonds of MS, and it is far from having a regular program of issuing European Bonds. It has limited resources (€750 billion), which are used in particular circumstances of crisis.

The OMT theoretically is even weaker than the ESM as far as permanent EU institutional guarantees are concerned. The OMT is neither based on a treaty nor guaranteed by EU institutions. It is mostly based on a famous speech of the ECB president, Mario Draghi, who, in the summer of 2012 in London, stated: "Within our mandate, the ECB is ready to do whatever it takes to preserve the euro. And believe me, it will be enough". Then, a program of OMT was officially announced in September 2012 as a program of conditional sovereign bond purchases on secondary markets without prior limits, subject to strict conditionality under the ESM programmes. The most important novelty of this program, which in the end was never really activated because the crisis circumstances attenuated, was the objective to buy MS bonds without limits. It was a speech of a president of a Central bank, which stated for the first time something extremely important and which proved to be extremely effective. However, everybody, and in particular the Germans who strongly objected Draghi's speech and informal strategy, knew that the statement was contrary to the spirit of the ECB statutes, which do not allow the ECB to act as a lender of last resort. Its unique objective is to stabilize prices and to guarantee against inflation spiral as the Germans prefer. However, this statement, more than any other policy was probably enough to guarantee markets, to increase trust in the euro, to stabilize and protect national bond markets of MS in crisis from speculators, to reduce the spread between South and North interest rates on treasury bonds, and to avoid further sovereign debt defaults (see Figure 6.12).

All this shows that a strong institution working as a lender of last resort, guaranteed by EU institutions and by the ECB statute, without conflicts, should be created for the EU or at least for the Eurozone as soon as possible.

For instance, Italy, in order to respect EU recommendations, reduced public spending, raised taxes, operated manoeuvers for deficit reduction, and stayed, even when not strictly necessary, as in recent years, under 3 per cent of the deficit (or close to the structural deficit of 0.5 per cent imposed by the new Treaty on Stability, Coordination and Governance). Today it is clear to many that these restrictive manoeuvers of austerity have not led to the two main advantages it was implemented for – i.e. reduction of public debt and economic growth. On the contrary, performances in this respect are quite negative as Table 6.1 shows.

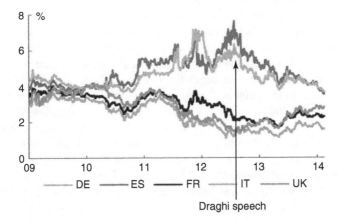

Figure 6.12 Ten-year treasury bonds yields – selected MS, 2009–14 (%).
Source: EU Commission.

Table 6.1 Italy's main macroeconomics indicators

	2012	*2013*	*2014*	*2015*
GDP growth	−2,5	−1,9	0,6	1,1
Deficit	−3,0	−3,0	−2,6	−2,3
Structural Deficit	−1,4	−0,8	−0,8	−0,7
Primary balance	2,5	2,3	2,7	3,1
Debt	127	133	135	135
Unemployment	10,7	12,2	12,6	13

Source: EU Commission.

The reason is simple: policies of deficit reduction, carried out during periods of recession, reduce further aggregate demand and thus contribute to the further decline of the GDP. The debt/GDP ratio then worsens as a result of the denominator of the fraction which decreases. In addition, it also contributes to lessening the reduction in tax revenues, due to a decline in income and employment. In recent years, countries in the EU such as Italy that have practiced austerity policies have seen worsening public debt and GDP dynamics. This process, which is well known as a "Keynesian multiplier", is very often undermined by policymakers and is not taken into account in the EU. Lately, however, the International Monetary Fund (which in the previous years had been very conservative on these issues) also stated that there is a positive Keynesian multiplier of the expenditure with a value between 1.5 and 2. In other words, economic policies that increase the public deficit may have an overall positive impact on growth, on the reduction of unemployment and also on the reduction of public debt because, with a multiplier of the expenditure bigger than 1, the positive effect on income is able to compensate the increase of deficit. Conversely, deficit reduction in recessions worsens through lower GDP dynamics and unemployment, also through the public debt.

Figure 6.13 is clear on this issue – as I repeated an exercise first conducted by Martin Wolf in 2012 with available data at that time (Wolf, 2012). The same exercise undertaken with today's data confirms Wolf's hypothesis: the bigger the structural tightening, the larger the fall in GDP. In 2012, Wolf estimated that every percentage point of structural fiscal tightening lowered the GDP by 1.5 per cent of its 2008 level. In my estimate, the results are essentially the same over a slightly different period of the crisis. First I calculated, among EA MS the structural balance adjustment from 2009 to 2014 (IMF, World Outlook Report, 2014).[11] Austerities policies started between 2009/2010; then, I evaluated their impact on economic growth from 2010 to 2014. The same negative relation is identified between structural balance adjustment and GDP: the tighter the fiscal adjustment (i.e. the deeper the austerity), the lower the GDP growth (or the deeper the recession).

Hence, austerity policies contribute to dramatically worsening the situation. They contribute to squeezing economies and to creating smaller ones, able to deliver fewer jobs. They contribute to destroying the capacity of production and reducing further industrial production. Moreover, from a social point of view, one can observe consequences of aging populations on social security systems and in many countries the real decline of welfare state instruments. The drop of fertility rates in most EU countries during the economic crisis may also significantly weaken the competitive potential of Europe. Effects of public spending

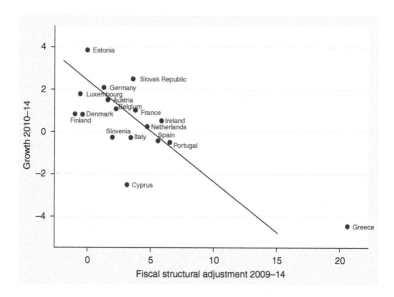

Figure 6.13 The impact of austerity on GDP growth in the Euro Area.
Source: Own elaboration on IMF data.

and related fiscal, budget and monetary policies should be calculated from the perspective of social aims such as poverty reduction or employment. Employment, specifically, requires decisive actions as in some EU countries like Spain and Greece where the unemployment rate among people younger than 25 years old is higher than 50 per cent and total unemployment is close to 25 per cent.

The long period of the current crisis also has a strong impact on citizens' state of mind and may lead to different kinds of frustrations and protests. We have observed in the last few years in Europe violent protests and riots in Spain and in Greece. Also in Central and Northern Europe, one can observe the emergence of anti-European and extreme right wing parties. These were obviously the consequences of disappointment, frustration, lower standards of living and above all mass unemployment in those countries. Hence, austerity not only proves to be ineffective in stimulating economic recovery, but it also increases social tensions within MS and anti-EU movements within the union.

In Europe, in the end, the biggest problem seems to be mass unemployment. On average, among all 28 MS, the unemployment rate is around 11 per cent, with strong differences among countries and huge variations: from 4 to 5 per cent in Germany and Austria, to around 25 per cent in Greece and Spain. Obviously the latter figures underline, in the South of Europe, the existence of problems related to lack of investments and insufficient aggregate demand. In the north of Europe, the very low unemployment rates underline different problems identified by the structural surplus in the balance of payments. These problems cannot be solved with a single agenda of structural reforms (i.e. labour market flexibility) and austerity policies that the EU has carried out. In the best case, labour flexibility will increase employee turnover and will probably bring about poorer performance of productivity. This will not increase the employment levels, in particular in the South of Europe. With this perspective, one can easily explain the very high youth unemployment rates in many countries in the EU, where the agenda of labour flexibility showed its complete failure. It contributed to creating no additional jobs; therefore, young people remain unemployed. In the EU a wide strategy, similar to the one implemented in US and in Japan, is needed, and it should be organised around the four following pillars:

- A Euro Area central budget of at least 5 to 10 per cent of GDP, which should allow for automatic compensation of macroeconomic imbalances due to the imperfections of the non-Optimal Currency Area of the EA
- Differentiated fiscal policies and budget flexibility for MS (beyond the current EU treaties) in recession time
- Buying operations without prior limits of treasury bonds by the ECB for MS in difficulty
- Issuing of EU bonds to back public investments in countries with unemployment higher than 10 per cent (A similar proposal, without the objective concerning public investments, and the limits of 10 per cent of unemployment, was made by Tremonti and Junker proposal.[12])

This strategy should also involve public investments along with public policies such as reform of labour markets (i.e. integration of labour and development policies), financial regulation, sustainable development, innovation stimuli, sound combinations of coordinated monetary and fiscal policies, and an institutional strategies towards a better governance for both public issues and private business. Moreover, this strategy should also be diversified at the MS level to give enough flexibility, in fiscal and budgetary terms, to MS and to allow them room for manoeuvres beyond the strict fiscal rules of the Stability and Growth Pact and of the even stricter TSCG.

In this context, labour market policies and development policies need to be considered "two sides of the same coin", and need to be faced with a single approach focusing on the demand side of the economy. As De Long (2010), Arestis and Pelagidis (2010), and many others underlined, surplus countries such as Germany, Austria and the Netherlands need to implement expansionary policies rather than austerity measures by spending more and taxing less. To sum up, in Europe, the ECB should practice a policy of zero interest rates for several years to come as modelled by the Fed and by the Bank of Japan. It also should start a regular program of buying national bonds. A program of issuing European Union Bonds should be introduced in the Euro Area as soon as possible. In order to overcome the German veto in this matter, the EU Bonds should focus merely on new productive investments in order to boost employment where needed in the EU.

Notes

1 The new behaviour of coordination and cooperation between BoJ and Government was heavily criticized by some orthodox analysts and economists, as this is a violation of the independence of the Central Bank (Reuters, 2013).
2 Bulgaria, Czech Rep., Denmark, Hungary, Poland, Romania, Sweden, Croatia and the UK are outside the Euro Area.
3 The currencies of Croatia, Bulgaria and Denmark are pegged to the euro.
4 Probably, the relations between the EU and the UK in the future will be more like the one between Norway and the EU. However, this is an evolving matter on which it is difficult to make projections, because it depends on political will and leader attitudes.
5 Only in September 2014, the ECB finally cut the interest rate to the historical low level of 0.05 per cent, overcoming the German resistance. This was an overdue measure, taken late, however welcomed.
6 The adjusted structural deficit refers to the deficit cyclically adjusted and it is calculated with respect to the potential rate of economic growth.
7 The reason it is preferred here to take into account a composite index rather than the GDP growth or the unemployment rate only is because the PI takes into consideration both employment and GDP aspects simultaneously. Using such an index would allow for better consideration of the performance of countries during the crisis, and it avoids biases and distortions such as the fact that countries could have experienced low recession but very bad unemployment or employment reduction (and vice versa).
8 Media pointed out how an election in the small Lander of Lower Saxon in Germany during the Greek crisis in the spring of 2010 was enough to keep German chancellor Angela Merkel far away from an idea of integration and financial solidarity, which populists in Germany objected.

9 The ESM is an EU agency created in October 2012 with the mission to safeguard financial stability in Europe by providing financial assistance to Euro Area member states. The ESM is a permanent institution, which followed the creation of the European Financial Stability Mechanism (EFSM), an EU institution created in April of 2010 and able to borrow on behalf of EU in capital markets and to lend to MS in difficulty. It was exceptionally created to save Ireland and Portugal, with a very limited resource of €60 billion. The EFSM was immediately followed by the European Financial Stability Facility (EFSF) which was a much bigger (but temporary) fund, also with the participation of private financial institutions, guaranteed by the Euro Area MS, created during the Greek crisis in the spring-summer of 2010, providing an initial support of €500 billion and with the objective to provide loans, bond purchases in primary markets, bank recapitalisation, secondary market interventions and financial assistance in particular to Greece, Portugal and Ireland. The EFSF borrows in capital markets, issues debt and then lends to MS in difficulty. It expired in June 2013. Both the EFSM and the EFSF involved the participation of the IMF.

10 In this period was also initiated a Banking Union (BU) among EU MS and negotiations are still continuing. The BU aims to set a single supervision and rescue mechanism for big banks at EU level, in order to reduce the vicious loop-circle between national sovereign debts and national banks whose cost of rescue (or of recapitalization) can sometimes be excessive for one country in isolation (UK, Czech Republic and Sweden chose to remain outside of this union).

11 The structural balance adjustment is the general government deficit cyclically adjusted. In this way, the change in fiscal policy represents the results of policy rather than cyclical effects.

12 Jean-Claude Juncker and Giulio Tremonti made a proposal on the *Financial Times* for a European Union bond, issued by a European Debt Agency (EDA). Each country can issue European bonds up to 40 per cent of GDP. This would create, over time, a sovereign bond market of similar size to the US one. Initially the EDA would finance 50 per cent of member states' debt issues – but this can be raised to 100 per cent during crises. The proposal also envisions a mechanism to switch between national and European bonds for countries in trouble at a discount rate. This would avoid the problem that secondary markets in many EU sovereign bonds are not sufficient liquid during crises.

7 Why some countries performed better than others during the initial phase of the crisis

Introduction

The objective of this chapter is to explore why some countries performed better than others in managing the crisis, during the initial phase of it, which was probably the worst (2007–11). I will elaborate on this question using the crisis management index (CMI), taking into consideration GDP and labour market performance among European Union member states. My findings conclude that countries that performed better during the initial phase of the crisis do not have a flexible labour market and have managed to keep stable employment levels. These countries combine a very good mix of economic policies and social institutions oriented to stabilize the level of consumption and the aggregate demand. Coordination mechanisms, higher levels of financial regulation and monitoring are also important features of these economies. Clearly, this group of countries identifies better, in the EU, a coordinated market economy model. Moreover, it can be stated, today, that countries that managed relatively better the initial phase of the crisis are the ones that had later a better recovery during 2012–15.

In EU, on average, GDP still is stagnating and the unemployment level is not declining (Fitoussi and Stiglitz, 2009; Barba and Pivetti, 2009). Besides the problem of imbalance in the current account and of the sovereign debt sustainability, the EU is strongly affected by economic problems such as mass unemployment and slow GDP growth which make imbalances and debt more severe issues. At the beginning of the crisis, among the EU member states, the situation was very variegated. As for the GDP performance, we can divide the (then) twenty-seven MS[1] into four groups:

- Group One: the worst one made up by countries that have experienced a deep recession with an average negative GDP performance during the period from 2007 to 2011 (Greece, Latvia, Ireland, Italy, Denmark, Portugal and Estonia).
- Group Two: countries whose GDP was just above 1 per cent between 2007 and 2011 (UK, Spain, France and Finland; this is also the average situation in the EU27).
- Group Three: countries that had an average GDP growth for the period between 2007 and 2011 between 1 and 2 per cent.

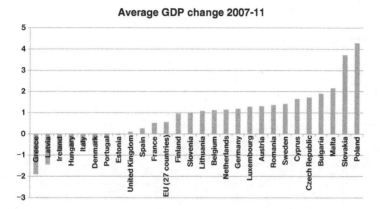

Figure 7.1 The initial phase of the economic crisis in the European Union.
Source: Eurostat (own elaboration).

• Group Four: Countries that had a relatively stronger performance in terms
  of GDP growth, with an average growth rate between 2.2 per cent (Malta)
  and 4.3 per cent (Poland, the best performer, which, contrary to all the other
  member states, did not experience a single year of recession during the period between 2007 and 2011).

Interestingly enough, initial conditions in terms of GDP per capita of the countries did not matter in the performance during the crisis, meaning that we did not
observe, as predicted by the neoclassical approach, that poorer countries grew
faster or richer countries grew slower. Instead, as Figure 7.2 shows, among the
best performers one can find both richer countries like Germany, Austria and
Luxemburg and poorer countries like Poland, Slovakia and Malta.

Hence, reasons for different performance and crisis management have to be
found elsewhere than initial conditions. In this chapter, I will also take into consideration labour market performance in order to rank overall EU country performances. This would allow for a deeper analysis of the crisis.

The crisis in the labour markets

Following the various performances of the EU economies, one can state that
EU labour markets were differently affected by the crisis. However, the performance in the labour market does not strictly reflect the performance of GDP.
In some countries where social institutions and trade unions were stronger,
unemployment increase was not dramatic and social costs of the crisis were less
significant. In particular, besides Poland and Malta (which experienced higher
growth of the GDP between 2007–11), this is the case of Germany, Austria and
Luxembourg, despite only a modest increase of GDP between 2007–11. Not surprisingly, in countries where labour flexibility was very high, unemployment

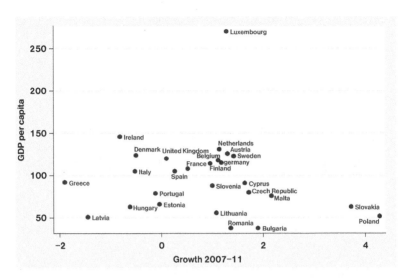

Figure 7.2 GDP per capita 2006 (EU27=100) and average growth, 2007–11.
Source: Eurostat (own elaboration).

increased dramatically. Even in the Scandinavian countries, which in the last decade adopted a so-called "flexicurity" model, like Denmark, Sweden and Finland, employment decreased and unemployment reached very high levels (around 7 per cent). However, the most dramatic figures in terms of unemployment and employment fall are in the countries where a flexibility model, *tout court*, was adopted or is more persistent, such as in Ireland, Estonia, Lithuania, Latvia, Spain and the UK.

At the same time, unemployment rates followed the same trend: in most of the EU countries, it increased enormously. It reached dramatic levels in Spain, around 20 per cent, and in Greece, Latvia, Lithuania, Estonia and Ireland, around 15 per cent. Such a dynamic is real and is not at all affected by demographic trends such as reductions of labour forces, chances in the population or reduction of people looking for jobs. Instead, absolute numbers such as employed and unemployed, in the Survey of EU Labour Forces, worsened. Figure 7.3 shows the dramatic increase of unemployment rates in most of the EU, with the exception of countries like Austria and Germany and some other few where unemployment declined.

Such a variegated situation underlines a different rate of elasticity of employment reduction to the recession of the GDP. Such elasticity is negative and higher in Spain, Estonia, the UK, Portugal, Ireland, and Lithuania. These countries are followed by Finland, Slovenia, Netherland, Sweden, Bulgaria, France, Cyprus, Czech Republic and Slovakia. In those countries, employment declined relatively more than the decline of GDP. Austria, Poland, Luxemburg and Malta, which are in general together with Germany the best performing countries, as we will see,

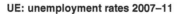

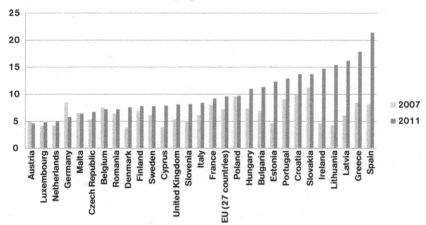

Figure 7.3 Mass unemployment in Europe.
Source: Eurostat (own elaboration).

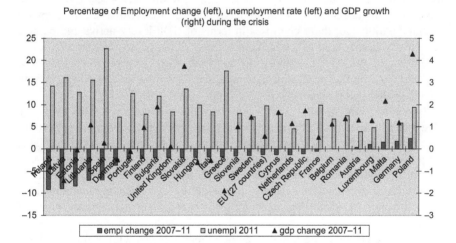

Figure 7.4 Employment, unemployment and GDP.
Source: Eurostat (own elaboration).

had a GDP growth relatively higher than employment growth. Finally, the case of Germany is extraordinary: this country experienced an employment growth relatively higher than the growth of GDP, and this highlights the importance of the labour nexus in Germany and the strategic role of trade unions in the industrial relations.[2]

Table 7.1 offers a general overview, country by country, with a detailed description of the impact of the crisis on the economy and on the labour market. Out of twenty-seven member states, only Poland did not experience a single year of recession during the critical period of 2007–11. Eight countries, such as Estonia, Spain, France, Italy, Portugal, Romania, Sweden and the UK experienced a so-called double dip, with a two-year recession in the same period. Ireland, Greece and Latvia experienced multiple dips, and the rest of the EU had at least one year of GDP recession (in 2009). From Table 7.1, the worst situation in terms of numbers of years of recession and magnitude of the fall was in the following groups of countries:

- Estonia, Latvia, Lithuania (Baltic countries – small and open economies strongly dependant on the outside and high deficit in the current account)
- UK and Ireland (Anglo-Saxon competitive capitalist countries – financially exposed, with very flexible labour market, inequality and lower public expenditure in social dimensions)
- Spain, Greece, Portugal and Italy (Mediterranean countries – which combine features of Figures 7.3 and 7.4)

To some extent also Denmark, Sweden and Finland were badly affected by the crisis in its initial phase. The reason is very likely attributed to the strong flexibility in the labour market,[3] which allowed firms to fire during recession, and so deepening the crisis from an employment point of view. However, the stronger initial conditions of those countries in terms of GDP levels, active and passive labour policies, as well as welfare made the crisis less costly in terms of social and human costs. This positioned the countries for a faster recovery, thanks to strong labour market programs, automatic stabilizers, better education, training and job-search programs.

In regard to the Mediterranean countries, the economic crisis is commonly deepened by structural problems such as low productivity, scarce innovation, exposure to the housing sector – badly affected by the crisis – and higher level of public debt. Moreover, poor labour market policies, higher inequality, and labour flexibility introduced massively in those four countries in the last decade, reduced consumption capacity, and made aggregate demand more unstable than in other EU countries, deepening the crisis from deflationary point of view.

When we consider the flows of employment changes with absolute values, the situation does not change much, meaning that the variation of the values goes in the same direction and magnitude as the variation of the rates. For instance, employment in Spain decreased more than 2 million while in Germany it increased more than 1.5 million; these figures correspond respectively to –11.8 per cent of employment in Spain and +4 per cent of employment in Germany. Consistently with our analysis, the top countries in maintaining positive employment flows are Luxembourg, Malta, Poland, Germany and Austria in that order. The bottom countries in losing jobs are Ireland, Latvia, Lithuania, Spain and Bulgaria.

Table 7.1 EU countries during the crisis, 2007–11

Countries with relatively higher cumulative GDP growth 2007–11	Countries with employment stable or increasing	Countries with employment reduction (2007–11)	Countries with high recession (cumulative 2007–11 below 0)	Countries with high unemployment (above 8%)	Countries with stagnating cumulative GDP 2007–11 (btw 0 and 1)	Countries with lower unemployment
Slovenia	Belgium	Ireland	Greece	UK	UK	Austria
Lithuania	Romania	Latvia	Latvia	Italy	Spain	Netherlands
Belgium	Austria	Estonia	Ireland	Poland	France	Luxembourg
Netherlands	Luxembourg	Lithuania	Hungary	Hungary	Finland	Germany
Germany	Malta	Spain	Italy	France		Czech Republic
Luxembourg	Germany	Denmark	Denmark	Bulgaria		Malta
Austria	Poland	Portugal	Portugal	Portugal		Belgium
Romania		Finland	Estonia	Estonia		Denmark
Sweden		Bulgaria		Slovakia		Sweden
Cyprus		United Kingdom		Ireland		Romania
Czech Republic		Slovakia		Lithuania		Finland
Bulgaria		Hungary		Latvia		Cyprus
Malta		Italy		Greece		Slovenia
Slovakia		Greece		Spain		
Poland		Slovenia				
		Sweden				
		Cyprus				
		Netherlands				
		Czech Republic				
		France				

Source: Own elaboration.

Measuring the crisis: the crisis management index

In order to evaluate the initial phase of the crisis on a cross-country basis, I have designed an index that would allow for an assessment of the impact of the crisis simultaneously on the GDP performance (recession and recovery) and on the labour market (employment, unemployment and labour productivity).

The crisis management index (CMI) takes into consideration both employment and GDP aspects. Using such an index would allow for a better consideration of the performance of countries during the crisis. This avoids biases and distortions such as the fact that countries could have experienced low recession but very bad unemployment or employment reduction. A situation like that for instance can be observed clearly in the US, where despite relatively lower recession than the EU in terms of GDP, during 2007–11, it experienced much worse performance in the labour market (Tridico, 2011b).

The CMI goes from a maximum of 0.4 (the best) for Austria to a minimum of –22 (the worst) for Spain. Values are assigned according to performances during 2007–11 in terms of magnitude and dynamics of the following: GDP fall, employment changes, unemployment, and employment elasticity effects. Since the first three variables capture all the same aggregate effects, I use only one of them – the unemployment – and I combine it with the elasticity variable ($CMI=U+g/n$). This also allows us to avoid collinearity in the building of the index.

Theoretically speaking, the building and the use of such an index is rather new. However, it's based on a strong empirical intuition. Moreover, the comparison is made with the same index for all the UE27 countries so that it can be considered a consistent method at least among the countries analysed. In other words, such an assessment allows for a consistent comparison solely between the twenty-seven member states and consequently for a rank where the situation of each country can be coherently analysed in comparison to other MS and does not aim to be a general theoretical framework of analysis for all countries in the world.

The CMI in the last column of Table 7.2 is the sum U plus the ratio g/n. The best values are for Austria, Luxembourg, Germany, Malta, Poland, the Netherlands and Belgium (the top seven). At the opposite spectrum (between –22 and –12.5) one can find Spain, Greece, Latvia, Lithuania, Ireland, Portugal and Estonia – the bottom seven. Figure 7.5 shows the rank and the CMI for all the countries.

The question that I will elaborate on, in regards to the CMI ranking, is what led these countries to perform so differently? Why are the worst-performing countries performing so poorly? What contributed to the better performance of the top seven countries – which by the way are not the usual suspects, meaning the Scandinavian countries? In order to answer these questions I have analysed data and correlations between selected variables and have elaborated on a model that estimates the CMI itself. The main hypotheses of my model are as follows:

- Labour flexibility worsened unemployment and employment levels during the crisis, since elasticity of employment reduction to recession, in countries with higher flexibility, is higher.

Table 7.2 Relevant dimensions for the CMI

Countries	GDP (g) change 2007–11	Employment (n) changes 2007–10	Unemployment 2011 (U)	Labour Elasticity / Labour Productivity* g/n	CMI = U + g/n
		BOTTOM 7 COUNTRIES			
Austria	1.3	0.3	–3.9	4.33	0–43
Luxembourg	1.28	1	–4.8	1.28	–3.52
Germany	1.18	1.7	–5.8	0.69	–5.11
Malta	2.16	1.5	–6.6	1.44	–5.16
Poland	4.9	2.3	–8	2.13	–5.87
Netherlands	1.14	–1.3	–5	–0.88	–5.88
Belgium	1.12	0	–6.7	0.00	–6.70
Denmark	–0.5	–3.7	–7.1	0.14	–6.96
Romania	1.36	0	–7.5	0.00	–7.50
Italy	–0.52	–1.8	–8.3	0.29	–8.01
Sweden	1.42	–1.5	–7.2	–0.95	–8.15
Czech Republic	1.72	–1.1	–6.6	–1.56	–8.16
Finland	0.96	–2.2	–7.8	–0.44	–8.24
United Kingdom	0.1	–2	–8.3	–0.05	–8.35
Slovenia	1	–1.6	–8	–0.63	–8.63
Cyprus	1.64	–1.3	–7.8	–1.26	–9.06
Hungary	–0.62	–1.9	–9.9	0.33	–9.57
France	0.52	–0.5	–9.9	–1.04	–10.94
Bulgaria	1.9	–2	–10.9	–0.95	–11.85
Slovakia	3.72	–1.9	–10.4	–1.96	–12.36
		BOTTOM 7 COUNTRIES			
Portugal	–0.12	–2.2	–12.5	0.05	–12.45
Estonia	–0.04	–8.4	–12.8	0.00	–12.80
Ireland	–0.82	–9.2	–14.2	0.09	–14.11
Lithuania	1.08	–7.1	–15.5	–0.15	–15.65
Latvia	–1.44	–9	–16.1	0.16	–15.94
Greece	–1.9	–1.8	–17.6	1.06	–16.54
Spain	0.26	–7	–22.6	–0.04	–22.64

Source: Own elaboration on Eurostat data.

Note: * a value >1 indicates that GDP increases more than employment; a value comprised between 1 and 0 indicates that the increase of employment (or its reductions) was bigger than the increase (or the decrease) of GDP; a negative value indicates that despite the increase of the GDP, employment decreased. This indicator can be considered a dynamic measure of labour productivity. However, its reverse is also an indicator of labour elasticity to GDP change.

- Inequality, in particular during the crisis, emerged as a detrimental variable, lowering income opportunities for middle class, weakening consumption and therefore leading to unstable aggregate demand, with further negative consequences on GDP performance.
- Exposure to foreign banks increased financial instability because with the crisis, foreign capital are the first to exit, leaving the country in danger of a

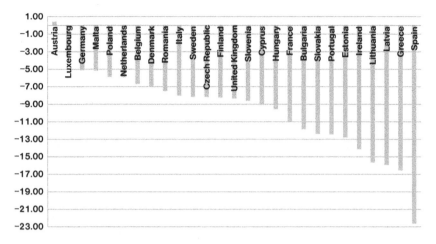

Figure 7.5 The CMI, 2007–11.
Source: Own elaboration on Eurostat data.

lack of liquidity, lack of additional investments and further negative conse-
quences on the GDP.
*   The higher the weight of the housing sector in the economy, the deeper the
    impact of the crisis in the GDP fall, since the first victim of the financial
    crisis was the housing sector and the building construction industry. Such a
    sector is usually very labour intensive, so consequences in terms of employ-
    ment can also be dramatic, as what was witnessed in Spain.
*   Active policies are very important for a fast recovery of the GDP since job
    training and education can help workers to easily transition to other sectors
    of the economy, with benefits for employment levels.
*   Trade unions are essential social institutions to cope with the panic and lack of
    trust that can emerge during a crisis. The objective of trade unions is usually to
    maintain higher levels of employment and to fight against mass firing tendency
    of firms. Such behaviour can be rational for firms during a crisis in order to
    minimize loss but can be detrimental for the negative recessive spiral of the
    economy, with further deflationary pressures and further recession of the GDP.
    A strong trade union that manages to maintain higher levels of employment,
    at the expense of profit erosion for firms, would contribute, at macro level, to
    reduce the negative impact of crisis on consumption, aggregate demand and on
    the GDP.
*   Passive policies are essential to introduce automatic stabilizers, which would
    avoid a collapse in consumption, a reduction in the aggregate demand and a
    further GDP decline.
*   A high level of credit in the system is a bad symptom, in particular if the
    level of savings is very low. Typically, the situation of the US and other

Anglo-Saxon economies shows that the magnitude of the bubble was high where credit was vast. Consequently, when the bubble bursts, then the negative consequences on the financial sector and on the banking system are at their worst.

- A low level of saving, in the long run, is detrimental for the sustainability of the appropriate level of investments that boosts economic growth.
- The financialisation of the economy shaped the regime of the economic system and may negatively affect the economic growth in the long run: a finance-led regime of growth, driven by consumption and credit only is not sustainable in the long run, because investments and savings are needed. A finance-led regime of growth may be able to guarantee growth thanks to credit for consumption and financial investments (as it happened in the US in the past twenty years) but in the long run may cause excess production, instability of the aggregate demand and deflationary pressures.

The hypotheses listed above are useful to build our model, where the dependent variable is the CMI and the independent variables are elements of those ten hypotheses.

Besides, we have deeply analysed two groups of countries: the countries that performed better during the crisis (the top seven countries in the order: Austria, Poland, Luxembourg, Malta, Germany, the Netherlands and Belgium) and the countries that performed the worst (the bottom seven countries in the order: Spain, Latvia, Ireland, Lithuania and Estonia, Greece and Portugal).[4] We have tried to show why the countries that performed better between 2007 and 2011 did so, and the division in two groups, best and worst, helps to this purpose, because it reveals clearly the main features of the best-performing countries and the main features of the worst-performing countries. In the following comparative correlations, we take into consideration the following variables: inequality, employment protection legislation, financialisation, active and passive labour market policies, savings, and trade unions density. All of these variables were correlated with the CMI for the worst and the best performing countries.

It appears very clear, from the correlation in Figure 7.6, that the top seven countries, with the highest CMI have the lowest inequality level, while on the opposite corner, with the highest inequality level (measured by the Gini coefficient in 2007) one can find the bottom seven countries.

A similar story can be found with the relation between the CMI and the Employment Protection Legislation (the EPL, 2008), the indicator of the OECD that measures the level of worker protection in the labour market and consequently the level of labour flexibility (OECD, 2004). The average indicator decreased consistently in the last two decades – which indicates more labour flexibility (Tridico, 2009; Leon and Realfonzo, 2008). The top seven, with the highest CMI, have the highest EPL level (lower labour flexibility), while, on the opposite corner, those with the lowest EPL (highest labour flexibility) are the bottom seven.

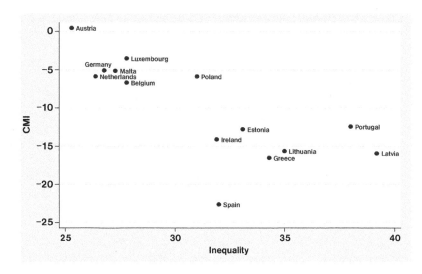

Figure 7.6 Correlation scatter plot CMI and inequality.
Source: Own elaboration.

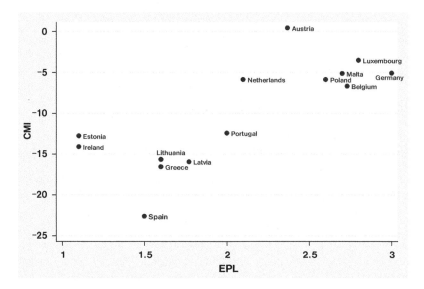

Figure 7.7 Correlation scatter plot CMI and EPL.
Source: Own elaboration.

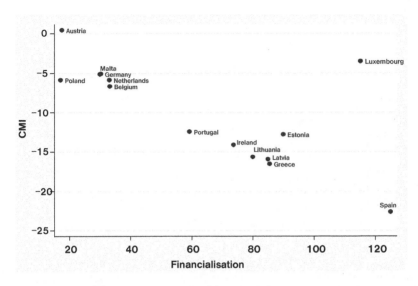

Figure 7.8 Correlation scatter plot CMI and financialisation.
Source: Own elaboration.

Interestingly enough, the correlation scatter plot between CMI and the level of financialisation of the economy just before the crisis in 2006–07 shows similar results with the bottom seven having the highest level of financialisation. The variable financialisation is the value of market capitalization in the stock exchange as a percentage of GDP. The market capitalization (also known as market value) is the share price multiplied by the number of shares outstanding (see p. 13 for a more in detail definition). Not surprisingly, the only exception among the top seven countries with the lowest levels of financialisation is Luxembourg.[5]

Active and passive labour market policies (% of GDP for expenditure on labour market policies 2008) are consistent with the hypothesis as they go in the expected direction. Poland is an exception as it spends relatively little in terms of labour market policies. The case of Poland is not unexpected because our hypothesis states that labour market policies help countries recover from crisis. Poland did not experience a recession during the period analysed so labour market policies were not required as strongly as what was needed in the rest of the EU. In Spain, on the contrary, with the extraordinary highest unemployment level in the EU, around 20 per cent, the active and passive labour market policies, as they are automatic stabilizers, were very consistent during the crisis.

Another relevant variable that appears in our hypothesis is the level of savings (in 2008). A low level of savings, in the long run, inhibits investment and growth.

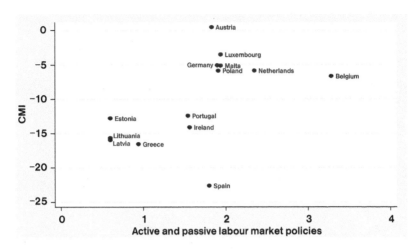

Figure 7.9 Correlation scatter plot CMI and active and passive labour market policies.
Source: Own elaboration.

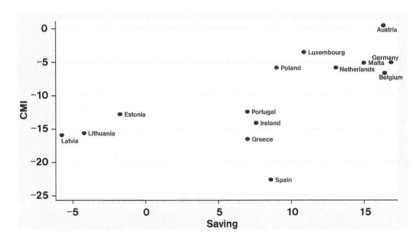

Figure 7.10 Correlation scatter plot CMI and savings.
Source: Own elaboration.

In this case, the only exception is Spain, which has a relatively high level of savings, equal to Poland, which has the lowest level among the top seven.

As I have argued above, among the ten hypotheses, trade union density is a relevant variable as well. In this case, without exception, the top seven have the highest trade union density level (membership average percentage 2006–10 of employees) and this has aided during the crisis to keep higher levels of employment, and of aggregate demand.

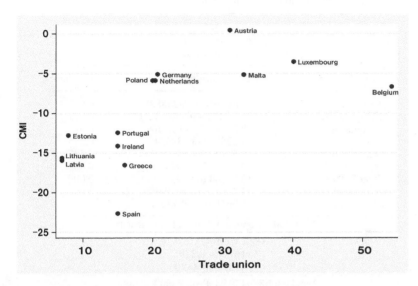

Figure 7.11 Correlation scatter plot CMI and trade union.
Source: Own elaboration.

The model: explaining the CMI

Following the hypotheses and correlation figures in the previous section, I am now able to put forward a model, with a simple regression analysis, investigating the variables that determined the highest CMI, considered as dependent variables.

The model is as follows:

$$CMI = \alpha + \beta_1 * EPL - \beta_2 * TW - \beta_3 * Ineq + e$$

where α is the constant; β_1, β_2, and β_3 are the coefficients of the correspondent variables; EPL is the Employment Protection Legislation Index (which measures the level of labour flexibility); TW is the percentage of temporary on the total of employment; and Ineq is the Gini coefficient, which indicates the income distribution and the inequality in the society.

I have tested this model in two ways: first, with a simple OLS cross-section regression, using average values of those variables, for the period 2007–11 (the crisis time) and twenty-seven observations (as many as the EU member states); and second, and more fundamentally, with a more sophisticated GLS model of a panel data of six years – 2006, 2007, 2008, 2009, 2010, and 2011 – and 162 observations (27×6). Results are very consistent to each other, robust and statistically significant, as Table 7.3 shows. I report data of the GLS model, which are more appropriate with a greater number of variables than the OLS model.

Table 7.3 Regression table, panel data

Variable	GLS Model. Random effects Dep Var. : CMI	
	Coeff. (standard errors)	*P-values*
EPL	1.615307 (0.7324882)	0.027
Temporary work	−0.1578564 (0.0694321)	0.023
Inequality	−0.2716993 (0.107862)	0.012
Constant	4.225772 (3.638554)	0.245
Year 2006	−0.5277289 (0.9971861)	0.597
Year 2008	−3.037997 (0.9973313)	0.002
Year 2009	−10.86284 (0.9978834)	0.000
Year 2010	−4.382909 (0.9970402)	0.000
Year 2011	−6.065116 (0.9974051)	0.000
Year 2007 dropped because of collinearity		
R-sq: within = 0.5610 between= 0.2293 overall = 0.4880		
Wald chi2(8) =170.93; Prob > chi2=0.0000		
Number of obs = 162. Number of groups = 27 **Panel 2006, 2007, 2008, 2009, 2010, 2011**		

Hausman Test (RE vs FE):
Ho: difference in coefficients not systematic
    $chi2(3) = (b-B)'[(V\_b-V\_B)^{\wedge}(-1)](b-B)$
      $= 20.75$
  Prob>chi2 = 0.0001
H (alternative) accepted

Source: Own elaboration.

This model, which should be analysed together with the correlation figures, indicates that a higher CMI is caused by a higher EPL index (lower labour flexibility) and a lower level of temporary work and a lower level of inequality. All the variables are very significant (most of them within 5 per cent levels) as one can see from the p-values in Table 7.3. The signs and the magnitude in both regressions go in the same directions. Moreover, in the panel, a random effect regression with dummy variables for each year was used, and the Hausman test proved the reliability of this effect.

These results call for reflection on the structure and on the situation of the labour market and give suggestions for policymaking towards a specific direction. In regard to policymaking, labour flexibility is a negative factor and contributes to deepening the effects of the crisis. At the same time, countries with higher shares of temporary work suffered more during the crisis and have a lower level of CMI. Inequality is also a bad factor, which increased the negative effects of the crisis: in fact, countries with higher levels of inequality have lower CMI. From a Keynesian point of view, this is quite obvious: societies with higher inequality have a middle class that suffers more in term of consumption possibilities and income, and they consume less. This worsens the aggregate demand, and consecutively the level of activity of the economy decreases; therefore, in our model, the CMI would decrease.

Labour flexibility has been increasing everywhere in Europe in the last two decades. However, some countries, like Austria, Germany, Malta, and Luxembourg and a few others, still maintain rigid labour markets. These are the countries that managed to better cope with the current economic crisis, as we saw, along with Poland, the Netherlands and Belgium. Labour flexibility allows for the reduction of the labour costs and thus wage saving at the expenses of wage earners (i.e. consumers). In such a situation, inequality increases and also the aggregate demand could curb since consumption decreases. As we observed earlier in Chapter 3 (Figure 3.6), there is an inverse relationship between inequality and labour flexibility. As usual in this analysis, countries like Germany and, in general, the rest of the top seven performed better: they have higher EPL (lower flexibility) and lower inequality. On the opposite side, countries that suffered the most during the crisis (Estonia, Lithuania, Latvia, Ireland, and Spain, followed by Portugal, Greece, Italy, the UK and some others) have higher inequality and lower EPL (higher flexibility).

The crisis itself proves that a Coordinated (or Corporative) Market Economy (CME), similar to the one found in Germany, may do more to shape a new global governance and may be more appropriate to help prevent further crises (Pontusson 2005; EuroMemorandum, 2010; Semmler *et al.*, 2010). The CME would guarantee a more stable path of development and accumulation, mitigating the risk of boom and bust cycles illustrated by Minsky (1986). Examples of CME can be found in the EU and in particular among continental economies (Germany and Austria in particular and also Belgium, Luxembourg and the Netherlands), which combine interesting and functional elements of competitive markets economies such as competition and private investments, with useful market coordination systems such as financial regulation, public strategies of investments and welfare and important public goods (Rochon and Rossi, 2010; Pitelis, 2010; Whelan, 2010).

In fact countries like Poland and Malta, it seems, are evolving towards a type of socioeconomic model similar to the one of Germany and Austria. These countries managed better in the crisis within all the dimensions analysed. On the contrary, countries that rely more on a liberal competitive market economy like Estonia, Lithuania, Latvia, Ireland, and the UK suffered the most during the crisis. This was also the case of the Mediterranean economies (Greece, Spain, Portugal and Italy), which, during the last fifteen to twenty years, strongly liberalized their labour markets, thus combining liberalized labour markets with inefficient social policies (Sapir, 2005). On a different note, Scandinavian economies, such as Denmark, Sweden and Finland, suffered during the crisis, in particular in terms of employment reduction. Most of this reduction can be attributed to the very flexible labour market that these economies have created during the last decade. However, it has to be said that these countries have a very efficient security model and safety net that prevent from inequality and poverty.

Discussion and implication for the economic recovery and inequality

In this chapter, I argued that countries that performed relatively better during the economic crisis of 2007–11 are those that do not have a strong flexible labour market and managed to keep stable employment levels. These countries are Germany, Austria, Poland, Belgium, the Netherlands, Malta and Luxembourg. On the contrary, along with a very strong flexible labour market, countries that performed the worst during the crisis also have a poor combination of high inequality levels, higher exposure to foreign banks, a stronger reliance on the housing sector, less incisive labour market policies and expenditure, less trade union density, higher levels of private indebtedness, strong financialisation and a lower level of savings. These countries are Latvia, Lithuania, Estonia, Spain, Ireland, Portugal, and Greece, followed by Italy, the UK and other EU members.

Clearly, the first group of countries identifies better, in the EU, with a coordinated or corporative market economy model, while the second group of countries identifies better with a (competitive market (or hybrid) economy. The regression model confirms such a result: the CMI is higher in the first group of countries and this is determined by higher levels of Employment Protection Legislation (lower flexibility), lower level of temporary work, and lower level of inequality.

The experience in the post-2011 era showed that austerity did not work. Second, economic recovery occurred actually faster in the countries that we classified as top seven, while the then bottom seven countries are still suffering and not recovering. This confirms that rather than curing the issue, labour flexibility is deepening the problem, causing further inequality, further squeeze of the aggregate demand and further stagnation in the GDP and lack of recovery in the labour market. Trade unions and other social institutions (unemployment subsidies, welfare, etc.) help to stabilize employment levels and aggregate demand, with benefit on GDP performance.

Income distribution and poverty worsened in the period after 2011 in most of the countries that had the worst initial phase, such as Greece, Spain, Portugal, Ireland and also in Baltic countries, followed by countries like Italy and the UK. While countries in the top-seven group had a different path, recovering faster from an economic point of view and also containing the social cost such as inequality and poverty. These different patterns indicate that our model has an important validity and explanatory capacity with respect to the further recovery of GDP in Europe.

Notes

1 Croatia is the twenty-eighth member state of EU and joined in 2013; and because we are considering the initial phase of the crisis in the EU (2007–11), it is excluded from this analysis.
2 This could also underline the fact that job creation in this period in Germany was characterized by low productivity. However, during recession time, it is probably better to stabilize employment level in order to avoid recession spiral.

3 These countries are characterized by a so-called "flexicurity" model.
4 In this group, I could have added most of the rest of the countries with very negative CMI (including Italy, Hungary, the UK, Bulgaria etc.), but since I have considered only seven countries on the top, for consistency I considered also only seven countries on the bottom.
5 Such an exception, about Luxembourg's higher level of financialisation, does not need further comments given the economy structure and the particular role and situation of the small economy of Luxembourg in the EU.

8 Global imbalances and declining hegemony

Looking for a new paradigm after the financial crisis

Introduction

The economic crisis and its negative consequences clearly indicate a declining trend for the most advanced economies in the world and a declining hegemony for the US (Clelland and Dunaway, 2010). On the contrary, emerging economies and in particular China and BRIC grow consistently and seem already far away from the 2007–09 crisis, which did not affect them so badly as the EU and the US.

The objective of this chapter is to show that the recovery from the crisis requires a new policy paradigm and a new global governance. The root of this crisis in the EU and in the US is strictly endogenous to their economic systems and concerns in particular the specific path that these two economies embarked since the end of the 1970s (as regards the US) and since the beginning of 1990s (as regards the EU). Such a path caused extreme financialisation in the US and in the EU, profits soared and wages stagnated (Tridico, 2012; Wolff, 2010; EuroMemorandum, 2010; Ivanova, 2010a; Posner, 2009). The idea of a minimalist state, which was coupled with a financial system completely deregulated, financial activities, portfolio investments, and speculation free to float around the globe, has been the main theoretical paradigm for the past thirty years (Petit, 2009). Such a paradigm eventually created bubbles and global Ponzi schemes in the financial markets, which inevitably burst in 2007–08 (Rasmus, 2010). In the real economy, this paradigm created a lack of productive investments in particular after the burst of the dot-com bubble (in 2001) in the West (mainly US and some EU countries), saving glut, and global imbalances, characterized by huge deficit in the Western economies and surplus in Asia (mainly China) and few other emerging economies (Obstfeld and Rogoff, 2009).

I argue that, contrary to the recent austerity policies in the EU and the US, a new level of government involvement is required in order to stabilize aggregate demand and create full employment, with a transparent financial sector, serving the real economy and encouraging productive investments. Moreover, at a global level, two main issues seem to negatively affect the markets: first, the lack of an independent international currency, and second, the instability of one of the biggest global markets, the Eurozone. The first needs a wider international solution; the latter needs a political response at EU level in order to deepen integration.

The governor of the Chinese People's Bank, Zhou Xiaochuan, has already argued against the use of the US dollar, and he has blamed its supremacy as reserve currency for the current imbalances and crisis. Zhou Xiaochuan seems to recommend the old Keynesian proposal of 1944 at Bretton Woods; with a global currency, the bancor, managed by an International Bank (the International Clearing Union) which would serve as the regulating institution of global surpluses and deficits. Zhou Xiaochuan (2009: 1) claimed that "the outbreak of the crisis and its spillover to the entire world reflect the inherent vulnerabilities and systemic risks in the existing international monetary system". The unique status of the US dollar underlines a latent political conflict and the need to revise the system of global financial governance which emerged immediately after World War II, when international politics and economics looked very different from now (Fuchita and Litan 2007).

In this context of reshaping international governance, EU and US relations seem to be stronger, although macroeconomic cooperation still remains limited. From one side, politics, in the post-Bush scenario, is showing more interest for multilateralism[1]; from another side, domestic constraints during crisis are tied and tend to impose national solutions for global problems. Nevertheless, a new geopolitical order is emerging and, as called for by international consensus within the United Nations or among emerging economies, G20 countries, and oil producers, progressive global responses are required (Stiglitz, 2010; Westbrook, 2010; Rasmus, 2010). However, the final outcome of this new wind of multilateralism is quite unclear.

US debts and international conflicts: a brief Monetarist and Keynesian view

Today, there is a growing consensus around the idea that the financial crisis of 2007–08 is strongly connected to the global imbalances and the saving glut issues (Skidelsky, 2009; Obstefeld and Rogoff, 2009; Bini Smaghi, 2008). The explanation that follows such a consensus is that the financial meltdown of 2007–08 is rooted in the US's main liabilities and debts. Since the 1990s, the amount of US government's debt grew impressively, reaching, on the eve of the crisis in 2006, more than $5 trillion.

Long-term data sets show that this public debt started to increase in the 1980s, increased dramatically during the 1990s, and was subject only to a small reduction in 2001, a drop that was not sufficient to offset the increasing trend. In the middle of the crisis the gross public debt was around 93 per cent of US GDP, and it was still increasing towards the record peak of the World War II period, with a public debt in 2010 almost of $9 trillion (see Figure 8.1). The international power of the US dollar favoured such indebtedness, which allows the US to consume and live above its production possibilities (Ivanova, 2010b).

In 2010, the US economy was affected by three separate $9 trillion debts: the national debt, the (non-bank) corporate debt, and the private mortgage debt. The financial institution's debt was even higher, with $12 trillion. Paralleling these

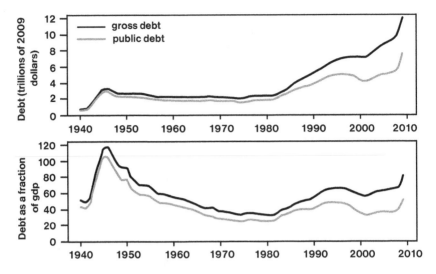

Figure 8.1 US government debt, 1940–2010.
Source: United States Treasury.

trends, both the unfunded Medicare liability and the unfunded Social Security liability were very high ($30 trillion and $12 trillion, respectively). Worse than that, America's net investment position with respect to the rest of the world deteriorated dramatically to –$2.5 trillion (this is around 20 per cent of US GDP) and the current account (CA) deficit reached the peak of $800 billion (over 6 per cent of GDP) on the eve of the financial crisis. This seems to be the most troubling data, since it speaks to the big issues of a saving glut and global imbalances, in particular with China.

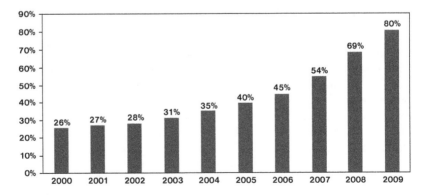

Figure 8.2 US trade deficit vs. China.
Source: US International Trade Commission and Economic Policy Institute.

Trade with China in particular is the Achilles' heel. China's share of the US non-oil goods trade deficit has tripled since 2000, as shown in Figure 8.2. Even during the crisis, although the American CA deficit decreased from the peak of $800 billion in 2006, the trade deficit with China has increased. China's share of the US non-oil goods trade deficit jumped from 68.6 per cent in 2008 to 80.2 per cent in 2009.

How all this debt, deficit and global imbalances are connected with the financial crisis is then simple to explain and is strongly connected with our main focus, inequality. During the process of financialisation, since the 1980s, wages in advanced economies and particularly in the US almost stagnated, and profits soared dramatically (Wolff, 2010; EuroMemorandum, 2010). Simultaneously, inequality increased sharply (OECD, 2010). In order to keep consumption up, the US manoeuvred economic policies: used cheap money that allowed bubbles in the housing sector and private debt soaring, and allowed huge amount of cheap imports from China. This eventually ended up with a huge CA deficit (IMF, 2009). US financed the CA debt issuing US bonds, which were bought in turn by Chinese, whose low level of consumption far compensates the American saving shortage. This scenario suggests a declining hegemony of the US economy, because policy options seem to be restricted and the supremacy of the US dollar as the main international currency started to be questioned (Zhou Xiaochuan, 2009). It also underlines a new weakness of the financial system on the basis of which the US economy nowadays seems to rotate (Clelland and Dunaway, 2010). When the bubbles burst, mortgage companies and lenders fell down and mortgage default correlations followed, since the securitization of mortgages and loans was an international, and opaque, issue. Credit markets seized up as risk increased and expectations worsened. Consequentially, the financial crisis floated in the real markets squeezing now also productive investments, economic activity and employment.

Looking in detail at the global saving glut, in 2008 the global aggregate excess over investment was over $2,000 billion (IMF, 2009). This discrepancy underlines the current account imbalances.

If in the East (China and Southeast Asia), where there are emerging economies and growing middle classes with theoretically high consumption potential, people save too much; in the West (mainly the US and the UK), advanced economies have to stimulate extra-consumption, and therefore monetary policies are enacted, which authorities hope will encourage spending. At least that is what the monetarists argue (Cooper, 2007; Caballero *et al.*, 2008). In this way, the claimed money glut is just a consequence of the saving glut. A more appropriate fiscal stimulus would be one based on increasing public investment following a Keynesian view. In the West (mainly in the US and the UK), a well-developed financial system allows for extra-consumption, mechanisms of future repayment, and sophisticated forms of saving with high risk. In the East, safe and ordinary saving tools guarantee low returns and low risks within the framework of an underdeveloped financial system. Unfortunately, high levels of savings in the East do not manifest in the West as high levels of investment that could compensate the lack of aggregate

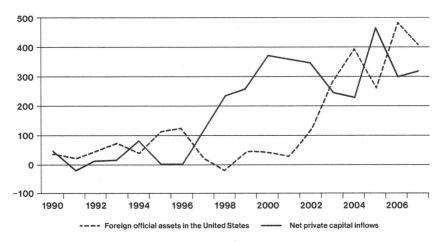

Figure 8.3 Net capital inflow to the US (US$ billion).
Source: Bureau of Economic Analysis, 2008.

demand. The lack of demand cannot be absorbed by the insufficient domestic in-vestments. Simultaneously net capital inflow to the US increased (see Figure 8.3), but this did not help productive investments but rather fed financial speculation and extra-consumption.

In the West, one can observe the increase in demand for finance from those goods and services which go un-bought because of high global saving (Lowen-stein, 2009). Consequently, financing for consumption and portfolio movement has increased massively since 2001.

The main criticism monetarists put forward in opposition to the saving glut is the following: if there is a surplus, there is a deficit, so deficit countries are as responsible as surplus countries. In the end, this is a matter of market efficiency, and natural re-adjustments will occur to cure temporary imbal-ances. This is because monetarists assume perfect capital, labour and goods markets; all tending towards equilibrium tendencies (Mendoza *et al.*, 2007; Greenspan, 2007).

Conversely, in the Keynesian view, policies matter; and, at a policy level, countries can decide to run a surplus current account with active policies or a deficit current account with passive policies, attitudes and blind trust in markets. Exchange rates, export-led institutions, state involvement, government subsidies, protectionism, and other policies are all functional for running a surplus or a balanced budget.[2] Deficits, on the other hand, can be the consequence of bad or neutral policies and attitudes. Furthermore, deficit countries have negative incen-tives to reduce their deficits by means such as reducing external demand, because this would bring about lower income and higher unemployment levels. Contrast this to surplus countries, which are incentivized to increase their surplus by in-creasing exports, and therefore aggregate demand, since they would generate higher income and employment levels.

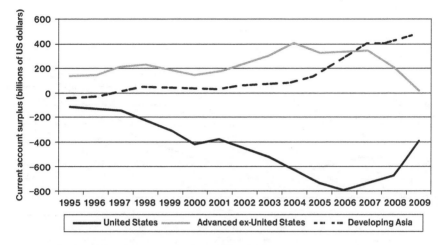

Figure 8.4 Global imbalances, the US and the rest, 1995–2009.
Source: IMF (2010), World Economic Outlook, online database.

A very good example of these tendencies was the Asian crisis of 1997 (see Figure 8.4). All of the Asian economies affected in 1997 (South Korea, Taiwan, Hong Kong, Singapore, Malaysia, Thailand, Indonesia) turned their current account balances from deficit to surplus (Walter, 2008).

These shifts were planned decisions, as policymakers in those countries had learned the downfalls of persistent current account deficits. In fact, the abrupt withdrawal of capital from Asia by foreign investors was one of the leading causes of that crisis (Bello, 2010). After the crisis, and after paying their debts to the IMF, Asian economies turned back to mercantilist policies: personified by high saving, high surplus, and low consumption, in particular of imports.

This is the same strategy that allowed the accumulation and the economic development of the Asian tigers in the 1970s and 1980s (Ha-Joon Chang, 2008) and of China since 2000s (see Figure 8.5). It was easier for them to operate with surpluses than to fall into deficit.

Paraphrasing Lowenstein (2010: 135), we can use an interesting metaphor to interpret conflicting relations between East and West, in particular between China and the US. Somebody from the East, Chang, is offering goods and services for free to John in the West, the only expense being that John has to run a deficit. John accepts, and now he works less (or is jobless). However, he enjoys an even higher standard of living than before, thanks to cheap goods from China and to a developed financial system in his home country. He uses credit (mainly from Chang) to make purchases and eventually to make financial speculations and generate profits. If he is able to make higher profits than the interest payments due on the debt he needed to run a deficit, he will be fine. If the available financing dries up, he will be in trouble, as the debt that he is responsible to pay tomorrow will lower the standard of living that he is enjoying today to an even lower level than before he entered into the Chinese deal with Chang.

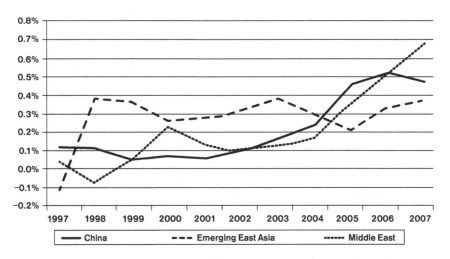

Figure 8.5 China and other emerging economies current account surpluses (% of world GDP).

Source: IMF 2010, World Economic Outlook, online database.

A need for a new international currency

At international level, global imbalances and the saving glut theory call into question the role of the US dollar as a global currency and raise the issue of a possible new global currency and/or governance.

Clearly, there can be a conflict between international and domestic objectives. As argued by Zhou Xiaochuan (2009), national monetary authorities may fail to meet growing global demand for money when they try to keep inflation low at home, and conversely, they may create an excess of liquidity at the global level when they try to overstimulate domestic demand (see Figure 8.6). The current crisis, Zhou Xiaochuan says, is an inevitable outcome of the current institutional flaws which have the US dollar acting as a global currency for debts and international transactions.

Many scholars, notably in the World System field, recognize the unique position of the US as a hegemonic borrower (Frasnk, 2005; Clelland and Dunaway, 2010). The US has the unique and indefinite capacity to sell Treasury notes for dollars, in massive quantities and practically without constraints, and became the key source of global liquidity. Obviously it has also the capacity to manufacture dollars indefinitely, in the last instance. The US's current account has been in massive deficit for the past thirty years. Therefore, every year, billions of dollars have been transferred from foreigners to US balance (Clelland and Dunaway, 2010). Debt could rise to finance practically everything – government expenditures, military operations, private debts – because the unique status of the US currency ensured an international stable demand of its debt. At the same time private finance created tools that allowed for the recycling of capital inflows

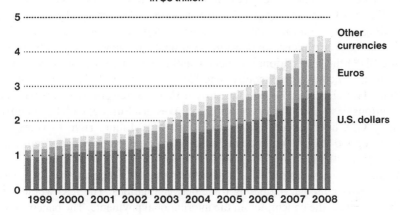

Figure 8.6 US dollar dominance over foreign debts.
Source: *Wall Street Journal.*

and for the mitigation of the US trade deficits. In this way, credit-consumption in US was guaranteed, even with stagnant wages (and profit soar) since the end of the 1970s (Wolff, 2010). The opacity of interconnection of massive transnational securitization and speculation brought eventually the financial implosion of 2007–08, which however was a natural outcome of such an institutional framework (Ivanova, 2010b).

Very interestingly in 1965, when General De Gaulle already denounced the "exorbitant privilege" of the international seigniorage of US currency, Rueff and Hirsch (1965: 3) wrote:

> [W]hen a country with a key currency has a deficit in its balance of payments – that is to say the United States, for example – it pays the creditor country dollars which end up with its central bank. But the dollars are of no use in Bonn, or in Tokyo, or in Paris. The very same day, they are re-lent to the New York money market, so that they return to the place of origin. Thus the debtor country does not lose what the creditor country has gained. So the key-currency country never feels the effect of a deficit in the balance of payments. And the main reason is that there is no reason whatever for the deficit to disappear, because it does not appear. Let me be more positive: if I had an agreement with my tailor (CHINA) that whatever money (IMPORTS) I pay him he returns to me the very same day as a loan, I (USA) would have no objection at all to ordering more suits from him (MORE IMPORTS).[3]

The solution, according to Zhou Xiaochuan, has to be found in an international currency disconnected from any single nation. He refers explicitly to the unaccepted Keynesian project at Bretton Woods of an International Bank and a global currency (the Bancor). This would make exchange rate policies more effective in both objectives: adjusting imbalances and decreasing deficits. He recalls an old, never fully implemented IMF project dating to 1969, intending to set up an international currency unit (the SDR)[4] based on a basket of national currencies. In these international currency projects, (the bancor or the SDR) the international monetary authorities should come from a wide consensus which exercises control and lends prestige to the new international system. This should go beyond the current IMF framework, which is based on institutions designed in North America and Western Europe, with big countries (mainly G7), having more power, more vetoes and more right to votes than others. A good starting point could be the G20 or any other wider organization (see Stiglitz, 2010).

In the Keynesian project of 1944, the International Clearing Union (ICU) was a global bank aimed at regulating trade between nations. The ICU would use a global currency, the bancor, for all the international payments. The bancor would have a fixed exchange rate against other national currencies and would measure the volume and the balance of trade among countries. Every good exported would add bancors to a country's account, every good imported would subtract them. Each nation would then be given large incentives to keep their bancor balance within an acceptable range. If a nation had too much bancor due to high export levels, surplus would arise and the ICU would take a percentage of that surplus and put it into the Clearing Union's Reserve Fund. This would encourage countries to maintain balance as close as possible to zero. Deficit nations, on the other hand, would have their currency devalued to encourage other nations to buy their products and make imports more expensive. A risk of inflation and a debt pressure would be an incentive for these countries to raise productivity and continue to strive for balance.

In regards to global imbalances, China would not volunteer, in the current institutional framework, to change from a quickly growing country to a slowly developing one in order to save international capitalism and eliminate global imbalances. China will not allow for an appreciation of the exchange rate and tight monetary and fiscal policies at the expenses of low employment. Moreover, China knows very well the causes of the Asian crisis in 1997, and with a population of almost 1.5 billion people and a delicate political situation, she prefers to stay on the safe side. International responsibilities should be passed to the richer countries, the ones that have already reached high living standards, unlike China. On this line, world systems scholars have already opened a debate (Wallerstein, 2008; Wallerstein, 2009; Clelland and Dunaway, 2010).

The crisis itself proves that a Coordinated Market Economy may do more to shape a new global governance and may be more appropriate to help prevent further crises (Pontusson, 2005). The CME would guarantee a more stable path of development and of accumulation, mitigating the risk of boom and bust cycles illustrated by Minsky (1986). Examples of CME can be found in the EU and in particular among continental and Scandinavian economies (the so-called

European social model). As we argued in the previous chapter, this model is better both in terms of efficiency and equity (Pontusson, 2005). However, when a new global governance needs to be put in place, global politics and power relations come into play, and this reveals that the EU's political position is weaker and less reliable than the US's position, which may appear, to the rest of the world at least, more convincing and backed by the voice of a unique and powerful government.

A new governance: old European tools for a global stable development

The essential truth of Keynes's ideas is that even the most productive economy can fail if consumers and/or investors spend too little. At the global level, it applies to the current crisis as follows: Asia, especially China, saves too much (and consumes too little), while the US saves and invests too little. Furthermore, at the policy level, the Keynesian theory states that sound money and balanced budgets are not always wisdom (Krugman, 2008; Arestis, and Pelagidis, 2010). Keynesianism is not a theory which has to be used during a specific phase of the economic cycle; it is a general theory which, if implemented correctly, helps to prevent crisis and to maintain a steady path of development.

For this reason, however, policymakers need to pay attention to two economic policies: aggregate demand management and labour market policy. The first should have the objective of stabilizing the level of activity and possibly to reach the full employment. The second, which is connected to the first, has to ensure that labour institutions are able to guarantee adequate wages and permanent income mechanisms to workers in order to sustain consumption and demand. In this respect, labour flexibility aimed at reducing labour cost would be inappropriate because it would put workers at the mercy of precarious jobs and unstable income and would lower or destabilize consumption. Wage shares on income would decrease, and consumption would then be obliged to rely on financial assistance and tools like credit and mortgage to be kept stable. These financial tools, however, could crash when workers do not have means (enough wages and jobs) to reimburse debts, and in turn the system could collapse.

In this light, one could find a good explanation for the beginning of the current financial crisis. The explosion of financial tools intended to sustain consumption, and the flexibility of labour markets in most of the advanced economies, two characteristics introduced during the last three decades, are two sides of the same coin. In the US, since the labour market is already very flexible, the main problem with regard to labour is that since 1975, wages have stopped increasing while productivity has increased consistently (Wolff, 2010). Overhauls to the financial sector must go hand in hand with a counter-flexibility agenda and wage increases in order to make jobs safer and income and consumption more stable to sustain aggregate demand.

What economies need today goes beyond monetary policies, fiscal stimulus, and the regulation of financial markets. We also need to create a stable accumulation regime that allows for productive investments and the increased sharing of productivity. This needs to be coupled with demand management policies and state intervention in order to keep the system on a path of stable development and full employment. The Welfare State is the necessary appendix of such a model, and it should provide for stable consumption, public goods, automatic mechanisms of wage compensation, and subsidies. In other words, to get out of the crisis, the solution cannot be found in temporary stimuli designed to rescue the economy from the current depression. The current financial-led model has been proven unstable. Therefore, any attempt to save this financial-led model by inflating liquidity and only temporarily raising the aggregate demand through fiscal stimulus will fail in the long run. What is needed is a complete restructuring of the economy, revising the fundamental institutional forms of the current financial-led regime with a stable demand management of the economy.

The new governance should address the fundamental issue of stable development, trying to avoid burst and bubble mechanisms, speculation, and unproductive investments. As I mentioned earlier, interesting parallels can be drawn between the different variations of the "old" European social model (German, Scandinavian) regarding stable development, as they all still have the important tools necessary, like Welfare States, social policies, and demand management coupled with a strongly regulated financial sector (Skidelsky, 2009). The EU may carry out a global governance proposal based on its own experience. The European model is in fact, in its different variations, an example for sustainable development in the long run. Table 8.1 is an ideal type representation of the kind of Coordinated Market Economy, which is drawn partially from the European experiences during Fordism and partially from the lessons of the current financial crisis.

Such a model would be a stable strategy for growth, led by three important features around which the other institutional forms would operate:

1   Secure jobs: increasing wages and full employment policy commitments to sustain consumption.
2   Macroeconomic and industrial policies aimed at stabilizing aggregate demand, investments, productivity, and innovation
3   Finance: regulated and transparent, which truly supports productive investments.

Following these "radical" changes, countries could better implement their economic policies, monetary ease, and fiscal stimulus, which would then produce more consistent results. This should, however, be decided within a complex framework of political economy, which would take into consideration the trade-offs, domestic and international constraints, social cohesion, and similar issues. Table A10 in the appendix, which would fit better for the political economy analysis of deficit countries, in particular the US, serves as a general representation of

Table 8.1 Post-financial model of accumulation and growth

	Coordinated Market Economies							
	Institutional forms					Policies		Finance
Wage relation	Form of competition	Monetary regime	Relationship between state and economy	International regime	Macroeconomic policy	Social policy		
Sharing productivity gains. Collective bargaining; Promotion of norms of sustainable production & consumption; full employment objectives.	Limited and controlled form of competition; redesign and re-regulate markets to reduce risks of and to avoid unlimited competition.	Soft money constraints coupled with fiscal policies; public credit management and credit money; state control over money.	Protection of strategic sectors; management of international economic relations; state interventionism in economy, State ownership, investment planning, stimulate	National competition; strategic protectionism; managing of exchange rate; "global" and stable currency; limited movement of short-term capitals.	Anti-cyclical policy; demand side policy; state interventionism; promotion of economies of scale and sustainable development; R&D and productivity growth incentives for firms; taxes to restore stability, public finances and stimulate growth	Income redistribution, progressive taxation; protection of welfare rights and social needs; strong Welfare State in health and education; promotion of inclusive policies.		Moderate finacialisation of the system; Developed finance for investments; extensive credit for firms; limited finance and credit for consumption; "Tobin tax" for financial transaction-speculation; financial regulation, transparency and protection of saving; higher taxes on financial corporation; Public entity status and for Credit Rating Agencies.

such a framework, and one could draw interesting observations from that. This is a synthetic classification of policy options that countries may put in place in order to cope with the crisis and to enact a recovery plan.

Notes

1 "The time has come to start thinking of an Atlantic Agenda for Globalization. We have the transatlantic marketplace, NATO, the Transatlantic Economic Council, and other instruments that we should continue to leverage for maximum mutual benefit. But we should move beyond this and set an agenda of common action for a new multilateralism that can benefit the whole world." European Commission President Jose Manuel Barroso, September 24, 2008. URL (March 4, 2009):.
2 Obviously not all countries in the world can simultaneously operate with surpluses. Therefore, temporary and small deficits across the world can be sustained.
3 Capitalized words in bracket are added to the authors' metaphor of the tailor, to emphasize the interesting parallel with today's situation between China and the US.
4 The SDR *(Special Drawing Rights)* is an international reserve asset, created by the IMF in 1969 to supplement its member countries' official reserves. Its value is based on a basket of four key international currencies, and SDRs can be exchanged for freely usable currencies.

9 Conclusion

This book investigated the reasons that are at the basis of the increase of income inequality in rich countries in the past three decades. These reasons have to do with the radical changes of the main features of the socioeconomic model in those countries. The change involves a shift towards financialisation, a pressure on labour through increased labour flexibility and other labour market institutions, the reduction of wage share, the expansion of capital through globalisation, the decline of trade unions' power and the retrenchment of public social spending. The mechanisms of these changes are tested on a sample composed of data for thirty-four OECD countries during the period between 1990 and 2013. The statistics and the econometric analysis produced very interesting results and the regressions confirmed our hypotheses. In particular, inequality increases when the level of labour flexibility and the level of financialisation of the economy increases, and when trade unions density and public social spending declines. The introduction of control variables, such as the unemployment rate, trade, economic growth, tertiary education level, does not alter the main results.

These results pose further challenging questions to governments and policy-makers, in particular around the supposed trade-off between inequality and economic performance. Recently important studies were carried out by Winkelmann and Winkelmann (2010), Larch (2012), Ostry *et al.* (2014), Cingano (2014). Their results, and also our analysis, suggest that the worsening of income distribution contributes to the secular stagnation via the compression of aggregate demand (since top income distribution have lower propensity to consume) and the consequent scarce GDP dynamics. High levels of inequality are associated with lower economic growth. Hence, the consensus around the supposed trade-off between equality and efficiency dissipated.

Moreover, inequality easily leads to economic instability and financial crisis, in particular when the financial sector tries to compensate the lack of consumption and aggregate demand with credit availability and debt-led growth as I have argued in the text, and as several studies show. The financialisation of advanced economies, as I discussed in the book, occurred since the end of the 1970s in the US and the UK and since the end of the 1980s in Western Europe and in other advanced economies. It increased rapidly in the 1990s and in the 2000s, with negative effects on inequality. Compensations in the financial sector soared enormously in the last two decades, beyond any reasonable link with labour productivity. Evidence shows that profits, since the end of 1970s, recovered as well, after a steady decline occurred after the Second World War. The globalisation of the economies, which occurred during the same period, as I argued, increased the power of capital in relation to labour, and trade unions lost power, contributing to the deterioration of labour market institutions. During the process of financialisation and globalisation of economies, which identifies the shift towards what I called "financial capitalism", labour markets were affected by radical changes, too, involving above all an increase in labour flexibility.

The main objective of this new model of financial capitalism, which started to emerge at the end of 1970s, was to restore both the profit rate, which did not increase between 1945 and 1975, and possibly the productivity rate. Through financialisation and globalisation the new capitalism could return to generate higher profits and rents, unbound from the limits previously imposed by the Keynesian paradigm. In financial capitalism, neoliberal policies such as financial deregulation, structural adjustments, capital mobility, flat and lower capital tax, capital attraction strategies, welfare retrenchments, labour flexibility and so forth became the main framework within which states aggressively compete with each other to attract capitals and to implement export-led strategies. Many examples in this context can be listed in West of Europe (Ireland, the UK, the Netherlands, and Switzerland for instance), in Central and Eastern Europe (Slovakia and Poland, among others) and in South of Europe (Spain or Cyprus), not to speak about emerging economies in Latin America or in Asia. Multi-national companies and big corporations get similar status as states and have the privilege to bargain advantageous fiscal and working conditions for their business directly with national governments. The cases of big companies (usually considered innovative and good) such as Apple, Google, Nike, Amazon, and De Beers, along with others (traditionally known for being internationally aggressive) such as Nestlé, Coca-Cola, BP, Vale, Pfizer, Monsanto, just to mention a few, were journalistically popularized in the last years for their aggressive outsourcing strategies, polluting production, fiscal privileges, bad working conditions, social dumping, precarious jobs, etc.

As I have argued, a flexible labour market with compressed and low wages needs to be supplemented by credit consumption and developed financial tools to sustain consumption. Hence, a strong correlation between financialisation and labour flexibility was identified in our empirical analysis, suggesting complementarities between these two phenomena. Labour market institutions (such as protections against firing and hiring) weakened, and contracts for temporary jobs increased. This process is captured in my book by the trend of the Employment Protection Legislation (EPL) indicator, which has decreased on average in OECD. In this context, labour was continuously under pressure, contributing to the worsening of income distribution and therefore to the increase in inequality. Finally, income distribution was worsened by the retrenchment of the welfare state (illustrated in my book by the stagnation in public social spending) in advanced economies mostly with the justification that firms would be more competitive and economies could attract more capitals as the so-called "efficiency thesis" would suggest.

On the contrary, I indicated that countries that reacted to the globalisation challenges by the implementation of the efficiency thesis, according to which globalisation needs to be accompanied by the retrenchment of welfare states in order for firms to be competitive, did not achieve better economic performance, and particularly during the current economic crisis suffered the most (these countries belong to the Anglo-Saxon and Mediterranean market economy models). Moreover, their income distribution worsened and inequality increased. On the contrary, our econometric exercises show that the "compensation thesis" (i.e. regulated globalisation and an expanded welfare state) was better able to produce higher economic growth along with better labour market performance and better income distribution.

On the basis of this, a new type of classification emerged between Welfare Capitalism and Financial Capitalism. Countries of the Continental and of the Scandinavian models may be aggregated in the first category, sharing similar values of the relevant variables (welfare spending, financialisation and Gini coefficients), while Anglo-Saxon and Mediterranean models fall into the second category, sharing similar values of the same relevant variables. Countries of the Welfare Capitalism category exhibit better economic performance (i.e. a better PI – composed by GDP growth and labour market indicators) and lower inequality; on the contrary, countries of the Financial Capitalism category have worse economic performance (a lower PI) and higher inequality.

My argument is not contrasting with the Piketty (2014), Atkinson *et al.* (2011) and with Facundo *et al.* (2013) arguments, who maintain that inequality rose since the 1970s mostly because taxation reduced progressivity in particular at the top of the distribution. The shift towards a model where trade unions are less important, social spending declines, financialisation becomes dominant and labour flexibility regulates industrial relations as main drivers of inequality, is very consistent with the lack of progressivity in taxation argument. All these policies and institutions are coherently part of the *financial capitalism* model in which income distribution worsened also because taxation became less progressive.

Obviously, there is a strong variation in the independent variables among the countries analysed, and strong variation also exists with regards to inequality. Usually, continental European countries, which have lower inequality levels, have lower levels of financialisation and labour flexibility and higher levels of trade union density and social spending. Conversely, Anglo-Saxon countries, which have higher inequality levels, have higher levels of financialisation and labour flexibility and lower levels of trade union density and social spending. Mediterranean countries, new European Union Member States (from Central and Eastern Europe) and emerging economies, which have increasing levels of inequality, are also increasing their levels of financialisation and of labour flexibility, while they are lowering their levels of trade union density and social spending.

The financial crisis was a test for advanced economies and their socioeconomic models. The background in which the current financial crisis emerged is the global saving glut and, particularly the imbalances between the US deficit and Asian (China in particular) surpluses in the current account. This was the state of the world economy on the eve of the crisis in 2007. However, the crisis is as complex as the financialisation process and finds its very roots in the uneven income distribution caused by wage stagnation, profits and financial rents soaring, and labour flexibility. The process of financialisation, measured as market capitalization, started in the US and the EU in the 1980s and appears to be strongly correlated with inequality and labour flexibility. As I argued in Chapter 8, workers in rich countries, whose wage is compressed, can however afford to buy cheap goods (imports) from China (or other emerging economies) and, thanks to huge credit-consumption and cheap money, expensive houses, cars, and other durable goods at home. The financial crash of 2007–08 proved the model to be unstable. In this sense, the causes of the crisis are internal: they lie within the financial-led model, which creates inequality and credit consumption, which in turn causes both its development and its failure.

In fact, the financialisation brought about a financial-led regime of accumulation, which begged for an agenda of deregulation, liberalization, and labour flexibility, causing a stagnation of real wage in the US (with productivity growth) and, to some extent, also in the EU. This agenda was also the demise of Keynesian policies. However, consumption kept increasing, even with stagnant wages, thanks to financing, the credit boom and readily available loans. A negative interaction between labour, finance, consumption, and investments took place, creating a model where finance is the main institutional form characterized by multi-bubbles and consequent bursts; wages are flexible, deregulated and compressed; consumption is sustained by finance; and real investments are lacking while portfolio movements and speculation prevail. Hence, unstable consumption, poor wages and uneven income distribution, with a fall in the wage share over GDP in the last thirty years in the US and the EU, weakened aggregate demand and threatened the advanced economic systems of capitalism. Monetary quantitative ease and cheap money, mortgage housing and credit boom, *Ponzi* financial schemes and *Minskyan* instabilities are the natural consequences of this economic model. This model is unstable. Therefore, a radical change is needed. My book suggests that Keynesian macroeconomics is not a theory that has to be used during a specific phase of the economic cycle. It is a general theory which, if implemented correctly, helps to prevent crises and to maintain a steady path of development.

Coherently, with the main argument put forward in the first part of the book, the argument developed in the empirical parts, confirms that the stagnation/decline of the aggregate demand, which in turn is caused by the worsening of income distribution, and by the change in the labour market, is the main cause for the lower dynamics of GDP (or better to say for its secular stagnation). This applies in most advanced economies. The mechanism follows this scheme:

$$FC = G + F \rightarrow \uparrow LF \rightarrow \uparrow IJ \rightarrow \downarrow W \rightarrow \uparrow Ineq \rightarrow \downarrow WS\,(+ \downarrow IW) \rightarrow$$
$$\downarrow C \rightarrow \downarrow AD \rightarrow \downarrow GDP$$

This scheme should be interpreted in this way. The lower GDP dynamics is the result of a stagnating/declining aggregate demand (AD). This is caused by a shrinking in the consumption (C) which in turn is caused by the deep reduction of wage share (WS) and the increase of income inequality (Ineq), coupled with a decline of the indirect wage (IW) – i.e. the public expenditure, in particular in social dimensions. This is the result of a pressure on employment and wages (W) caused by a strong labour flexibility (LF) and by its correlated creation of unstable jobs (IJ). The pressure on labour is determined by financialisation (F) and globalisation (G), two processes that emerge in financial capitalism (FC).

A finance-led regime of growth, driven by consumption and credit, which was (and still is) in place in advanced economies to sustain the otherwise shrinking consumption, is not sustainable in the long run, because productive investments are needed. A stable economic growth path occurs when growth is driven by the aggregate demand and in particular by investments and consumption. The first may also be supported by finance and the second should be supported by wage increases, which should follow labour productivity growth.

In the same vein as Kindleberger (2005), I argued that if there are manias governing financial systems, which are far from rational and efficient, then governments should intervene and regulate. Monetary policy could go further to discourage manias by implementing a financial transaction tax. Beyond that, however, governments need to do something more: guarantee an appropriate level of consumption which could be sustained by an appropriate level of wage in order to maintain an appropriate level of aggregate demand. Finance, regulated under the supervision of the state, should serve productive investments. On the other side, an appropriate level of aggregate demand is guaranteed by a demand management policy which relies on an appropriate level of public investments. Nevertheless, as I have argued, the most recent austerity policies, both in Europe and the US, go just in the opposite direction. Lessons can be drawn from Keynes and from the Fordist model of production, where finance had a secondary role in the economic system, and it was a tool that guaranteed credit for firms and productive investments, while wage, which guaranteed consumption, was the main nexus around which other institutional forms gravitated.

As far as the European Union is concerned, it has to be said that despite the Euro currency crisis, the Eurozone, when treated as a single entity, looks to be in a slightly better position than the US, as the synthetic vulnerability index in the book showed, at least in the initial phase of the crisis. In fact, in the US, deficit issues of Federal States such as California, Nevada and others are not treated separately as one could treat separately similar issues in Greece, Ireland and Portugal. Such a political bias brings commentators to consider European issues more vulnerable than US issues. Besides that, in the EU, institutional forms are more anchored to the wage nexus; unemployment does not increase dramatically as in the US during crisis, and finance is not yet the main institutional form, although the past twenty years in Europe have seen deregulation of finance and liberalization which brought about strong financialisation in the economic system and greater systemic risk. The main problem in Europe remains the deflationary policies initiated with the Maastricht Treaty, and the flaw in the institutional architecture of the Eurozone. The EU, and in particular the countries of the European social model, would be able to combine, better than the US, efficiency (GDP growth) and social performance (inequality, poverty, mass education and life expectancy). After the Second World War, the countries of the Eurozone grew faster than the US and reached better social conditions. Only in the last two decades has the US had slightly faster GDP growth, with further worsening social indicators. However, that GDP growth in the US was led by the kind of financialisation that caused the big crash and the Great Recession of 2007–09. In this light, the US model, led by finance, raises many doubts and should be radically reformed. I suggested this has to be done along with the original ideas of the old European social model. Despite the fact that GDP recession was deeper in the EU than in the US, social costs are greater than in the EU. Moreover, as I argued, the US recovery still seems to be affected by structural problems of income distribution, consumption-driven components and huge compensation in the financial sector. This in the end will generate an unstable economic growth which favours again the top decile of the income distribution and which is keen to cause bubble and burst cycles.

The EU and US efforts toward financial regulation in the last years have to be welcomed, although they still seem insufficient to bring the whole system to a path of stable and sustainable development. In the US, the Frank-Dodd Act was an inferior compromise which would need to be improved in order to give real stability to the system and eliminate, or simply reduce, the systemic risk. Too many carve-outs and ambiguities remain, in particular regarding the oversight role of the Fed towards large firms, the almost unchanged regulation for Rating Agencies and hedge funds, the objections against a financial tax, and the opposition to Basel III. Though it does seem interesting, the attempt to introduce the Volcker Rule, which separates the dangerous coexistence between investment and commercial banks and limits banks in engaging proprietary trading, occurred in the US. However, complex implementation and creation of new vigilant agencies can still be obstructed by lobby actions and Wall Street deregulation supporters (*The Economist,* 2011).

In Europe, the main difficulties are at the operational level of the new EU financial regulatory systems introduced. Too much fragmentation exists among member states, divisions between Eurozone and non-Eurozone, and most importantly, a very different strategic position between the French-German axe and the British one, whose distance has clearly deepened by the result of the "Brexit" Referendum in June 2016. Such strategic differences pose obstacles to the very important questions, such as a financial transaction tax, hedge fund regulation, and the introduction of a sort of Volcker Rule, not to mention the differences over the general framework of the kind of the socioeconomic model required. Financial stability (1), financial integration (2), and national supervisory autonomy (3) cannot be achieved simultaneously. The EU must decide what it wants to achieve, knowing that only two out of those three objectives can be achieved simultaneously.

With the return of austerity in Europe, inequality has increased further. Poverty increased tremendously as well as crime, political instability and disaffection towards politics with dangerous increase of populism, nationalisms and xenophobia. These dangerous feelings increased in coincidence also of the huge flow of migration, which exploded since the Arab spring, in 2010, and the Syria war. Welfare retrenchments, austerity and lack of redistribution policies, I believe, will only worsen inequality and exacerbate problems linked to it such as migration, north-south dualisms, reinforcing in turn, in a vicious circle, populism and xenophobia.

Europe and more precisely the Euro Area, suffered the most from the lack of recovery after the financial crisis of 2007–08 in particular with respect to Japan and the US. These three "countries" (the Euro Area was considered a "country", meaning that aggregate average data were used for the Euro Area) implemented very different polices in the past years. Japan and the US followed a policy of monetary expansion and fiscal stimuli continuously since 2008. In Japan this rule became more consistent after 2011 and was characterized by quantitative easing, currency devaluation, higher inflation targeting, buying of Treasury bonds and public spending to support investments. In the US after the TARP (implemented by the Bush administration in 2008 mainly to save banks and financial institutions), a second plan called ARRA was implemented by the Obama administration in 2009 to sustain investments and jobs. These two plans together accounted for about 7 per cent of US GDP. Moreover, the Fed during the whole period of crisis, until today, has been continuously practicing a policy of zero interest rates, buying operations of US Treasury bonds, and huge inflows of money into the system through a quantitative easing approach.

In Europe, instead, the situation looked very different. After a brief period of fiscal and monetary expansion in 2008–09, the consensus turned back towards more conservative policies which became clear austerity measures after 2009. The ECB, pressed in particular by Germany and other North and Central European Countries, remained worried mainly about inflation, and implemented more prudent monetary policies. Only in September 2014 did the interest rate in the Euro Area reach the same level as the one in the US (0.05 per cent). At the same time, severe austerity policies were implemented in Europe, in particular in the South, with dramatic and negative effects on the GDP performance and on the unemployment rate. The DDC index (a proxy for policies implemented) and the Performance Index both used in the book for Japan, the US and the Euro Area showed clear differences in policies and subsequent poor performances in the Euro Area during the crisis.

The ECB cannot issue European Bonds nor buy MS national bonds, and this had very negative consequences on the sovereign debt of Euro Area member states during the crisis. They were left practically without a lender of last resort. This contributed dramatically to increasing the cost of debt repayment and debt allocation by member states in difficulty like Portugal, Italy, Ireland, Greece and Spain, with further negative consequences on the public budgets of these countries. A very limited, conditioned and complex, operation of buying national bonds within strict rules was indirectly practiced by the ECB during the period of austerity in Europe. This was done through the cooperation of national banks, which borrowed cheap money from the ECB and eventually (but not always) bought Treasury bonds of Member States in difficulty. A new institution was created, the European Stability Mechanism, to save countries in difficulty, and a new program of OMT was announced but never really implemented by the ECB. The very recent program of Quantitative Easing introduced by Draghi seems to have little or no effects on economic growth. All these measures contributed to "save the euro" from a default which would have resulted from the exit strategy from the Eurozone of the member states in the South of Europe. However, these measures are far from being a definite solution. They did not boost economic growth and will not avoid further crises. They do not intervene on the main *virus* which caused the *disease*. They did not solve the structural problems and the worsening of income distribution. Moreover, these measures do not solve the main flaws of the architecture of the Euro Area which is a non-Optimal Currency Area, and are far from useful for economic recovery and restoring growth and employment in Europe. I have proposed some solutions and I have also showed that austerity policies worsened the situation caused by the financial crisis. These solutions require a new form of governance in the Euro Area, which should be organized around four pillars: a Euro Area central budget of at least 5 to 10 per cent of GDP; differentiated fiscal policies for member states; buying operations of treasury bonds without prior limits or conditions; and the creation of EU bonds to back public investments in countries with unemployment higher than 10 per cent.

As regard the countries of the EU that performed relatively better during the initial phase of the economic crisis (2007–11), as it was showed in Chapter 7, these are countries which do not have a strong flexible labour market and managed to keep stable employment levels. These countries combine a very good mix of economic policies and social institutions oriented to stabilize the level of consumption and the aggregate demand. Coordination mechanisms, higher levels of financial regulation and monitoring are also important features of these economies. On the contrary, along with a very strong flexible labour market, countries which performed the worst during the crisis also have a poor combination of high inequality levels, higher exposure to foreign banks, a stronger reliance on the housing sector, less incisive labour market policies and expenditure, less trade union density, higher levels of private indebtedness, strong financialisation and a lower level of savings.

Nevertheless, the problems of the European Union should find a solution within its own club. Since it would be practically impossible for poorer member states to enact mercantilist and protectionist policies within the context of the European Union, imbalances should be accepted within the EU. Germany enjoys a better position since it historically has a competitive and technological advantage and enjoys free trade and free movement within the union at much less cost. This cannot be the position of Greece, Portugal, and other Mediterranean countries, along with Ireland, France, and some others EU members. They could offset the German advantage if they could operate on the exchange rate or use monetary policies. But within the EMU this is not possible. Moreover, since withdrawal from the union is not politically practical and convenient, the reasonable solution must be found in a central budget; a common fiscal policy aimed, in solidarity among MS, at eliminating differences and at increasing cohesion (rather than aimed at fiscal discipline); and the toleration of reasonable unbalances within the EU. In the end, Germany cannot run a surplus if Mediterranean member states cannot run a deficit. In Europe, more than in the rest of the world, coordination and solidarity is needed.

On the global level, a lot needs to be done, at least within the new framework of the G20 countries. The economic institutions created for the post-World War II are no longer adequate to address international issues and to manage global crises. In particular, issues such as the contradiction and the tensions created by the US dollar as an international currency and the management of global imbalances need to be addressed. The creation of a new international currency as called for by the Bank of China's governor and the institution of an international bank of payment are issues to be addressed. As argued in the book, an international bank could work to large extent automatically, in order to deal with imbalances and crises, rather than operate on the conditions decided on by a few members.

My analysis suggests that more (and not less) state involvement and public policy in the economy is required in order to eradicate inequality, and consequently in order get out of the crisis and the secular stagnation. This should be coupled with a new global governance and a radical change of the international order, introducing, possibly, a new global currency. In the US and the EU a wide program of aggregate demand management, appropriate labour policies, and public employment are needed. This should allow for full employment and shared productivity gains. A coordinated market economy, similar to the one existing in some continental European countries and the Scandinavian economies, can be considered good examples on the basis of which national solutions and global governance can draw interesting lessons. The recent McKinsey report (2016) stated that in Sweden only 2 per cent of population remains in poverty after the welfare contribution, and inequality level is one of the lowest in the world, while in the rest of the advanced economies, the poverty level is between 20 and 25 per cent, and the situation worsened since the 2007 crisis. The McKinsey report (which does not have a reputation of being radical) explains in detail the reasons for the Swedish success, which have to be found in its special model. This is characterised by strongly coordinated industrial relations (68 per cent of Swedish workers is unionised), the particular social dialogue among social forces and government, and by important welfare interventions which determines the power relations and the distribution of income. These features allow for an equal and fair income distribution and a positive impact on the aggregate demand dynamics. Moreover, thanks to an appropriate and high tax level, public debt in Sweden remains lower than 40 per cent, one of the lowest levels among advanced economies.

The worrying changes, captured in the book, which occurred since the end of the 1970s in the economic models of advanced economies, and the last financial crisis, constitute strong signals for policymakers who wish to reduce income inequality. This study in fact indicates that policymakers should address specific variables in order to reverse these changes and decrease inequality – first of all, labour flexibility. Restoring higher levels of labour protections would help to stop the declining trend of wage share along with the instability of consumption. Stable and higher wage share would be strongly helped also by a change in the financial sector regulation, aiming at limiting the shareholder principle "downsizing and distribute" and at protecting size of workforce and employment levels. This latter aim could be reached only if corporations and their boards of directors involve trade unions and workers in distributional and ownership decisions. This obviously requires new management models, which should be promoted and supported by governments. Last but not least, the crucial role of welfare state should be reconsidered. The welfare state is not only the major tool for income support for people without a job and the provider of essential social services which otherwise would be inaccessible for most workers. The welfare state is also the major public institution for income re-distribution, and as such should be used. It can be the source and the regulator of employment levels, and it is the major institution able to reconcile the conflict between capital and labour.

Appendix

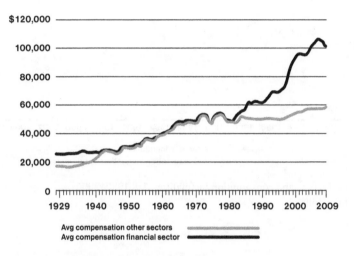

Figure A1 Compensation financial sector and other sectors.
Source: Financial Crisis Inquiry Commission (2011).

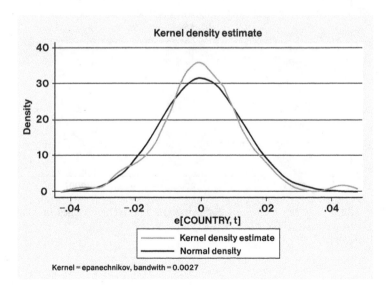

Figure A2 Residual normality test.
Source: Own elaboration.

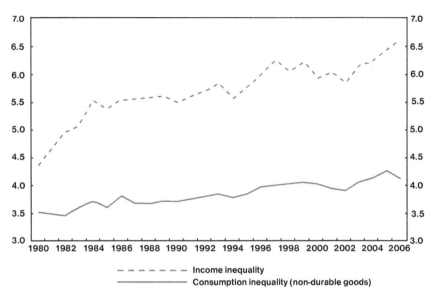

Figure A3 Income and consumption inequalities, US 1980–2006.
Source: IMF (2010).

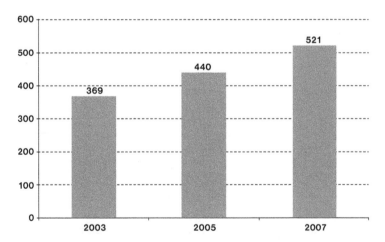

Figure A4 Ratio between manager's compensation and average wages of blue-collar
workers, US 2003–07.
Source: ILO (2008).

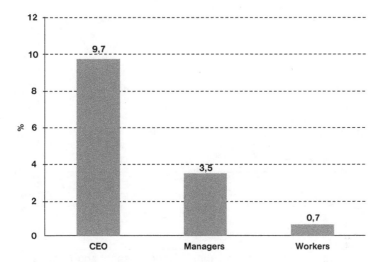

Figure A5 Average wage increases, US 2003–07.
Source: ILO (2008).

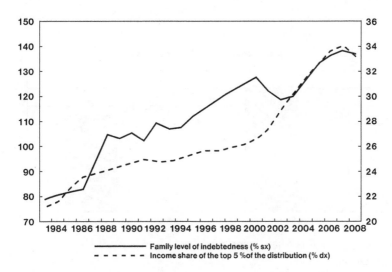

Figure A6 Family debts and income inequality, US 1984–2008.
Source: IMF, 2010.

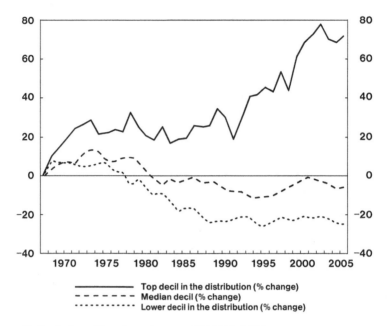

Figure A7 Evolution of hourly real wages, US 1967–2005.
Source: IMF (2010).

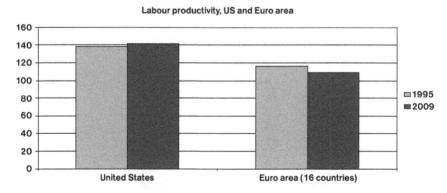

Figure A8 Labour productivity, 1995–2009.
Source: Eurostat.

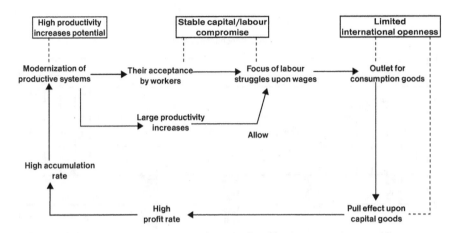

Figure A9 The mechanism of the Fordist Growth Model.
Source: Boyer, 2000.

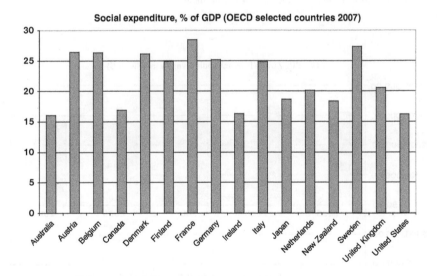

Figure A10 EU and US social expenditures.
Source: OECD 2010, Employment Outlook (online database).

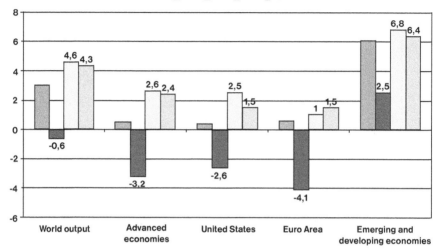

Figure A11 The 2008–11 recession.
Source: IMF, 2010 World Economic Outlook (online database).

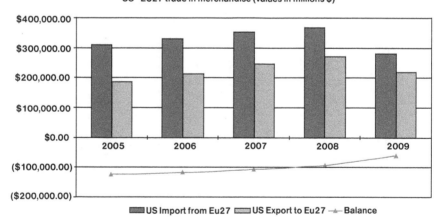

Figure A12 US-EU27 trade balance.
Source: US International Trade Commission, online database, 2010.

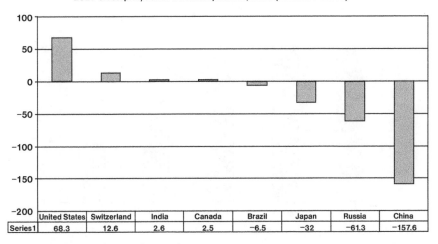

Figure A13 EU current account balance with selected partners.
Source: Eurostat.

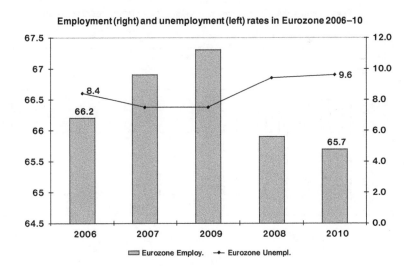

Figure A14 Labour market evolution in the Eurozone.
Source: Eurostat.

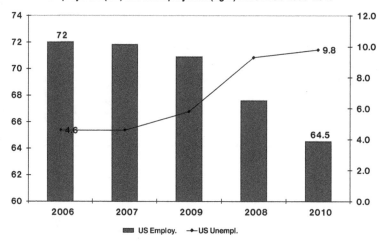

Figure A15 Labour market evolution in the US.
Source: US Bureau of Labour Statistics.

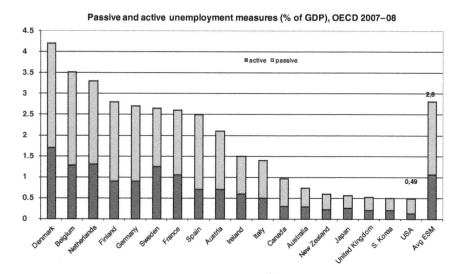

Figure A16 Public expenditure on unemployment, OECD countries.
Source: OECD 2010, Employment outlook (online database).

Table A1 Labour market indicators

	Active policy 2012 (% of GDP)	Passive policy 2012 (% of GDP)	Coverage (in % of workers) of trade unions 2009–11	Level of coordinate bargaining wage	Length unempl. subsidies (months) 2011	Substitut. rate for unempl. subsidies (% 2009 11)	Minimum wage, hourly (US$ PPP)	Scores of the principal component analysis
Australia	0.29	0.51	99.00	6.00	9	0.55	10.5	–0.75
Austria	0.75	1.29	60.00	0.00	48	0.22		0.65
Belgium	0.81	2.08	96.00	0.33	48	0.59	10.1	2.07
Canada	0.24	0.59	31.50	0.00	11	0.59	7.8	–1.41
Chile	0.1	0.23	48.00	0.00	18	0.71	2.9	2.07
Denmark	2.1	1.7	82.00	0.00	24	0.55		3.19
Estonia	0.29	0.44	80.00	4.00	24	0.49	2.8	–1.15
Finland	1.03	1.45	90.00	1.67	23	0.54		1.93
France	0.9	1.45	95.00	3.33	24	0.69	10.7	0.43
Germany	0.69	0.98	63.00	0.00	12	0.60		–0.28
Ireland	0.91	0.57	44.00	0.00	12	0.36	9.0	1.53
Italy	0.45	0.34	80.00	0.67	8	0.63		–0.19
Netherlands	0.98	0.37	82.00	3.67	38	0.68	9.5	1.09
New Zealand	0.29	0.35	17.00	0.00	48	0.23	8.7	–1.49
Norway	0.54	0.3	72.00	0.00	24	0.67		–0.31
Portugal	0.49	0.44	62.00	0.00	24	0.78	4.0	–0.010
Sweden	1.33	0.59	92.00	0.00	35	0.60		1.67
UK	0.41		34.80	0.00	6	0.17	8.0	–1.15
US	0.12		13.10	0.00	23	0.57	7.3	–2.20

Source: Own elaboration on OECD data.

Note: data concerning most of these labour market indicators, on the basis of which the factor analysis was run, and the score of PC in the last column was extracted, are not available for all thirty-four OECD countries, but only for nineteen as this table suggests.

Table A2 Descriptive statistics for the regression of Table 2.2 (Chapter 2)

	Financialis 2013 (% GDP)	Financialis avg (% GDP)	EPL 2013	EPL avg	TU density 2013	TU density avg	Social spending 2013 (% gdp)	Social spending avg (% gdp)	Inequality (Gini 2013)	Inequality (Gini avg)
Austral.	85	92	1.27	1.11	17	26	19	15.2	0.32	0.32
Austria	27	21	1.84	1.94	27	36	28.3	25.5	0.28	0.27
Belgium	62	57	2.09	2.46	55	54	30.9	26.3	0.26	0.27
Canada	111	95	0.59	0.59	27	30	17.2	16.9	0.32	0.31
Chile	117	97	2.81	2.81	15	15	10	10.8	0.50	0.51
Czech R	19	23	2.18	2.01	13	25	20.5	18.0	0.26	0.25
Denm.	72	54	1.79	1.95	67	72	30.2	26.9	0.25	0.23
Estonia	11	23	2.40	2.09	6	14	16.1	15.9	0.32	0.34
Finland	63	85	1.86	1.88	69	74	30.6	25.6	0.26	0.25
France	70	64	3.00	2.99	8	8	32	27.9	0.31	0.29
German	44	40	2.00	2.34	18	25	25.6	24.5	0.29	0.27
Greece	18	41	2.18	3.29	21	27	24.3	18.7	0.34	0.34
Hung	17	19	1.42	1.42	11	21	22.1	22.1	0.29	0.29
Iceland	21	62	1.18	1.18	83	88	17.1	15.7	0.25	0.26
Ireland	52	54	1.01	0.90	30	39	21.9	18.6	0.30	0.31
Israel	57	61	1.46	1.46	32	55	15	15.9	0.38	0.36
Italy	24	31	2.26	2.97	37	36	28.7	23.1	0.32	0.32
Japan	62	74	1.12	1.40	18	21	23	14.4	0.34	0.33
Korea R	105	60	2.25	2.55	10	12	10.2	5.7	0.31	0.31
Luxemb	123	149	3.00	3.00	33	41	23.4	20.9	0.28	0.27
Mexico	45	31	2.05	3.05	14	16	7.9	4.5	0.48	0.49
Netherla	84	92	1.88	2.00	18	22	24.6	23.8	0.28	0.29
NewZea	48	42	1.20	1.06	19	25	20.8	19.1	0.32	0.33
Norway	51	43	2.67	2.67	54	55	22	20.8	0.25	0.26

Poland	36	20	1.99	1.69	13	20	20.7	20.0	0.30	0.33
Portugal	31	32	2.50	3.57	21	23	25.8	17.0	0.34	0.37
Slovak	5	6	1.80	1.81	17	29	18.7	18.3	0.26	0.26
Sloven.	14	18	2.21	2.22	23	42	23.8	14.5	0.25	0.25
Spain	74	65	2.31	2.91	17	17	27.3	21.2	0.34	0.33
Sweden	107	92	1.71	2.17	68	77	28.2	28.8	0.27	0.24
Switzerl	171	187	1.36	1.36	16	20	19.9	16.5	0.29	0.30
Turkey	39	25	3.59	3.62	5	11	12.5	6.8	0.41	0.44
UK	124	128	0.70	0.71	25	30	22.5	19.4	0.34	0.34
US	119	115	0.25	0.25	11	13	18.6	15.1	0.39	0.37
OECD	62	62	1.88	1.11	17	21	21.7	15.2	0.32	0.32

Source: Own elaboration on OECD data.

Note: The average (avg) is for the whole period (1990–2013).

Table A3 Correlation matrix

	gini	EPL	TU_dens.	SocSpend	Financ.	FDI_IN	import	growth	Unemploy.	3th_Edu.L
gini	1.0000									
EPL	0.2721	1.0000								
TU_density	-0.4535	-0.0640	1.0000							
SocSpend	-0.6734	-0.0973	0.4489	1.0000						
Financializ.	-0.1215	-0.3800	-0.0052	0.0938	1.0000					
FDI_in	-0.0301	-0.0449	0.0266	0.0737	-0.0258	1.0000				
import	-0.3201	0.0846	0.0344	0.2808	-0.0122	0.1158	1.0000			
growth	0.0726	-0.0198	-0.0649	-0.2520	0.0976	0.0386	-0.0424	1.0000		
unemployment	0.0265	0.1894	-0.0247	0.1909	-0.2615	-0.0130	0.0408	-0.1132	1.0000	
3th_Edu.L	-0.2507	-0.5556	0.1603	0.1372	0.4599	0.0109	-0.0719	-0.0978	-0.1940	1.0000

Source: Own elaboration.

Table A4 Multicollinearity test

Variable	VIF	1/VIF
Third_Edu	1.72	0.581160
socspend	1.62	0.618468
EPL	1.52	0.657412
Financiali~n	1.43	0.700823
TU_density	1.33	0.749221
unemployment	1.18	0.848148
import	1.13	0.883048
growth	1.13	0.886945
FDI_IN	1.03	0.975215
Mean VIF	1.34	

Source: Own elaboration.

Table A5 Unit roots test (stationarity of the panel)

```
Levin-Lin-Chu unit-root test for Inequality (Gini)
-----------------------------------------
Ho: Panels contain unit roots        Number of panels =   34
Ha: Panels are stationary            Number of periods =   24

AR parameter: Common                 Asymptotics: N/T -> 0
Panel means: Included
Time trend:  Not included

ADF regressions: 1 lag
LR variance:   Bartlett kernel, 9.00 lags average (chosen by LLC)
------------------------------------------------------------------------
---
          Statistic   p-value
------------------------------------------------------------------------
---
 Unadjusted t    -8.0045
 Adjusted t*     -2.9023      0.0019
------------------------------------------------------------------------
---
```

Source: Own elaboration.

Table A6 US and Eurozone comparison on main features

	Eurozone 2009	US 2009
World share of GDP	14.8% (EU27: 21%)	20.2%
Global market share (exports, world %)	15% (EU27: 20%)	13%
Population	328 mln: (EU 27: 498mln)	317mln
Inequality - Gini coefficient	0.29%	41%
GDP per capita $ ppp	33,452	46,653
Life expectancy at birth	81	79
Poverty (50% of median income) 2006	10%	17.1%
Combined education rate (primary,	95%	92%
secondary & tertiary levels, % of pop)		88%
Secondary enrolment ratio (% of	91%	91%
secondary school-age population)		15
Primary enrolment ratio (% of primary	97%	
school-age population)		
Expected years of schooling (children)	16	

Source: IMF, 2010 World Economic Outlook; UNDP (online database).

Table A7 Varieties of capitalism

Varieties of capitalism within the enlarged European Union (19 Eurozone members, with *)			*Competitive Market Economies (Anglo-Saxon model)*
European social model:	**Hybrid model (mixed between ESM and LME)**	**Competitive Market Economies (CME)**	US, UK, Ireland, Canada, New Zealand, Australia
Austria*	Cyprus*	UK	
Belgium*	Malta*	Ireland*	
Finland*	Latvia*		
France*	Lithuania*		
German*	Poland		
Netherlands*	Romania		
Slovenia*	Bulgaria		
Denmark	Estonia*		
Sweden	Slovakia*		
Luxemburg*			
Hungary			
Czech Rep			
Greece*			
Italy*			
Portugal*			
Spain*			

Source: Adapted from Pontusson (2005), Tridico (2011).

Note: Norway and Switzerland are not part of the EU but would fit very well in the ESM (Pontusson, 2005). Greece, Italy, Portugal and Spain sometimes classified as Mediterranean model with typical characteristics of the ESM such as consistent Welfare States and Public expenditure, coupled with inefficiency, debt and corruption (which usually are not found in the ESM).

Table A8 Governmental bank rescues, 2007–09

US (bailing out, saving plans or govmt shares for firms and financial institutions)	EU
AIG Fannie Mae Freddie Mac Merril Lynch Goldman Sachs Morgan Stanley Washington Mutual Bank of America Maiden Lane Citigroup	**Govmt shares** ING (Netherlands) BNP Paribas (France) Unicredit (Italy) Swedebank (Sweden) Alpha (Greece) Lloyds and RBS (UK) Commerzbank (Germany) **Nationalisation** Fortis (Belgium) Anglo Irish (Ireland) Northern Rock (UK) Hypo Real Estate (Germany)

Source: IMF (2008); Wahl, 2010.

Table A9 Stimulus packages, 2007–09

	Germany	UK	Netherlands	Italy	France	Spain	Tot EU	US
Bn. Euro	82	31	8.5	9	26	40	200 (approx)	775 USbn$
% GDP	3.3	2.2	1.4	0.6	1.3	3.7	1.5% (approx)	2.7%

Source: IMF (2008).

Table A10 Political economy issues and trade-offs: recovery plans and fiscal stimuli

Policies / Effects	Monetary expansion	Fiscal stimulus	Direct public employment	Exchange r. devaluation/ protectionism	Price targeting	Industrial policies & incentives
Positive outcomes	Keynes' effect: ↓r ↑I ↑E ↑trust	↑I, Ag Demand ↑E & Income	Employment (E) & Income	↑Ex ↑Ag Demand ↑E & Income ↓Im	Price stability no deflation & inflation	Boost in the industrial yield, ↑E&technology ↑Hedge tax on labour
Negative outcomes	Risk of inflation; Liquidity trap	↑Tax and/or deficit	Risk of low efficiency and tax	Beggar my neighbour and risk of currency wars		
Domestic Constraints	Debt: creditors do not want their real credits devaluated	Debt sustainability and lender availability	Sustainability of general taxation	Risk of imported Inflation; Imports become too expensive		Budget and tax
International constraints	With inflation int.nal debt becomes cheaper and int.nal lenders lose (this applies to US since int. nal debts are in its own currency, $. However this increases int. nal tensions)			Loss of int.nal credibility; No one is going to lend money anymore		WTO and other int. nal organization may claim for State aid end and fair competition; However all States may prefer industrial policies and state aids in crisis time

Firm issues and State/Market relations	Risk that the firms just hold money and do not do investments, if they do not trust	Crowding-out (very limited given the fact that firms during crisis do not invest anyway); On the other side, during crisis time, firms prefer to lend money to the state (buying national bonds) for deficit spending, and not to invest or make corporate profits to be taxed	Downsizing of private sector (which however is not employing anyway during crisis)	National Firms abroad want fair exchange rate (for instance, US firms in China which export back to US)	Enforcement issues: govmt control and inspection over firms price policies	Cooperation and partnership for better technology, public incentives for innovation, easier access to finance for firms and productive investments
Workers and industrial relations	Inflation ↓purchasing power of wage; Distributional conflict over stagnant GDP	Fiscal stimulus is considered superior, first best. Repayment issue: paid by upper classes or general taxation	Help to sustain fair industrial relations and higher employm.	Income differences with the rest of the world worsens (at the new devaluate level of exchange rate) ↑domestic goods ↓foreign goods	Help to keep purchasing power stable	↑Productivity gains Wage to sustain consumption (not finance)
Consumers	Liquidity may ↑ wealth and consumption (Pigou's effect) or may postpone consumption, waiting for further ↓prices	Consumption ↑(Keynesians) Or Saving may ↑(neoclassicals)	↑Consumption		↑Consumption eliminating saving increases risk and Pigou's effects	↑Consumption (not financial tools to sustain consumption)

References

Abramovitz, M. (1986). "The Tasks of Economic History". *The Journal of Economic History*, 46(2), (Jun., 1986): 385–406.

Acemoglu, D. (2011). *Thoughts on inequality and the financial crisis.* Presentation held at the American Economic Association. Available at: http://economics.mit.edu/files/6348 [Accessed 7 Nov. 2013].

Adema, W. and M. Ladaique (2009). "How Expensive is the Welfare State?: Gross and Net Indicators in the OECD Social Expenditure Database (SOCX)". OECD Social, Employment and Migration Working Papers, No. 92, OECD Publishing. Available at: www.oecd-ilibrary.org/social-issues-migration-health/how-expensive-is-the-welfare-state_220615515052.

Adema, W., P. Fron and M. Ladaique (2011). "Is the European Welfare State Really More Expensive?: Indicators on Social Spending, 1980–2012 and a Manual to the OECD Social Expenditure Database (SOCX)". OECD Social, Employment and Migration Working Papers, No. 124, OECD Publishing.

Aglietta, M. (1979). *A theory of capitalist regulation: the US experience.* London: Verso Classics.

Ahluwalia, M.S. (1976). "Inequality, Poverty and Development". *Journal of Development Economics*, 3(4): 307–342.

Akerlof, G.A. and J.L. Yellen (eds.) (1986). *Efficiency wage models of the labor market.* Cambridge: Cambridge University Press.

Alesina, A. and Perotti, R. (1996). "Income Distribution, Political Instability and Investment". *European Economic Review*, 40: 1203–1228.

Allan, J.P. and Scruggs, L. (2004). "Political Partisanship and Welfare State Reform in Advanced Industrial Societies". *American Journal of Political Science*, 48(3): 496–512.

Allen, R.E. (2009). *Financial crises and recession in the global economy.* Cheltenham: Edward Elgar.

Allison, C., Fleisje, E., Glevey, W. and Johannes, W. L. (2014). "Trends and Key Drivers of Income Inequality". Working Paper, The Marshall Society, Cambridge. Available at: http://marshallresearch.co.uk/publications/Oxford_Economics_Trends_and_Key_Drivers_of_Income_Inequality.pdf.

Altman, M. (1998). "A High Wage Path to Economic Growth and Development". *Challenge*, 41(1): 91–104.

Amable, B. (2003). *The diversity of modern capitalism.* Oxford: Oxford University Press.

Amoroso, B. (2003). "Globalization and Welfare". Working Paper, University of Roskilde.

Andersen, J.G. (2007). "Impact of Public Policies: Economic Effects, Social Effects and Policy Feedback. A Framework for Analysis". CCWS Working Paper, No. 2007–53, Aalborg University.

Arestis, P. and Pelagidis, T. (2010). "The Case Against Deficit Hawks. Absurd Austerity Policies in Europe". *Challenge*, 53(6): 54–61.

Arestis, P., Charles, A. and Fontana, G. (2013). "Financialization, the Great Recession, and the Stratification of the US Labor Market". *Feminist Economics*, 19(3): 152–80.

Arrighi, G. (1994). *The long twentieth century: money, power, and the origins of our times.* London: Verso.

Arrighi, G. (2014). *Il lungo XX secolo. Denaro, potere e le origini del nostro tempo.* Milano: Il Saggiatore.

Arrighi, G., Po-keung Hui, Ho-Fung Hung and Selden, M. (2003). "Historical Capitalism, East and West". In: G.Arrighi, T. Hamashita and M. Selden, eds, *The Resurgence of East Asia: 500, 150, 50 Year Perspectives.* London and New York: Routledge.

Arts, W. and Gelissen, J. (2002). "Three Worlds of Welfare State Capitalism or More? A State-of-the-Art Report". *Journal of European Social Policy*, 12(2): 137–58.

Atkinson, A.B. (1999). *Is rising inequality inevitable? A critique of the transatlantic consensus.* WIDER Annual Lectures, No. 3, Helsinki.

Atkinson, A.B. (2015). *Inequality. What can be done?* Harvard University Press.

Atkinson, A.B., Piketty, T. and Saez, E. (2011). "Top Incomes in the Long Run of History". *Journal of Economic Literature*, 49(1): 3–71.

Autor, D., Manning, A. and Smith, C. (2015). "The Contribution of the Minimum Wage to US Wage Inequality over Three Decades: A Reassessment". *American Economic Journal.* Available at: http://economics.mit.edu/files/3279.

Bank of Japan (2014). *Bank of Japan official website.* [online] Available at: www.boj.or.jp/en/mopo/outline/other.htm/.

Barba, A. and Pivetti, M. (2009). "Rising Household Debt: Its Causes and Macroeconomic Implications. Along-Period Analysis". *Cambridge Journal of Economics*, 33(1): 113–37.

Barro, R. J. (1989), "The Ricardian Approach to Budget Deficits". *Journal of Economic Perspectives*, 3(2): 37–54.

Bartlett, B. (2010). "The Great Stimulus Debate". *The International Economy.* Summer 2010, Washington, DC.

Basili, M., Franzini, M. and Vercelli, A. (2006). *Environment, inequality and collective action.* Abingdon: Routledge.

Basso, P. (1998). *Tempi moderni, orari antichi. Il tempo di lavoro a fine secolo.* Milano: FrancoAngeli.

Bastia, T. (2013). *Migration and inequality.* London: Routledge.

Baten, J., Ma, D., Morgan, S. and Wang, Q. (2010). "Evolution of Living Standards and Human Capital in China in the 18–20th Centuries: Evidences from Real Wages, Age-Heaping, and Anthropometrics". *Explorations in Economic History*, 47(3): 347–59.

Bello, W. (2010). *All fall down: ten years after the Asian Financial Crisis.* Published on Transnational Institute. Available at: www.tni.org.

Bernanke, Ben S. (2005). *The global saving glut and the U.S. current account deficit.* Remarks by Governor Ben S. Bernanke: The Sandridge Lecture, Virginia Association of Economists, Richmond, VA (10 March 2005). Available at: www.federalreserve.gov/boarddocs/speeches/2005/20050414/default.htm.

Bernanke, Ben S. (2009). *Financial reform to address systemic risk*. Speech at the Council on Foreign Relations, Washington, DC (10 March 2009). Available at: www.federalreserve. gov/newsevents/speech/bernanke20090310a.htm.

Bhagwati, J. (2004). *In defense of globalization*, Oxford: Oxford University Press.

Bibow, J. and Terzi, A. (eds) (2007). *Euroland and the world economy. Global player or global drag?* New York: Palgrave.

Bini Smaghi, L. (2008). *The financial crisis and global imbalances: two sides of the same coin*. Speech at the Asia Europe Economic Forum, Beijing (9 December 2008). Available at: www.bis.org/review/r081212d.pdf.

Birdsall, N. and Sabot, R. (1994). "Inequality as a Constraint on Growth in Latin America, Development Policy". Newsletter on Policy Research, Inter-American Development Bank.

Birdsong, N. (2015). "The consequences of economic inequality". Seven Pillars Institute series, February 2015.

BIS – Bank for International Settlements (2010). *Semi-annual OTC derivatives statistics*. Available at: www.bis.org/statistics/otcder/dt1920a.pdf.

BIS – Bank for International Settlements (2013). Triennial Central Bank Survey, Bank for International Settlements, Monetary and Economic Department, Basel.

Blackmon, P. (2006). "The State: Back in the Center of the Globalization Debate". *International Studies Review*, 8(1): 116–119.

Bogliacino, F. and Lucchese, M. (2015). "Endogenous skill biased technical change: testing for demand pull effect". *Industrial and Corporate Change*, first published online April 2014, doi:10.1093/icc/dtv010.

Bogliacino, F. and Maestri, V. (2014). "Increasing economic inequalities?" In: W. Salverda, B. Nolan, D. Checchi, I. Marx, A. McKnight, and I. Tóth, eds, *Changing Inequalities in Rich Countries: Analytical and Comparative Perspectives*, Oxford University Press, 15–48.

Bonoli, G. (1997). "Classifying Welfare States: A Two-dimensional Approach". *Journal of Social Policy*, 26(3): 351–72.

Borjas, G.J. and Ramey, V.A. (1995). "Foreign Competition, Market Power, and Wage Inequality". *The Quarterly Journal of Economics*, 110(4): 1075–1110.

Bourguignon, F. and Morrisson, C. (2002). "Inequality among World Citizens: 1820–1992". *The American Economic Review*, 92(4) (Sep., 2002): 727–44.

Boyer, R. (2000). "Is a Finance-Led Growth Regime a Viable Alternative to Fordism? A Preliminary Analysis". *Economy and Society*, 29(1): 111–45.

Boyer, R. (2005). "Coherence, Diversity, and the Evolution of Capitalisms: The Institutional Complementarity Hypothesis". CNRS-CEPREMAP discussion paper No. 076.

Boyer, R. (2009). "Come conciliare la solidarietà sociale e l'efficienza economica nell'era della globalizzazione: un punto di vista regolazioni sta". *Argomenti*, N. 1 gennaio/maggio, 5–31.

Boyer, R. and Saillard, Y. (eds) (2002). *Regulation theory: the state of the art*. London: Routledge.

Brancaccio, E. and Fontana, G. (2011). "The Global Economic Crisis (Introduction)". In: E., Brancaccio and G., Fontana, eds, *The Global Economic Crisis. New Perspective on the Critique of Economic Theory and Policy*. London: Routledge.

Braudel, F. (1982). *Civilization and capitalism, 15th–18th century: the wheels of commerce*. Oakland: University of California Press.

Butcher, T., Dickens, R. and Manning, A. (2012). "Minimum Wages and Wage Inequality: Some Theory and an Application to the UK". CEP discussion paper, No. 1177.

Caballero, R., Farhi, E. and Gourinchas, P.O. (2008). "An Equilibrium Model of 'Global Imbalances' and Low Interest Rates". *American Economic Review*, 98 (March): 358–93.

Caramani, D. (ed) (2008). *Comparative politics.* Oxford University Press.

Card, D., Lemieux, T. and Craig Riddell, W. (2004). "Unions and Wage Inequality", *Journal of Labor Research*, 25(4): 519–62.

Castells, M. (2004). "Global Informational Capitalism". In: D. Held, and A.G. McGrew, eds, *The Global Transformations Reader: An Introduction to the Globalization Debate.* Malden: Blackwell.

Cesaratto, S. (2011). "Europe, German Mercantilism and the Current Crisis". In: E. Brancaccio, and G. Fontana, eds, *The Global Economic Crisis. New Perspectives on the Critique of Economic Theory and Policy.* London: Routledge.

Chenery, H.B. and Syrquin, M. (1975). *Patterns of development, 1950–1960.* Oxford University Press.

Chong Ju Choi (2004). "Communitarian Capitalism and the Social Market Economy: An Application to China". In: J. Kidd and F. Richter, eds, *Development Models, Globalization and Economies.* Palgrave.

Chorafas, Dimitris N. (2009). *Capitalism without capital.* Houndmills: Palgrave.

Choudhry, M.T., Signorelli, M. and Marelli, E. (2010). "The Labour Market Impact of Financial Crises". COST Workshop, University of Rome III, Italy, 9 July.

Chusseau, N. and Dumont, M. (2012). "Growing income inequalities in advanced countries". ECINEQ WP 2012 – 260, Paris.

Cingano, F. (2014). "Trends in Income Inequality and Its Impact on Economic Growth". OECD Working Papers, No. 163. OECD Publishing.

Clelland, D.A. and Dunaway, W.A. (2010). "The Current Economic Crisis: What Insights Does the Word System Perspective Offer?" Paper presented at the Annual Meeting of the American Sociological Association, August 2010.

Cobb, C.W. and Douglas, P.H. (1928). "A Theory of Production". *American Economic Review,* 18: 139–65.

Cochrane, J. (2001). "Understanding Fiscal and Monetary Policy in the Great Recession: Some Unpleasant Fiscal Arithmetic". *European Economic Review,* 55: 2–30.

Conzelmann, T., Rodriguez, P.I., Kiiver, P. and Spendzharova, A. (2010). "Regulatory Overhaul in the EU and the US Following the Financial Crisis – What Role for Accountability?" Paper prepared for the ECPR Standing Group on International Relations Conference, 9–11 September 2010, Stockholm.

Cooper, R.N. (2007). "Living with Global Imbalances". *Brookings Papers on Economic Activity,* 2: 91–110.

Cynamon, B. Z. and Fazzari, S. M. (2013). "Inequality and Household Finance during the Consumer Age". Working Paper, No. 752, Levy Economics Institute, Annandale-on-Hudson, NY.

D'Apice, V. and Ferri, G. (2010). *Financial instability. Toolkit for interpreting boom and bust cycles.* Hundmills: Palgrave.

Deaton, A. (2013). *The great escape: health, wealth, and the origins of inequality.* Princeton: Princeton University Press.

Delli Gatti, D., Gallegati, M., Greenwaldc, B., Russo, A. and Stiglitz, J. (2012). "Mobility Constraints, Productivity Trends, and Extended Crises". *Journal of Economic Behavior & Organization,* 83: 375–93.

De Larosière (2009). Report from The High-Level Group on Financial Supervision in the EU. Brussels, 25 February 2009.

De Long, B. (2010). "It Is Far Too Soon to End Expansion". *Financial Times,* June 19. Available at: www.ft.com/cms/s/0/f74bb844-9369-11df-bb9a-00144feab49a.html.

De Muro, P. (2016). "Not Just Slicing the Pie: The Need for a Broader Approach to Economic Inequality". In: S. Fadda and P. Tridico, eds, *Varieties of Economic Inequality.* London: Routledge.

Dunaway, S. (2009). *Global imbalances and the financial crisis.* Council Special Report. No. 44, March.

Dymarsky, W. (2008). "Labour market deregulation and performance of the economy. What do these two things actually have in common?" EAEPE Conference 2008, University of Roma Tre, Rome.

Easterly, W. (2001). "The Middle Class Consensus and Economic Development". *Journal of Economic Growth,* 6: 317–35.

ECB (2010). Monthly Bulletin, June 06/2010, June. Frankfurter.

Economic Policy Institute Research and Ideas for Shared Prosperity. *Economic Policy Institute Official Website.* [online] Available at: www.epi.org/.

EFILWC – European Foundation for the Improvement of Living and Working Condition. (2006). European Opinion Research Group EEIG, Dublin.

Engelen, E., Konings, M. and Fernandez, R. (2008) "The Rise of Activist Investors and Patters of Political Responses: Lessons on Agency". *Socio-Economic Review,* 6(4): 611–36.

Engelen, E., Konings, M. and Fernandez, R. (2010). "Geographies of Financialisation in Disarray: The Dutch Case in Comparative Perspective". *Economic Geography,* 86(1): 53–73.

Epstein, G. (2005). *Financialization and the world economy.* Cheltenham: Edward Elgar.

Erturk, I., Froud, J., Johal, S., Leaver, A. and Williams K. (eds). *Financialisation at work: key texts and commentary.* London: Routledge.

Esping-Andersen, G. (1990). *The three worlds of welfare capitalism.* Cambridge: Polity.

EU (2009a). Regulation of the European Parliament and of the Council on Credit Rating Agencies. 2008/0217 (COD). 14 July 2009.

EU (2009b). Proposal for a Regulation of the European Parliament and of the Council Establishing a European Banking Authority. COM(2009) 501 final.2009/0142 (COD).

——— Proposal for a Regulation of the European Parliament and of the Council Establishing a European Insurance and Occupational Pensions Authority. 23.9.2009 COM. (2009) 502 final. 2009/0143 (COD).

——— Proposal for a Regulation of the European Parliament and of the Council Establishing a European Securities and Markets Authority. COM (2009) 503 final. 2009/0144 (COD).

——— Proposal for a Regulation of the European Parliament and of the Council on Community macro prudential oversight of the financial system and establishing a European Systemic Risk Board. COM (2009) 499 final. 2009/0140 (COD).

EU (2009c). Proposal for a Directive of the European Parliament and of the Council on Alternative Investment Fund Managers and amending Directives 2004/39/EC and 2009/.../EC. 30.4.2009 COM (2009) 207 final. 2009/0064 (COD) C7-0040/09. Brussels.

EU (2010a). Proposal for a Regulation of the European Parliament and of the Council on OTC derivatives, central counterparties and trade repositories. COM (2010) 484/5. 2010/0250 (COD). Brussels.

EU (2010b). Proposal for a Directive of the European Parliament and of the Council amending Directives 2006/48/EC and 2006/49/EC as regards capital requirements for the trading book 38 and for re-securitisations, and the supervisory review of remuneration policies COM (2010) XXX final. Brussels.

EuroMemorandum (2010). *Confronting the Crisis: Austerity or Solidarity.* European Economists for an Alternative Economic Policy in Europe - EuroMemo Group 2010/11. Available at: www.euromemo.eu.

European Commission (2003). "Impact Evaluation of the EES. Italian Employment Policy in Recent Years". Final Report, Provisional Version, Brussels.

European Commission, (2008). Economic Forecast, Directorate-General for Economic and Financial Affairs, No. 6. Autumn, Brussels.

European Commission (2009). *Employment in Europe 2009.* November, Brussels.

European Council (2009). Council Conclusions on Strengthening EU Financial Supervision. Available at: www.consilium.europa.eu/uedocs/cms_data/docs/pressdata/en/ecofin/108389.pdf.

European Council (2010). Short Selling and certain aspects of Credit Default Swaps, COM (2010) 482. 2010/xxxx (COD). Brussels.

Eurostat (2010). Structural Indicators (online statistics).

Eurostat (2011). Structural Indicators (online statistics).

Eurostat (2014). Structural Indicators (online statistics).

Facundo, A., Atkinson, A.B., Piketty, T. and Saez, E. (2013). "The Top 1 Percent in International and Historical Perspective". *Journal of Economic Perspectives*, 27(3): 3–20.

Fadda S. (2016). "What Causes it and How to Curb it". In: S. Fadda and P. Tridico, eds, *Varieties of Economic Inequality.* London: Routledge.

Feenstra, R.C. (1998). "Integration of Trade and Disintegration of Production in the Global Economy". *Journal of Economic Perspectives*, 12(4): 31–50.

Feenstra, R.C. (2004). *Advanced international trade: theory and evidence.* Princeton: Princeton University Press.

Feng, S. and Hu, Y. (2010). "Misclassification Errors and the Underestimation of U.S. Unemployment Rates". IZA DP, No. 5057, July.

Ferrera, M. (1996). "The 'Southern Model' of Welfare in Social Europe". *Journal of European Social Policy*, 6: 17–37.

Financial Crisis Inquiry Commission (2011). *The Financial Crisis Inquiry Report.* Washington, DC: US Government.

Fitoussi, J.P. (1992). *Il Dibattito proibito.* Bologna: Il Mulino.

Fitoussi, J.P. (2005). "Macroeconomic Policies and Institutions". *Rivista di Politica Economica.* Novembre-Dicembre, 2005.

Fitoussi, J.P. and Saraceno, F. (2010). "Inequality and Macroeconomic Performance". Documents de Travail OFCE 2010–13, Observatoire Francais des Conjonctures Economiques.

Fitoussi, J.P. and Stiglitz, J. (2009). *The ways out of the crisis and the building of a more cohesive world.* The Shadow GN, Chair's Summary, LUISS Guido Carli, Rome, May 6–7.

Frangakis, M. (2010). "Rising sovereign debt in the EU – Implications for economic policy". Nicos Poulantzas Institute, Athens, Greece, mimeo.

Frank, A.G. (2005). "The naked hegemon: why the emperor has no clothes". *Asia Times*, (January 11). Available at: www.asiatime.com.

Franzini, M. (2016). "Meno crescita e più disuguaglianza: effetti (straordinari) delle politiche neoliberiste secondo il FMI". Menabò n 45, Etica e Economia.

Fraser, N. (1995). "From Redistribution to Recognition? Dilemmas of Justice in a 'Post-Socialist' Age". *New Left Review,* I/212: 68–93.

Fraser, N. (2005). "Mapping the Feminist Imagination: From Redistribution to Recognition to Representation". *Constellations,* 12(3): 295–307.

Fuchita, Y. and Litan, E. R. (2007). *New financial instruments and institutions: opportunities and policy challenges.* Baltimore Brooking Institutions Press.

Galbraith, J. K. (2012). *Inequality and instability.* Oxford: Oxford University Press.

Garegnani, P. (1966). "Switching of Techniques". *The Quarterly Journal of Economics,* 80(4): 554–67.

Gastaldi, F. and Liberati, P. (2011). "Economic Integration and Government Size: A Review of the Empirical Literature". *Financial Theory and Practice,* 35(3): 328–84.

Giavazzi, F. and Pagano, M. (1990). "Can Severe Fiscal Contractions Be Expansionary? Tales of Two Small European Countries". *NBER Macroeconomics Annual 1990.*

Gillingham, J. (2003). *European integration, 1950–2003: superstate or new market economy?* Cambridge: Cambridge University Press.

Goda, T. and Lysandrou, P. (2014). "The Contribution of Wealth Concentration to the Subprime Crisis: A Quantitative Estimation". *Cambridge Journal of Economics,* 38(2): 301–27.

Goldstein, M. and Veron, N. (2010). "Too Big To Fail: The Transatlantic Debate". Prepared for Conference on Transatlantic Relationships in an Era of Growing Economic Multipolarity, Organized by Bruegel and the Peterson Institute for International Economics Sponsored by the European Commission Washington, DC, October 8, 2010.

Gordon, C. (2012). "Union decline and rising inequality in two charts". *Economic Policy Institute.* Available at: www.epi.org/blog/union-decline-rising-inequality-charts/.

Greenspan, A. (2005). *Remarks by Chairman Alan Greenspan: current account.* Speech at Advancing Enterprise 2005 Conference, London (February 4). Available at: www.federalreserve.gov/boarddocs/speeches/2005/20050204/default.htm.

Greenspan, A. (2007). *The age of turbulence: adventures in a new world.* Allen Lane.

Ha, E. (2008). "Globalization, Veto Players, and Welfare Spending". *Comparative Political Studies,* 48(6): 783–813.

Hague, D.C. (ed). *The theory of capital.* New York: St. Martin's Press, 177–222.

Haidar, J.I. and Hoshi, T. (2014). "Implementing Structural Reforms in Abenomics: How to Reduce the Cost of Doing Business in Japan". Stanford University FSI Working Paper, June 2014.

Ha-Joon Chang (2008). *Bad Samaritans: the myth of free trade and the secret history of capitalism.* Bloomsbury Press.

Hancké, B., Rhodes, M. and Thatcher, M. (eds) (2007). *Beyond varieties of capitalism – conflict, contradictions, and complementarities in the European economy.* Oxford: Oxford University Press.

Hay, C. and Wincott, D. (2012). *The political economy of European welfare capitalism.* Palgrave Macmillan.

Hein, E. (2015). "Secular Stagnation or Stagnation Policy?" Working Paper, No. 846, Levy Economics Institute.

Held, D., McGrew, A., Goldblatt, D. and Perraton, J. (1999). *Global transformations: politics, economics and culture.* Cambridge: Polity.

Hemerijck, H., Keune, M. and Rodhes, M. (2006). "European Welfare States: Diversity, Challenges and Reforms". In: P. Heywood, E. Jones, M. Rodhes and U. Sedelmeir, eds, *Development in European Politics.* New York: Palgrave.

Hoshi, T. and Patrick, H. T. (2000). *Crisis and change in the Japanese financial system.* Norwell: Kluwer Academic Publisher.

ILO (2010). *Global employment trends.* International Labor Office, Geneva, January.

ILO (2013). Global Wage Report 2012/13. Wages and equitable growth. International Labour Office, Geneva.

IMF – International Monetary Fund (1995). "Gender Issues in Economic Adjustment", IMF Survey, September 25: 286–88.

IMF – International Monetary Fund (2008). "Fiscal Policy for the Crisis". Staff Position Note (by Antonio Spilimbergo, Steve Symansky, Olivier Blanchard, and Carlo Cottarelli), Washington, DC.

IMF – International Monetary Fund (2009a). "Global Financial Stability Report. Navigating Challenges Ahead", October 2009. Washington, DC.

IMF – International Monetary Fund (2009b). World Economic Outlook. Washington, DC.

IMF – International Monetary Fund (2010). World Economic Outlook (online database).

IMF – International Monetary Fund (2013). "Japan: 2013 Article IV Consultation". Country Report, No. 13/253, International Monetary Fund, Washington, DC.

IMF – International Monetary Fund (2014). The IMF's approach to capital account liberalization, Washington, DC.

IMF – International Monetary Fund (2015). World Economic Outlook (online database), Washington, DC.

Irwin, N. (2013). "Toyota is crushing it. Abenomics is the reason". *Washington Post*. August 2, 2013.

Ivanova, M.N. (2010a). "Consumerism and the Crisis: the American Dream?" *Critical Sociology*, XX(X): 1–22.

Ivanova, M.N. (2010b). "Hegemony and Seigniorage: The Planned Spontaneity of the U.S. Current Account Deficit". *International Journal of Political Economy*, 39(1): 93–130.

Jessop, B. (2001). "What follows Fordism? On the periodization of capitalism and its regulation". In: R. Albritton *et al.*, eds, *Phases of Capitalist Development: Booms, Crises, and Globalization.* Basingstoke: Palgrave, 282–99.

Jessop, B. (2002). *The future of the capitalist state.* Cambridge: Polity.

Jha, P. and Golder, S. (2008). "Labour Market Regulation and Economic Performance: A Critical Review of Arguments and Some Plausible Lessons for India: International Labour Office, Geneva.

Kaldor, N. (1956). "Alternative Theories of Distribution". *The Review of Economic Studies*, 23(2): 83–100.

Kaldor, N. (1961). "Capital, accumulation and economic growth". In: F.A. Lutz and D.C. Hague, eds, *The Theory of Capital*, New York: St. Martin's Press, 177–222

Kalecki, M. (1965). *Theory of economic dynamics.* Unwin University Books.

Kindleberger, C. (2005). *Manias, panics, and crashes.* New York: John Wiley & Sons.

Kok Report (2004). "Facing the challenge. The Lisbon Strategy for Employment and Growth". Report from the High Level Group, chaired by Wim Kok.

Krippner, G.R. (2005). "The Financialisation of the American Economy". *Socio-Economic Review*, 3(2): 173–208.

Krugman, P. (2008). *The return of depression economics and the crisis of 2008.* New York: W.W. Norton & Company.

Krugman, P. (2010). "Fiscal Fantasies". The Conscience of a Liberal blog. Available at: http://krugman.blogs.nytimes.com/ [June 18].

Kuznets, S. (1933). "National income". *Encyclopaedia of the Social Sciences*, vol. 11. New York: Macmillan. Reprinted in Readings in the *Theory of Income Distribution*, selected by a committee of the American Economic Association. Philadelphia: Blakiston, 1946.

Kuznets, S. (1955). "Economic Growth and Income Inequality". *American Economic Review*, 45(1): 1–28.

Kuznets, S. (1965). *Economic growth and structure: selected essays*. New York: W.W. Norton & Company.

Larch, M. (2012). "Fiscal Performance and Income Inequality: Are Unequal Societies More Deficit-Prone?" *Kyklos*, 65(1): 53–80.

Lavoie, M. (2014). *Post-Keynesian economics: new foundations*. Cheltenham: Edward Elgar.

Lavoie, M. and Stockhammer, E. (eds) (2013). *Wage-led growth: an equitable strategy for economic recovery*. Basingstoke: Palgrave Macmillan.

Leamer, E. (1996). "Wage Inequality from International Competition and Technological Changes: Theory and Country Experience". *The American Economic Review*, 86(2): 309–14.

Lee, E. (1996). "Globalization and Employment: Is Anxiety Justified?". *International Labour Review*, 135(5): 485–97.

Lemieux, T., MacLeod, W.B. and Parent, D. (2009). "Performance Pay and Wage Inequality". *Quarterly Journal of Economics*, 124(1): 1–49.

Leon, P. and Realfonzo, R. (2008), a cura di, *L'Economia della Precarietà*. Manifestolibri.

Lewis, A. (1980). "The Slowing Down of the Engine of Growth: Nobel Lecture". *American Economic Review*, 70(4): 555–64.

Liberati, P. (2007). "Trade Openness, Capital Openness and Government Size". *Journal of Public Policy*. 27(2): 215–47.

Lin, K.H. and Tomaskovic-Devey, D. (2011). Financialization and US Income Inequality, 1970–2008, mimeo. Available at: http://papers.ssrn.com/sol3/papers.cfm?abstract_id= 1954129.

Lipietz, A. (1992). *Towards a new economic order. Postfordim, ecology and democracy*. Polity Press.

Lowenstein, Roger (2010). *The end of wall street*. Penguin Press.

Lucas, R. (1993). "Making a Miracle". *Econometrica*, 61(2): 251–57.

Lysandrou, P. (2011b). "Global Inequality, Wealth Concentration and the Subprime Crisis: A Marxian Commodity Theory Analysis". *Development and Change*, 42(1): 183–208.

Maddison A., database project. Available at: www.ggdc.net/maddison/maddison-project/ data.htm.

Mazzucato, M. (2013). *The entrepreneurial state: debunking public vs private sector myths*. London: Anthem Press.

McKeown, T.J. (1999). "The Global Economy, Post-Fordism, and Trade Policy in Advanced Capitalist States". In: H. Kitschelt, P. Lange, G. Marks, and J. Stephens, eds, *Continuity and Change in Contemporary Capitalism*. Cambridge: Cambridge University Press.

McKinsey Report (2016). "Poorer than their parents? Flat or falling income in advanced economies". McKinsey Global Institute, July 2016.

Mendoza, Enrique G., Vincenzo Quadrini and José-Victor Rios-Rull (2007). "Financial Integration, Financial Deepness, and Global Imbalances". Working Paper 12909, National Bureau of Economic Research (February).

Milanovic, B. (1994). "Determinants of Cross-Country Income Inequality: An Augmented Kuznets Hypothesis". Policy Research Working Paper Series 1246.

Milanovic, B. (1998). "Explaining the Increase in Inequality During the Transition". Policy Research Working Paper Series 1935, The World Bank.

Milanovic, B. (2011). "Global Inequality and the Global Inequality Extraction Ratio: The Story of the Past Two Centuries". *Explorations in Economic History*, 48(4): 494–506.

Milanovic, B. (2016). *Global inequality: a new approach for the age of globalization*. Harvard: Harvard University Press.

Minsky, H.P. (1986). *Stabilizing an unstable economy*. New Haven: Yale University Press.

Mishel, L., Shierolz, H. and Edwards, K. (2010). "Reasons for Skepticism about Structural Unemployment Examining the Demand-Side Evidence". EPI, Briefing Paper 279, 22 September.

Mundell, R. (2009). "Financial Crises and the International Monetary System". New York: Columbia University, mimeo.

Nickell, S.G. (1997). "Labour Market Rigidities and Unemployment: Europe versus North America". *Journal of Economic Perspectives*, 11(3): 55–74.

Nölke, A. and Vliegenthart, A. (2009). "Enlarging the Varieties of Capitalism: The Emergence of Dependent Market Economies in East Central Europe". *World Politics*, 61(4): 670–702.

Obstfeld, M. and Rogoff, K. (2009). "Global Imbalances and the Financial Crisis: Products of Common Causes". CEPR Discussion Paper, No. 7606.

OECD (2004). Employment Outlook, Chapter 2, *Employment Protection Regulation and Labour Market Performance*.

OECD (2010). Employment outlook (online database).

OECD (2012). Social expenditure database. Available at: www.oecd.org/els/social/expenditure.

OECD (2011). "Divided We Stand: Why Inequality Keeps Rising". Paris: OECD Publishing.

OECD (2013). "Protecting Jobs, Enhancing Flexibility: A New Look at the Employment Protection Legislation". In: *OECD Employment Outlook*. Paris: OECD Publishing.

OECD (2014). "Focus on Inequality and Growth". Paris: OECD Publishing.

OECD (various years). Employment outlook (online database).

Ostry, J.D., Berg, A. and Tsangarides, C.G. (2014). "Redistribution, Inequality, and Growth". IMF Staff discussion paper, Washington, DC.

Ostry, J.D., Loungani, P. and Furceri D. (2016). "Neoliberalism: Oversold?" *Finance & Development*, June 2016, 53(2).

Padoa-Schioppa, T. (2004). *Financial stability review: December 2004*. Powerpoint presentation. ECB, Frankfurt (December 15). Available at: www.ecb.int/press/key/date/2004/html/sp041215_annex.en.pdf.

Palley, T.I. (2012). *From financial crisis to stagnation: the destruction of shared prosperity and the role of economics*. Cambridge: Cambridge University Press.

Palma, G. (2009). "The Revenge of the Market on The Rentiers: Why Neo-Liberal Reports of the End of History Turned Out to be Premature". *Cambridge Journal of Economics*, 33(4): 829–66.

Pariboni, R. and Tridico, P. (2016). "Inequality, financialisation and economic decline". Roma Tre University, mimeo.

Peck, J. and Tickell, A. (1992). "Local Modes of Social Regulation? Regulation Theory, Thacherism and Uneven Development". *Geoforum*, 23(3): 347–63.

Peece, D. (2009). *Dismantling social Europe. The political economy of social policy in the EU*. London: First Forum Press.

Peet, J. and La Guardia, A. (2014). *Unhappy Union how the euro crisis – and Europe can be fixed. The Economist*. London.

Peet, R. (2011). "Inequality, Crisis and Austerity in Finance Capitalism". *Cambridge Journal of Regions, Economy and Society*, 4: 383–99.

Perugini, C., Hölscher, J. and Collie, S. (2015). "Inequality, Credit and Financial Crises". *Cambridge Journal of Economics*, 39(1): 1–31.

Petit, P. (2003). "Large network services and the organisation of contemporary capitalism". CNRS-CEPREMAP, WP, No. 2003–14. Aglietta, 1979.

Petit, P. (2009). "Financial Globalisation and Innovation: Lessons of a lost Decade for the OECD Economies". CNRS Working Paper No. 2009–14.

Pianta, M. (2014). Presentazione of the book: *Il lungo XX secolo. Denaro, potere e le origini del nostro tempo* by Arrighi Giovanni, 2014, Il Saggiatore.

Pianta, M. and Tancioni M. (2008). "Innovations, Profits and Wages". *Journal of Post Keynesian Economics*, 31(1): 103–23.

Piketty, T. (2014). *Capital in the twenty-first century.* Cambridge, MA: Belknap Press, 2014.

Pitelis, C. (2010). "From Bust to Boom: an Introduction". *Contribution to Political Economy*, 29: 1–8.

Pontusson, J. (2005). *Inequality and Prosperity. Social Europe vs. Liberal America.* Ithaca and London: Cornell University Press.

Posner, R.A. (2009). *A failure of capitalism.* Cambridge: Harvard University Press.

Qian, Y. (2003). "How Reform Worked in China". In: D. Rodrik, ed, *In Search of Prosperity.* Princeton: Princeton University Press.

Rajan, R.G. (2010). *Fault lines: how hidden fractures still threaten the world economy.* Princeton University Press.

Rasmus, J. (2010). *Epic recession. Prelude to global depression.* New York: Pluto Press.

Rawls, J. (1971). *A theory of justice.* Cambridge: Harvard University Press.

Reuters (2013). "ECB's Weidmann: Pressure on Central Banks Risks FX Competition". Frankfurt, 21 Jan 2013.

Rochon, L.P. and Rossi, S. (2010). "Has 'It' Happened Again?" *International Journal of Political Economy*, 39(2): 5–9.

Rodrik, D. (1996). "Why Do More Open Economies Have Bigger Governments?" NBER Working Papers 5537. Cambridge: National Bureau of Economic Research.

Rodrik, D. (1998). "Why Do More Open Economies Have Bigger Governments?". *Journal of Political Economy*, 106(5): 997–1032.

Rodrik, D. (1999). *Making openness work.* John Hopkins University Press.

Rodrik, D. (2004). "Rethinking Growth Policies in Developing World". Working paper, Harvard University, mimeo.

Rodrik, D. (2011). *The globalization paradox. Democracy and the father of the world economy.* New York and London: W.W. Norton & Company.

Rodrik, D., Subramanian, A. and Trebbi, F. (2004). "Institutions Rule: the primacy of Institutions over Geography and Integration in Economic Development". *Journal of Economic Growth*, 9(2): 131–165.

Romer, C. and Bernestein, J. (2009). "The Job impact of the American Recovery and Reinvestment Plan". Council of Economic Advisers and Office of the Vice President Elect, White House, Washington, DC, January 9.

Rueff, J. and Hirsch, F. (1965). "The Role and Rule of Gold: An Argument". Princeton Essays in International Finance, No. 47, Princeton University International Finance Section.

Saez, E. (2013). "Striking it Richer. The Evolution of Top Income in the United States". University of Berkley, mimeo.

Sapir, A. (2005). "Globalization and the Reform of European Social Models". Bruegel Policy brief. Issue 2005/01, November.

Sawyer, M. (2010). "'It' Keeps Almost Happening: Post Keynesian Perspectives on the Financial Crisis and the Great Recession". June 2010, University of Leeds, mimeo.

Schulmeister, S., Schratzenstaller, M. and Picek, O. (2008). "A General Financial Transaction Tax. Motives, Revenues, Feasibility and Effects". Vienna: WIFO Publication.

Semmler, W. and Young, B. (2010). "Lost in Temptation of Risk: Financial Market Liberalization, Financial Market Meltdown and Regulatory Reforms". *Comparative European Politics.*

Sen, A. (1973). *On economic inequality.* Oxford: Clarendon Press.

Shapiro, C. and J.E. Stiglitz (1984). "Equilibrium Unemployment as a Worker Discipline Device". *The American Economic Review,* 74 (3), 433–44.

Shield, S. (2012). *The international political economy of transition. Neoliberal hegemony and Eastern Central's Europe transformation.* Abingdon: Routledge.

Skidelsky, R. (2009). *Keynes: The return of the master.* New York: Public Affairs.

Smith, A. (1976 [1776]). *An inquiry into the nature and causes of the wealth of nations.* Oxford: Oxford University Press.

Sokoloff, K. and Engerman, S. (2000). "History Lessons. Institutions, Factor Endowments, and Paths of Development in the New World". *Journal of Economic Perspectives,* 14: 217–232.

Soskice, D. and Hall, P. (2001). *Varieties of capitalism.* Oxford University Press.

Stiglitz, J. (1998). *More instruments and broader goals: moving toward the post-Washington consensus.* WIDER Annual Lecture.

Stiglitz, J. (2002). *Globalization and its discontents.* New York: W.W. Norton & Company.

Stiglitz, J. (2006). *Making globalization work.* New York: W.W. Norton & Company.

Stiglitz, J. (2010). "Recommendations by the Commission of Experts of the President of the General Assembly of United Nations on Reforms of the International Monetary and Financial System". UN, New York.

Stiglitz, J. (2012). *The price of inequality, how today's divided society endangers our future.* New York: W.W. Norton & Company.

Stockhammer, E. (2013) "Why Have Wage Shares Fallen? A Panel Analysis of the Determinants of the Functional Income Distribution". Condition of work and employment N 35, International Labour Organization, Geneva.

Stockhammer, E. (2015). "Rising Inequality as a Cause of the Present Crisis". *Cambridge Journal of Economics,* 39(3): 935–58.

Stolper, W.F. and Samuelson, P.A. (1941). "Protection and Real Wages". *Review of Economic Studies,* 9(1): 58–73.

Summers, L. (2016). "The Age of Secular Stagnation. What it is and what to do about it". *Foreign Affairs,* 95(2): 2–9.

Swank, D. (2002). *Global capital, political institutions, and policy change in developed welfare states.* New York: Cambridge University Press.

Taylor, J.B. (2009). *Getting off track.* Stanford: Hoover Institution Press.

Taylor, J.B. (2010). Testimony before the House Budget Committee, US Congress, Washington, DC. July 1.

The Economist (2011). Special Report on International Banking, May 14–20, London.

The Economist (2013a). "Abe's master plan". [18 May 2013].

The Economist (2013b). "Japan and Abenomics'. [5 Oct. 2013].

Tisdell, C. and Svizzero, S. (2003). "Globalization, Social Welfare, and Labour Market Inequality". Working Paper No. 20, The University of Queensland.

Tobin, J. (1978). "A Proposal for International Monetary Reform". *Eastern Economic Journal* (Eastern Economic Association), 153–59.

Tridico, P. (2009). "Flessibilità e istituzioni nel mercato del lavoro: dagli economisti classici agli economisti istituzionalisti". In: *Lavoro&Economia,* N. 1, gennaio/maggio, 113–39.

Tridico, P. (2010). "Growth, Inequality and Poverty in Emerging and Transition Economies". *Review of Transition Studies,* 16(4).

Tridico, P. (2011a). *Institutions, human development and economic growth in transition economies.* London: Palgrave.

Tridico, P. (2011b). "Varieties of Capitalism and Responses to the Financial Crisis: The European Social Model Versus the US Model". Working Paper No. 129, Dipartimento di Economia, Università Roma Tre.

Tridico, P. (2012). "Financial Crisis and Global Imbalances: Its Labor Market Origins and the Aftermath". *Cambridge Journal of Economics,* 36(1): 17–42.

Tridico, P. (2013). "The Impact of the Economic Crisis on the EU Labour Market: A Comparative Perspective". *International Labour Review,* 152(2).

Tridico, P. (2014). "From Economic Decline to the Current crisis in Italy". *International Review of Applied Economics,* (29)2: 164–93.

Tridico, P. (2016). "Labour Productivity", in Bernardi A. and Monni S., *The Co-operative Firm Keywords,* Roma Tre University Press, Rome

Tropeano, D. (2010). "The Current Financial Crisis, Monetary Policy, and Minsky's Structural Instability Hypothesis". *International Journal of Political Economy,* 39(2): 41–57.

Tsebelis, G. (2002). *Veto players: how political institutions work.* Princeton: Princeton University Press.

Turner Review (2009). "A regulatory response to the global banking crisis". Financial Services Authority, March, 2009. Available at: www.fsa.gov.uk/pubs/other/turner_review.pdf.

UK Treasury Committee (2010). Summary of Treasury Committee opinions on EU Regulatory reform proposals. London.

Van der Zwan, N. (2014). "Making Sense of Financialization". *Socioeconomic Review,* 12 (1): 99–129.

Van Reenen, J. (2011). "Wage Inequality, Technology and Trade: 21st Century Evidence". *Labour Economics,* 18(6): 730–41.

Van Treeck, T. (2014). "Did Inequality Cause the U.S. Financial Crisis?" In: *Journal of Economic Surveys,* 28(3): 421–48.

Vis, B., van Kersbergen, K. and Hylands, T. (2011). "To What Extent Did the Financial Crisis Intensify the Pressure to Reform the Welfare State?" *Social Policy & Administration,* 45(4): 338–53.

Wahl, P. (2010). "Fighting Fire with Buckets. A Guide to European Regulation of Financial Markets Weltwirtschaft, Okologie & Entwicklung (World Economy, Ecology & Development), Berlin.

Wallerstein, I. (2008). "The Depression: A Long-Term View". Commentary No. 243, Fernand Braudel Center, Binghamton University.

Wallerstein, I. (2009). "Crisis of the Capitalist System: Where Do We Go From Here?" Harold Wolpe Lecture, University of Kwa Zulu-Natal, 5 November 2009. Online at Fernand Braudel Center, Binghamton University.

Walsh, P. and Whelan, C. (2000). "The Importance of Structural Change in Industry For Growth", *Journal of the Statistical and Social Inquiry Society of Ireland,* 29: 1–32.

Walter, A. (2008). *Governing finance. East Asia's adoption of international standards.* Ithaca: Cornell University Press.

Webb, S. (1912). "The Economic Theory of a Legal Minimum Wage". *Journal of Political Economy,* 20(10): 973–98.

Westbrook, D.A. (2010). *Out of crisis. Rethinking our financial markets.* Boulder: Paradigm publisher.

Whelan, K. (2010). *Global imbalances and the financial crisis.* General Directorate for Internal Policies. European Parliament, Brussels.

Winkelmann, L. and Winkelmann, R. (2010). "Does Inequality Harm the Middle Class?" *Kyklos*, 63(2): 301–16.

Wisman, J.D. (2013). "Wage Stagnation, Rising Inequality and the Financial Crisis of 2008". *Cambridge Journal of Economics*, 37(4): 921–45.

Wolf, M. (2012). "The Impact of Fiscal Austerity in the Eurozone". *Financial Times,* 27 April 2012.

Wolf, M. (2013). "Japan Can Put People Before Profits". *Financial Times,* 6 Feb 2013.

Wolff, R. (2010). *Capitalism hits the fan. The global economic meltdown and what to do about it.* New York: Pluto Press.

Wolfson, M. (2010). "Neoliberalism and the Social Structure of Accummulation". *Review of Radical Political Economics*, 35(3): 255–63.

Wolfson, M. H. (1994). *Financial crises. Understanding the postwar US experience.* Armonk: M.E., Sharpe.

Wood, A. (1994). *North-south trade, employment and inequality.* Oxford: Clarendon Press.

World Bank (2010). Statistical Indicators (online database).

Wray, L.R. (2000). *The neo-chartalist approach to money.* Center for Full Employment and Price Stability. Available at: www.cfeps.org/pubs/wp/wp10.html.

Yeager, J.T. (2004). *Institutions, Transition Economies and Economic Development.* Boulder: Westview Press.

Voitchovsky, S. (2005). "Does the profile of income inequality matter for economic growth? Distinguishing between the effects of inequality in different parts of the income distribution". *Journal of Economic Growth*, 10: 273–96.

Zandi, M. (2010). Testimony before the House Budget Committee, US Congress, Washington, DC, July 1.

Zhou X. (2009). "Reform the international monetary system". Essay by Dr Zhou Xiaochuan, Governor of the People's Bank of China, 23 March 2009. BIS Review 41/2009.

Index